D1547512

The Ends of Modernization

Nicaragua and the United States
in the Cold War Era

David Johnson Lee

Cornell University Press
Ithaca and London

First published 2021 by Cornell University Press

Library of Congress Cataloging-in-Publication Data

Names: Lee, David Johnson, 1978– author.
Title: The ends of modernization : Nicaragua and the United States in the Cold War era / David Johnson Lee.
Description: Ithaca, New York : Cornell University Press, 2021. | Series: The United States in the world | Includes bibliographical references and index.
Identifiers: LCCN 2020043168 (print) | LCCN 2020043169 (ebook) | ISBN 9781501756214 (hardcover) | ISBN 9781501756238 (ebook) | ISBN 9781501756221 (pdf)
Subjects: LCSH: United States—Foreign relations—Nicaragua. | Nicaragua—Foreign relations—United States. | Nicaragua—Politics and government—1937-1979. | Nicaragua—Politics and government—1979-1990. | Nicaragua—Politics and government—1990-
Classification: LCC E183.8.N5 L44 2021 (print) | LCC E183.8.N5 (ebook) | DDC 327.7307285/0904—dc23
LC record available at https://lccn.loc.gov/2020043168
LC ebook record available at https://lccn.loc.gov/2020043169

Contents

Acknowledgments

This book would have been impossible without the generosity of many people. I was fortunate to study and work at Temple University during a golden age of historical scholarship and teaching and owe everything to my mentors there. Richard Immerman provided inspiration and encouragement from the early stages of my interest in the history of the United States and Latin America. David Farber, Arthur Schmidt, and Harvey Neptune all helped me conceive and fulfill this project over many years of writing and rewriting. Michel Gobat provided outside support as both a model of scholarship and invaluable guidance.

My long stays in Central America and trips to archives around the United States, Latin America, and Europe were made possible by many travel grants and scholarships. These included grants from Temple University's Graduate School, the Center for Force and Diplomacy, the Center for the Humanities, and the College of Liberal Arts. The Society of Historians of American Foreign Relations also provided travel funding. Many people and institutions provided venues to share my ideas both within my home university and abroad. I am especially grateful for the efforts of scholars at the Universidad Centroamericana de Nicaragua, the Universität Tübingen, the Universität Wuppertal, the University of Leiden, and the London School of Economics for fostering international conversation.

The work of a historian is impossible without the labor of archivists, and historians of Nicaragua have the benefit of an exceptional group within and outside the country. I am especially grateful for the kind and patient staff at the archive and library at the Instituto de Historia de Nicaragua y Centroamérica in Managua, especially María Auxiliadora Estrada, Lissette Ruiz, María Ligia Garay, and Margarita Vannini. Archivists at Archivo General de la Nación were also tremendously helpful in navigating the papers of the Somoza administration. Archivists in the national archives of Mexico, the Dominican Republic, the United Kingdom, Panama, and Costa Rica generously shared their work with me. In the United States, the staff at the National Archives and Records Administration in College Park, Maryland, as well as at the presidential libraries of Franklin Delano Roosevelt, Jimmy Carter, John F. Kennedy, Lyndon Baines Johnson, Richard M. Nixon, and Ronald Reagan, all provided indispensable assistance. Many university collections also opened their materials to me, especially Rutgers University, Princeton University, Swarthmore College, the University of Miami, the University of California at Berkeley, the University of Texas at Austin, and Universidad Centroamericana in San Salvador. I also benefited from the collections at the Hoover Institution and the International Institute of Social History in Amsterdam.

I am grateful for the inspiration and editorial assistance that made this book possible. David Engerman provided unfailing support throughout the process. At Cornell University Press, Michael McGandy and Clare Jones patiently worked to help see the book to completion. Matt Farish, David Monteyne, and the editors at *Urban History* helped publish a version of a chapter of this book, which gave my work much-needed momentum in its earliest stages.

Many friends assisted at all stages of this project, providing a world of conversation and collaboration that made my work worthwhile. Alex Elkins was an indispensable intellectual ally. Aria Finkelstein provided a fresh sense of perspective. Colbert Root helped plumb the meaning of everything. Jared Brey, Juliana Rausch, Aaron Frey, Benji Davis, Leanne Fallon, Ben Webster, and Dave Mesing all helped create a community of learning and camaraderie in Philadelphia. Phil Lewin, Madalyn Freedman, Julia Cantuária, and Noelle Egan accompanied me in my travels in the Nicaraguan countryside. Lara Gunderson and Leah Trangen helped me explore Managua. Kelsey Baack helped me find the castle.

My work would have been impossible without the friends and acquaintances in Nicaragua who provided places to stay, conversation, and inside information to help me navigate their native or adopted land. I benefited enormously from the insights on Nicaraguan life of Aynn Setright and Lillian Hall, who helped orient me in the country to which they devoted so much work and affection. Casa Ben Linder provided a welcoming space to meet other people as fascinated by Nicaragua as I was. Claudia Hueppmeier helped me learn to navigate Managua. Eimeel Castillo shared her affection and knowledge of her beloved city. Lenin Flores Rossman was an unfailingly kind host and companion. María José González and Margarita Loring opened their home to me in Barrio Monseñor Lezcano, *dos y media abajo*.

I am thankful for the love and support of my family—Ellen and Steve Lee, Jeff and Jenna, and the newest generation of Nik, Ada, and Martha. Above all I am grateful to my students at Temple University, the College of New Jersey, Jefferson University, Holy Family University, Garden State Youth Correctional Facility, and Albert C. Wagner Youth Correctional Facility. All of them helped fulfill the primary goal of my scholarship, to build shared spaces of inquiry and learning that make the world a less lonely place.

The Ends of Modernization

Introduction

Development, Ideology, and Catastrophe in the Americas

> Catastrophes, then, they're our history?—Worse than that. We
> ourselves are a catastrophe product of a sum of catastrophes, because
> when these strike other peoples they sweep away countryside and city,
> but the people's identity remains. This hasn't happened here.
>
> Pedro Joaquín Chamorro

"We are ourselves a catastrophe product of a sum of catastrophes."[1] Pedro Joaquín Chamorro's words in the epigraph were written in response to the devastation brought by the 1972 earthquake that destroyed the city of Managua. The earthquake itself was a disaster, causing the immediate loss of thousands of lives and the destruction of a vibrant metropolis. The disaster became a catastrophe, a total overturning of a previously coherent system, when the US government and the regime of Anastasio Somoza Debayle used the disaster to try to rewrite the history of Nicaragua. They reshaped the city of Managua around plans to modernize both the metropolis and the lives of the millions of Nicaraguans whose fates were centered there. This most proximate catastrophe, Chamorro argued, was just the latest consequence of a prior catastrophe, the US Marine occupation of Nicaragua from 1912 to 1933, which put the Somoza dynasty in power and postponed the possibility for national self-determination. For Chamorro—who was a member of one of his country's most powerful families and the editor of its most prominent newspaper—although the catastrophes Nicaragua underwent were undoubtedly destructive, they also had a productive nature. They produced a battered nation, but one in which he saw a readiness to overturn Nicaragua's tragic fate.

The catastrophes Chamorro described would help bring about another set of catastrophes in the sense of radical overturnings, with the 1979 Nicaraguan revolution, the decade-long Contra War, and the end of the Cold War in Latin America, which replaced a catastrophe-prone interstate system built around the promise of modernization with one shaped by neoliberalism. The term "catastrophe" should not be taken to designate simply a disastrous turn of events, because "disaster" connotes a fate written in the stars. Nor does the word necessarily imply tragedy, though the language of tragedy runs like a scarlet thread through the history of US global relations.[2] "Catastrophe" refers to the final turning, or strophe, of the chorus in Greek drama, whether comedy or tragedy, in which the outcome of the play is revealed to the audience. The positive or negative character of a catastrophe is inseparable from the process of narration. The idea of modernization at the center of Nicaragua's Cold War history inspired an acute form of narrative contestation, as both opponents and proponents recognized modernization's catastrophic character. Expanding this understanding of catastrophe more broadly to the Cold War, in which the revolutionary transformations in Nicaragua played a formative role, means understanding the Cold War as a process of contestation between a chorus of actors all over the world vying to shape the outcome.

This book traces relations between the United States and Nicaragua in the age of development, from the pinnacle of modernization as ideology in the 1960s through the end of the Cold War in the 1990s.[3] The book examines US plans for development as they changed in reaction to events in the global South, beginning with the Cuban revolution, that set off a global program of anticommunist modernization. The book shows how Nicaragua played an important role in US plans for Latin America thanks to its leaders' close affinities with the United States and the two countries' long interconnected histories. This close relationship made Nicaragua central to new development practices promoted by the United States through the 1970s, until the 1979 Nicaraguan revolution became the catalyst for a new reconfiguring of global development in the 1980s. The US-sponsored Contra War and postrevolutionary transition in 1990 attempted to make Nicaragua an archetypal neoliberal republic, though local elites reshaped US-centric paradigms around their own interests, with further destabilizing consequences.

While requiring attention to interests and imaginings emanating from the United States, this study also follows closely the circulation of development ideas between North and South. This book examines how elite Nicaraguans especially responded to US programs for development. From the Alliance for Progress onward, US officials made Latin American ideas, networks, and individuals an intimate part of programs for reshaping the region's political and economic life. US policymakers frequently remarked on Nicaraguan willingness to court US intervention, as well as to turn local struggles into international ones. This affinity between US and Nicaraguan aims did not breed harmony and stability—it created the grounds for contestation that led Nicaraguans to challenge US power in their country and beyond.

The changes in the theories and practices of development described here are concurrent with the growing forces of globalization and neoliberalization beginning in the early 1970s.[4] Even as the imperatives of capital and finance restructured state power and territorial sovereignty worldwide, Nicaragua's story shows how contests grounded in national territory shaped the global dynamics propelled by US global power. Until the 1970s, the US government in its role as sometime anticolonial power supported a vision of self-determination and national autonomy that culminated in the development decade of the 1960s. After that, support for national autonomy, manifest in support for strong central governments built around long-term planning, would transform, especially in response to the collective threat of a New International Economic Order. The threat of collective action by the states of the Third World was accompanied by a resurgence of national liberation movements in Central America. Thanks to Nicaragua's growing and eventually successful revolutionary movement and US attempts to counter its influence, the country would play a key role in changing the premises and practices of US development policy.

The transformation of the modernization paradigm to which Nicaragua was central arose from that paradigm's failures to manage the paradox of sovereign equality and manifest inequality at the international level. Modernization failed to provide just and equitable growth; instead it brought dictatorship, inequality, human rights abuse, ethnocide, patriarchy, environmental degradation, and ultimately nationalist revolt. Development institutions transformed as well, assimilating critiques into their practice, in the process creating a new form of international governance that transformed the relations between central state authority and international power. The piecemeal changes in development thinking described in the chapters to follow correspond not to a single catastrophic shift but rather obeyed a catastrophic logic of democratic empire in which imperial modes of governing the internal and international relations of states like Nicaragua changed in reaction to contestation from the empire's subjects.

The instability at the heart of US policy toward Nicaragua is a direct consequence of the paradoxes of an empire run by democracy. The quadrennial cycles of US presidential elections brought in new regimes that inherited the machinery of development but altered their ends. The division of powers of the US government also bred instability, and Nicaraguan political actors could seek to shape US foreign policy by addressing its Congress, citizens, and international public opinion to reshape the ideas that structured the relations between these various actors. The terms of debate about Nicaragua's future refused to hold still; the language of modernization gave way to human rights, basic human needs, pluralism, indigenous rights, and sustainable development. Walter Benjamin called the ruling concepts of progress "the mirrors by which an 'order' came about," a kaleidoscope that "must be smashed" to bring about a more just world.[5] But it was in this process of smashing—the political and military struggle between the United States, local elites, and insurgent forces—that a new panoply of concepts came to define a new international order.[6] At the end of the Cold War, nations of the global South consisted of the same territory as before, but the ways of seeing that territory had changed dramatically. There was not, however, one dramatic change but rather a series of changes, as modernization was repurposed for the political ends of actors in the global North and South.

Emphasizing the dispersed origins of the ideas that would govern the post–Cold War order means imagining history in the form of a dialogue and contestation between North and South. To emphasize the importance of dialogue does not discount the importance of power and brute force but instead takes seriously the sense in which power and force were mediated by ideas and politics. José Coronel Urtecho wrote that Carlos Cuadra Pasos, a key Nicaraguan politician and intellectual of the early twentieth century, was the only thinker of his era to understand history as a dialogue. Other intellectuals saw history in the form of civil war, a zero-sum game in which intellect was in service of power, but Cuadra Pasos urged his disciples to put power to the service of knowledge to bring an end to Nicaragua's continual internal strife since independence. Doing so meant in part actively attempting to turn US power to their own ends and sometimes courting intervention in local struggles. The Nicaraguan intellectuals who attempted to shape their country's international relations engaged in both an internal and international dialogue of power and knowledge without predetermined ends: Coronel Urtecho would become an important intellectual influence on the Nicaraguan revolution, and Cuadra Pasos's son Pablo Antonio Cuadra Cardenal would become the intellectual standard-bearer of counterrevolution. To emphasize the dialogic nature of history for these thinkers was not to erase conflict but rather to embody it in the "living and reliving of history."[7] In the process of "living and reliving" described hereafter, Nicaraguans sought to escape from the binary logic of civil war, which the United States had long helped foster, turning to the whole world to mend the fissures created by their territory's precarious position as a meeting place of oceans, tectonic plates, cultures, ecosystems, and empires.

Nicaragua, the United States, and Revolution

As early as the Monroe Doctrine, Latin America was the object of visionary imaginings by US politicians. Beginning with the 1847 conquest of Mexico, the crowning achievement of the idea of Manifest Destiny, Latin America played an essential role in the expansion of US global power. The expansion of US economic and military power into what would later be called the Caribbean Basin made the region a staging post and essential bulwark for US global expansion. The creation of the Panama Canal marked a high point of US ability to harness geopolitical power to redraw political boundaries and to use engineering know-how to engrave that power into Latin American territory. Nicaragua's location as transit point in the westward expansion of the United States linked Nicaraguan and US history by drawing closer the Atlantic and Pacific Oceans.[8] The brief but catastrophic moment of conquest in the 1850s during which William Walker became president of Nicaragua made manifest in the minds of Nicaraguans the perpetual possibility of US intervention.[9] Nicaragua's status as the site of a possible transoceanic canal, and after the creation of the Panama Canal the site of a possible second route, assured that Nicaragua's future remained closely linked to the United States.

The successive occupations of Nicaragua in the early twentieth century continued US involvement with the country, culminating in the war of Augusto Sandino against the Marine occupation in the 1920s. International outcry against US policy helped encourage the creation of Franklin D. Roosevelt's Good Neighbor policy.[10] Rather than marking a reform of US relations with Nicaragua, this moment brought to power Anastasio Somoza García, who along with his sons would assume an iconic position as both authoritarian strongman and arch-capitalist. The recurring family affair of Nicaragua and the United States with the Somozas, sometimes tragic sometimes farcical, would in the 1960s conjugate with the romance of economic development, thanks to Cold War competition between the capitalist and socialist superpowers for the affection of the people, setting the stage for the last act of the age of national revolution.

During a long and catastrophe-ridden relationship with the United States, from Nicaragua's independence to the present, the country became the site of an experiment to manage catastrophe, the Alliance for Progress, that was epoch-making in defining the promise and perils of the 1960s as the "development decade." The Alliance itself was built around the idea that the forces of modernity were inevitably encroaching on and overturning traditional systems of power in Latin America. Those who conceived the Alliance knew that modernization was disruptive, as it reshaped people's lives, and also destructive, as it annihilated traditional ways of life forever. US policymakers and their allies tasked themselves with guiding this catastrophic process in alliance with both Latin American elites and their nations.

In Nicaragua, the Alliance quickly achieved its goal of rapid economic growth but at the price of entrenching military autocracy. The destruction of Managua, brought by the collusion of the forces of nature and political power, set in motion the events that would cause another overturning, the 1979 revolution that would replace the Somoza regime with the Sandinista government. Many people, in Nicaragua and around the world, saw this radical overturning not as a calamity but as a fortuitous possibility of renewing the promise of revolution in the Americas. The revolution created new stirrings of radical democracy and social justice, mobilizing a worldwide network of solidarity activists, people for whom the Nicaraguan revolution would become the center of their lives. Their work in Managua was preparation for work in San Salvador and points beyond. The revolution also mobilized groups worldwide seeking to counter the revolutionary movement in the Americas and brought constitutional crisis to the United States itself.

Critics of the Reagan administration accused it of exaggerating the threat of a rising red tide in Latin America.[11] Nonetheless, the revolutionary situation in Central America prompted one of the largest foreign aid programs since the Marshall Plan, despite the marked lack of Reaganite fervor for what many conservatives considered international welfare. Scholars have asserted that the Reagan administration's publicly touted program for channeling private aid to the Contras was a cover for the US government to continue illegal covert aid after it was prohibited by Congress.[12] The motley cowboys' charge up San Juan Hill that was the US-backed counterrevolution had effects far beyond the carnage it created in the mountains of Central America. The counterrevolution facilitated the restructuring of US foreign aid to the entire Caribbean region and altered the balance of power in favor of entrepreneurial elites who shared US goals for restructuring states. Like Cuba before it, Nicaragua was a locus of concern that set in motion profound changes in US foreign policy, with global consequences.

Development Policy in Latin America

The Cuban Revolution marked the beginning of a profound shift in US foreign policy toward Latin America. Like the Haitian Revolution, the Cuban Revolution provided an example of how small and weak nations could assert independence from imperial power, while also providing aid for like-minded revolutionaries. The chief US response was the creation of the Alliance for Progress, aiming to subvert revolution by appropriating the rhetoric of social transformation while also boosting military power in the region. The Alliance was more than just the creation of a Marshall Plan for Latin America, something that Latin American elites had been calling for since the end of World War II and a desire that Truman's Point IV program had failed to fulfill. The Alliance marked the coming together of social scientific expertise with US foreign policy under the aegis of modernization theory and the union of pan-Americanism with a vision of national autonomy.

When Kennedy met Latin American leaders at the Uruguayan resort of Punta del Este in 1961, he proposed a vast increase of US aid, $1 billion the first year and a projected inflow of $20 billion over the next decade. Many of the goals of the Charter of Punta del Este were well defined: a regional growth rate of 2.5 percent, elimination of illiteracy, increase of life expectancy, and overall increase in quality of life and employment. But these goals were also elusive. The Alliance was imagined as a "counter-mystique" to the appeals of the Cuban Revolution.[13] As such, the Alliance wedded the hegemonic ideal of US power with a promise of individual autonomy for the nations involved. Several nations were designated as "showcases" for Alliance goals; Brazil, Colombia, Chile, and the Dominican Republic were singled out as places where receptive governments and widespread poverty could make possible rapid and far-reaching change.[14] Nicaragua was a special case, as its rulers were especially receptive to the Alliance's anticommunism, though those rulers were precisely what the Alliance purported to replace.

Many of the early policy formulations of the Alliance contained radical implications. Arthur Schlesinger Jr. warned that Latin Americans saw themselves as Ariel to the US Caliban and that a program to remake the hemisphere in the US image was bound to fail. Instead, he counseled that "we should give every dictator a sense of impermanence" and that "social justice" was the "basic human want" of much of the hemisphere. Obstacles to these goals were internal to the United States as much as external, as "the special interests of the military are distorting our Latin American policy today much as the special interests of the private corporations were distorting it 35 years ago."

Schlesinger, Walt Rostow, and Lincoln Gordon were aware that in a time of emergency austerity was not the answer and warned of the "baleful influence" of bankers like those at the International Monetary Fund, whose imperative for financial stabilization brought "economic stagnation, lowered living standards, and . . . an entirely predictable pro-Communist reaction."[15]

Seen from the south, despite the blandishments of democracy and social justice, the Alliance for Progress was at its heart a program for creating a managed revolution or, as many Latin Americans saw it, a catastrophe. An essential element of this managerial component was the creation of linguistic and bureaucratic structures with which to understand and shape development, institutionalizing the encounter between actors in the United States and Latin America. As Sergio Ramírez put it, the Alliance established

> a verbal imperium, no less abundant than in the nineteenth century but more technicized . . . : national development, industrial progress, process of change, green revolution, peaceful revolution, structural transformation, agrarian reform, tax reform, technicization of production, resource planning, words taken out of their context and carried to their maximum elasticity forming a lexicon to enrich others like national diet, minimum wage, rural education, environmental health, techniques of cultivation, all the terms members of a single sterile family.

Acknowledging that the technocratic language was co-opting older language of revolution, he stated that such phrases "don't fill the radical newspapers and proclamations as of old, but the innumerable technical reports, feasibility studies, intergovernmental covenants, investment projects, contracts of microloans. These word games are used to justify economic integration . . . but constitute only one vertex of the blueprint, which is enclosed also by lines of political, military, and cultural domination."[16]

Ramírez, who would help plan and execute the Sandinista insurgency against the Somozas, captures the implicit lines of force that accompanied the anodyne rhetoric of bureaucratic revolution. Alongside the inert phraseology of development, however, was another rhetoric that summoned the telluric energies that animated past revolutions, as when Teodoro Moscoso, charged by the Kennedy administration with coordinating the Alliance for Progress, called the Alliance a "*peaceful* revolution on a Hemisphere scale" while equating it with military enterprises such as the American Revolution and the D-Day landing in Normandy.[17] Quoting former Costa Rican president José Figueres, Moscoso warned that "it is one minute to midnight in Latin America" and that "there is no time for dialectic exercises or philosophical musings." While distinguishing the Alliance from the communist-inspired revolution, he spoke of a "social revolution welling up with tremendous force," propelling changes in Latin America.

The development programs of the Alliance era were plotted on two axes that planners hoped would contain these "powerful historical forces." The first was between "community development" and large-scale economic growth. Community development involved programs like health and education designed to improve the quality of life of poor Latin Americans. Such programs were imagined to improve, not only the livelihood of poor people, but also the functioning of government by teaching the poor to both help themselves and to demand improved services from their governments. Programs of land reform, economic cooperatives, and home ownership fell under community development as well, encouraging small-scale farm production that could help create a class of middle peasants and workers who could provide the foundation for a middle class.[18] On the other end of the spectrum were programs to promote macroeconomic growth. Although small-scale agriculture and health programs could educate citizens, large-scale export agriculture was necessary to import technology necessary for capitalist development.

The second set of contradictory imperatives the Alliance set out to balance, Ramírez's other "vertex of the blueprint," was between dictatorship and democracy. Though calls for an antidictatorial campaign animated the Alliance's conception, enthusiasm for democratization waned in the Kennedy administration after opposition groups began overturning governments such as that of Rafael Trujillo in the Dominican Republic. Advocates for an end to the Somoza dynasty in Nicaragua, such as Moscoso and Adolf Berle, were sidelined, and Alliance energy was focused on steering elections in the short term and relying on the subtle work of modernization in the long term. As Secretary of State Dean Rusk put it, "Our first objective . . . is to help preserve the independence of the modernization process, meanwhile working to help build the conditions which will make consent increasingly a reality and to encourage those who would remain steadfast to their own version of the democratic objective."[19]

In Nicaragua in the early 1960s, despite the abstract invocation of impersonal laws of development, Rusk's "independence of the modernization process" had a face, or more accurately two faces, epitomizing the twin poles of the Alliance: the two sons of General Anastasio Somoza García, Luis and Anastasio Somoza Debayle. Luis, president of Nicaragua from his father's assassination in 1956 until 1963, was an exponent of technocratic modernization.

Trained in agronomy at Louisiana State University, Luis echoed the rhetoric of the Alliance about the need for land reform and self-help. Rather than parrot the words of President Kennedy, however, Luis translated them to his own vision of Nicaraguan reality, arguing that the primary restraint on Nicaraguan development was not military rule but the greed of Nicaragua's traditional aristocracy, against whom General Somoza García had built a base of support among Nicaragua's workers and farmers.[20] It was Luis's presence in power that made it possible for the architects of the Alliance for Progress to imagine Nicaragua to be a "test case" for the democratizing influence of the United States, and Luis complied with the wishes of Washington in passing the mantle of governance to a handpicked successor in 1963.

The other face of the "independence of the modernization process," Anastasio Somoza Debayle, embodied the other facet of the Alliance, the mailed fist of military power that accompanied the rapid economic growth that Nicaragua did in fact achieve. As head of the Guardia Nacional, the ostensibly politically neutral military force created by the United States in the 1920s, Anastasio preserved his family's power and the influence of the United States in Nicaragua. His assumption of the presidency in 1967 with US approval marked an end to attempts to replace the face of governance in Nicaragua with anyone other than a member of the Somoza family. US officials had long acknowledged that their aim was not to remove the Somozas completely from power in Nicaragua, an impossible task without wholesale revolution, but to foster the alternation of governments under the imprimatur of relatively free elections. The US ambassadors encouraged the Conservative Party, which was the only electoral competitor to the Somozas' Liberal Party, to contest elections, while also urging Conservatives to quietly take their allotted seats in the Assembly when they inevitably lost these contests.[21]

By the end of the 1960s, many argued that the Alliance was a failure. The large showcase countries for the Alliance for Progress, such as Colombia and Brazil, proved less tractable to both the forces of history and the emoluments of aid than hoped, and efforts to keep radicals like Chile's Salvador Allende from power through development aid and covert action were in vain. Nicaragua, however, turned out to be a star of the Alliance once the pretensions of democratization were lifted. Already at the beginning of the 1960s, per capita aid to Nicaragua was twice that to Latin America as a whole and would grow to be ten times as much by the 1970s.[22] Nicaragua's economy boomed while the economies of its neighbors stagnated. This significance would grow as programs for large-scale modernization faded. Awareness of the importance of foreign aid, both for the Somoza regime and its opponents, prompted outsized efforts to court the various competing power centers in the United States, from the president and Congress to the American people themselves.

Even though the rhetoric of the Alliance waned by the end of the 1960s, the infusion of US capital and technocratic expertise into Nicaragua helped accelerate social and economic changes that would radically reshape the country. The simulacra of democratic governance that US officials helped create convinced them of the essential pliability of Nicaraguan politics and the emptiness of Nicaraguan culture outside the influence of the United States. Outside of the awareness of US officials, a cultural ferment was reshaping the country as both Conservative and radical critics of Nicaragua's relationship with the United States began in the 1960s to try to formulate an alternative ending to the drama scripted in Washington. The Frente Sandinista de Liberación Nacional (FSLN) would attempt to re-create the feats of the Cuban Revolution by creating a vanguard guerrilla movement to rally the population against the government. Simultaneously, cultural elites grouped around the opposition newspaper *La Prensa* would attempt to articulate a future for Nicaragua beholden neither to the socialist bloc nor to the United States. The circumstances of the 1960s, and especially the 1972 earthquake, would cause these forces to converge. Their alliance would make possible the 1979 revolution, and the dissolution of this alliance would fuel the Reagan administration's Contra War. The re-creation of this convergence once again in the early 1990s would make possible the "transition to democracy" that the Alliance for Progress had imagined, while alienating the US government and institutionalizing Nicaragua's precarious international position.

Intellectuals and Power in Nicaragua

Just as Cold War intellectuals provided the essential narrative structures that formed the contours of US ideas about modernization, Nicaraguan elites carried out debates about universality and particularity while attempting to turn US power to their own ends. Unlike in the United States, where the language of social science dominated, in Nicaragua the privileged voices were those of poets and essayists, who like their counterparts in the North circulated between the fringes and centers of power. While much of the literature on Latin America's Cold War centers on collaboration and resistance to US power, Nicaraguan intellectual life was shaped by an autochthonous tradition that structured Nicaragua's internal and international conflicts from the Cold War through the twenty-first century. The behavior of this intellectual elite shows how international power relations are not formed solely by collaboration and resistance; the independent imperatives of these actors shaped the contours of the Cold War.

Nicaraguan cultural nationalism was rooted in early twentieth-century literary and political modernism that spawned both political and artistic vanguards. In the 1920s Pablo Antonio Cuadra and José Coronel Urtecho, members of the Granada-based Conservative elite that governed Nicaragua for much of the postindependence period, founded a poetic vanguard movement of young aristocrats who hoped to renovate Nicaraguan political and cultural life they believed had been corrupted by a "bourgeois spirit" linked to US influence.[23] The movement paradoxically embraced the anti-imperialist rebellion of Augusto Sandino in the Segovias against the US Marine occupation, as well as the military dictatorship of Anastasio Somoza García. In both figures the members of this movement sought a political and cultural bulwark against the corrosive influence of the United States. They attempted to combine the power of cultural modernism with their own Catholic and Hispanic tradition to foment a political and cultural awakening throughout Latin America around their own version of authoritarian corporatism. They rejected the pan-Americanism advocated by the burgeoning US empire, under which Cuadra believed "we Americans have only succeeded in becoming tributaries of the Great Nation of the North."[24] Instead of a hemispheric identity, Cuadra and his compatriots called for a revival of the Spanish American imperium. Cuadra critiqued a *yanquizante* or "yankeefying" spirit in the youth of his time, which sought the mediocrity of physical ease, sexual pleasure, and comfort.[25] Instead he advocated a return to the rigors of the conquistadors, who brought civilization to the Americas by the sword and the cross, and he believed that each was indispensable to the other.[26] When Cuadra looked back on these years in later life after his views had moderated, he said he had imagined society "like an immense column—a fullness of faith," crowned by the aristocracy of the spirit he imagined himself and his peers to be.[27]

Cuadra also encouraged a Nicaraguan version of the myth of *mestizaje* that distinguished Latin American racial ideals from those of the United States by emphasizing mixture over racial exclusion.[28] What began as a critique of US racism became in the hands of Latin American intellectuals a justification for the nation-building projects of Europeanizing and Americanizing elites.[29] During the age of development following World War II, the *mestizaje* promoted by Latin American elites converged with the modernizing goals of the Alliance for Progress and underwrote the power of authoritarian states like that of the Somozas and insurgent forces such as those sponsored by Cuba.[30] Revolution, counterrevolution, and post–Cold War nation-building would be shaped by the problem of *mestizaje* formulated by Cuadra and his peers.

This book traces the lasting influence of the Conservative critique of both US power and the Somozas. After their early support, Conservatives became disillusioned with the dictatorship of Anastasio Somoza García and his relations with the United States. This disillusionment led to opposing orientations toward US influence that manifested in different styles of subaltern diplomacy. Conservatives dubbed the Somozas as *herodianos*, or followers of the biblical Herod of Judea, drawing the idea from Arnold Toynbee's description of how traditional societies manage foreign influence. For Toynbee, contemporary dilemmas of modernization had ancient roots, and countries as diverse as Turkey and Japan faced persistent questions of subjection and confrontation in seeking autonomy in the face of European imperial power.[31] To their critics, the Somozas were like the vassal king of Judea under Roman rule, using public flattery to associate Nicaragua with the foreign policy goals of the United States and embracing the cultural products of empire. Conservatives attacked the Somozas for basing their rule on US sponsorship and claiming a special relationship with the northern colossus that boosted their family fortunes through development aid during the Good Neighbor era and beyond.[32]

Conservatives in turn preferred the role of *zelotes*, or anti-Roman Zealots, openly confronting both the Somozas and the United States while using their own cosmopolitan connections with US and European culture to garner international allies.[33] The generation of Conservative intellectuals after the vanguard, such as Pedro Joaquín Chamorro and Ernesto Cardenal, used their cultural prestige and access to means of disseminating the printed word to promote their brand of cultural nationalism against the Somozas. In the 1960s, they welcomed US development policy in hopes that its democratizing promises could be turned against the Somozas. In the process, they accommodated themselves to US-oriented modernizing goals, assimilating their vision of the redemptive possibilities of contact between their country's elite and its poor peasants to the promise of development. After the Alliance for Progress helped bolster the power of the second generation of Somozas under Luis and Anastasio Somoza Debayle, and the reconstruction of Managua engraved a disfigured modernity on their nation's capital, many Conservatives turned to radicalism.

The convergence of Conservative cultural nationalism and the radical FSLN gave the Nicaraguan revolution much of its distinctive character.[34] The FSLN's insurrectionary strategy promised to overcome the political and economic backwardness that both radicals and Conservatives believed US power had created. Cultural nationalism influenced the FSLN's successful solidarity campaign and its international diplomacy that attempted to overcome US influence by diversifying the country's international relationships. When the counter-revolution took off in the 1980s, members of a third generation of Conservatives turned against the FSLN and joined the Contra movement. After the revolution exhausted its international and domestic alliances by the end of the 1980s, elite cooperation would re-create a tactical alliance of Conservatives and radicals around the idea of *concertación*, an elite compact to manage democracy. Conservative cultural nationalism and the style of diplomacy created by Conservative interactions with both the Somozas and the FSLN would continue to influence Nicaraguan politics through the era of the "pink tide" resurgence of the Latin American Left and into the present.

Plan for the Book

This first three chapters of this book describe how Nicaragua went from development success story to crucible of socialist revolution. Chapter 1 begins by discussing the origins of the Alliance for Progress in Latin American ideas and political networks. The earliest version of the Alliance was premised on promoting drastic political and economic change as an antidote to the spreading of a Cuban revolutionary model. US planners originally hoped to overturn the Nicaraguan government after fostering regime change in Cuba and the Dominican Republic, building on the efforts of Latin America's anticommunist democratic movement. When these initiatives faltered, Nicaragua became a key site for new programs to manage political and economic development built around the Central American Common Market (CACM). Promotion of regional development replaced immediate regime change, and US programs worked to integrate Nicaraguan elites by using community and regional development programs to win Conservative support for the Liberal-controlled central government. Elite Nicaraguans continued to lobby for overt US intervention, until the election of Anastasio Somoza Debayle and the 1967 massacre in Managua led many of them to turn to the more radical politics promoted by the Cuba-inspired FSLN.

Chapter 2 examines the aftermath of the 1972 earthquake that destroyed Managua. Though the US government under President Nixon turned away from the developmental premises of the Alliance for Progress, the planners who implemented Managua's reconstruction nonetheless planned a new city modeled on US urban space that implemented the belief that structural transformation could beget economic and political change. The plan for a decentralized metropolis created an unlikely consensus: US planners, many of whom were less comfortable than Nixon with Somoza's dictatorship, as well as Nicaragua's anti-Somoza opposition, believed that decentralization could diminish the power of the dictator, while Somoza and his staunchest supporters in the United States believed that the tools of urban planning would cement the dictator's economic and political control. The reality of the new city—a blighted downtown, the growth of new consumer development, and model housing projects that became urban slums—cemented an alliance of FSLN radicals with Nicaragua's anti-Somoza elite.

While the failed reconstruction of Managua was convincing many Nicaraguans that social revolution was necessary, chapter 3 shows how politicians and planners reacted to the realization that US development was not working as planned, and not only in Nicaragua. Under pressure from a growing network of nongovernmental organizations (NGOs) and activists, the US Congress mandated that all US aid must benefit the "poorest of the poor," rather than corrupt elites such as the Somozas. As the FSLN's rebellion grew, the United States made Nicaragua the site for a new program of "integrated rural development." As US planners used Nicaragua to reconfigure development around a new form of "benign counterinsurgency," radicalized Nicaraguans used the image of peasant victims of human rights abuse to mobilize an international human rights campaign. The imagery of peasants as victims of a repressive developmental order united Nicaraguan nationalists, radical socialists, and international human rights activists around the idea that peasants were both modernization's victims and potential revolutionary subjects.

The next three chapters show how Nicaragua served as bridge between Cold War development ideologies and the post–Cold War world. Chapter 4 traces the successful 1979 revolution to international alliance formation by the FSLN and shows how the Reagan administration reshaped international development policy in reaction. The revolution took place at a moment when Latin American and European politicians pushed for "ideological pluralism" to recognize the possibility of multiple paths to development worldwide while simultaneously advocating global economic restructuring. The FSLN tried to harness global dissatisfaction with the reactionary order linked to the United States, using diplomacy to transform dependency into revolutionary solidarity. The Reagan administration used confrontation with Nicaragua to encourage a restructuring of economic and political development in the region. The administration harnessed ideas and structures created by the revolution to undermine the alliance between socialists and capitalists while placing Nicaragua at the center of the administration's own response to the challenge of global solidarity.

Chapter 5 explores conflict on Nicaragua's eastern coast in the context of global critiques of the effects of both socialist and capitalist development on indigenous peoples. The FSLN's vision of social development through national integration came into conflict with indigenous and Afro-descendant desires for autonomy. The US government encouraged groups that would begin their own revolutionary movement in the east, causing fractures in the international solidarity movement cultivated by the FSLN. Miskito activists and their international allies cast their struggle against the revolutionary government in Managua as part of a "fourth world" movement outside the Cold War. This movement was made possible by new ideas about ethnic pluralism and environmental sustainability that were transforming international development and would impact indigenous rights struggles worldwide.

Chapter 6 assesses the conflicts between the US and Nicaraguan visions of political and economic development amid global post–Cold War transformation. After the 1990 election brought an end to the revolutionary order, US plans for Nicaragua as a prototypical neoliberal republic and new doctrines of sustainable development reshaped the country's economic and political horizons. The transition generated local forms of adaptation to structural transformation, as elites used the Latin American model of *concertación* to manage local conflict in the face of US power. In response to continued local resistance, US policies created new forms of intervention to oversee local politics, institutionalizing new forms of precarity in the new post-development world.

The epilogue situates the return of the FSLN to power in the 2000s within Latin America's "pink tide" and the longer history of international development and intervention described here. Nicaragua's precarious neoliberal present brought about a new process of alliance formation that recapitulated many of the aspirations of the early days of modernization while pushing Nicaragua's history once again to the brink of catastrophe.

Chapter 1

The Alliance for Progress
on the Doubtful Strait

"The country is beautiful," Christopher Columbus's cartographer Paolo Toscanelli tells him in the opening line of Ernesto Cardenal's *El estrecho dudoso*. The long exteriorist poem, published in 1966 and compiled of fragments of texts written by the explorers and conquerors of the Americas, narrates the coming of Europeans to the Central American isthmus in the sixteenth century. The Europeans came to the beautiful country of Nicaragua searching, Cardenal relates, not for gold but for the fabled transoceanic route that would allow them to reach the Spice Islands in East Asia, cementing the dominance of the Spanish Empire over the burgeoning system of world trade. Instead of discovering this "doubtful strait," they discovered that "the strait was of land, not water," and their search would lead them to murderous confrontations with one another and the native peoples who inhabited the territory between the Caribbean and the Pacific. Cardenal calls the victor in this bloody battle on the dubious isthmus, Pedro Arias (Pedrarias) Dávila, "the first 'promoter of progress' in Nicaragua, and the first dictator."[1]

If readers missed Cardenal's unsubtle connections between the battle over the doubtful strait and contemporary events in Nicaragua, poet José Coronel Urtecho made them clear in his prologue. If, "by disgrace—or luck, depending on how you see the question," all of the conquistadors had been like Pedrarias, the enterprising conqueror who turned the isthmus into his own feudal domain, the countries of Hispano-America would be not be "underdeveloped," but rather "already would have achieved their 'take-off,'" the Rostovian end point of modernization as self-sustaining growth.[2] The confluence of feudalism and entrepreneurship of the past, Cardenal and Coronel's readers were to understand, was now embodied in the latest promoter of progress in Nicaragua, the Somoza family regime, backed by the power of the United States and its mission to create an Alliance for Progress in the hemisphere. For Nicaragua's Conservative elite, among whom Cardenal and Coronel were distinguished members who would soon become partisans of social revolution, the paradoxes of the Alliance for Progress were both an expression of the power of the United States and an outgrowth of Nicaragua's own history.

The correlation between authoritarianism and US foreign aid was not a foregone conclusion at the beginning of the development decade announced by John F. Kennedy. Nor was it, as Coronel and Cardenal recognized, simply the product of US designs. The Alliance for Progress attempted to implement a vision of the mutually constitutive nature of economic development and political democracy rooted in the US experience. Latin Americans such as Fidel Castro asserted that democratization was a sham and critiqued the Alliance ratified at Punta del Este as US neo-imperialism driven by economic exploitation, an updated version of the lust for gold driving the conquistadors.[3] Others argued that the ideals were sincere, but elites North and South failed to hold fast to the transformational promise that underlay hemispheric cooperation.[4] Thanks to their own complex relationship with the United States, from the William Walker invasion to the Sandino rebellion and the rise of the Somoza dynasty, many Nicaraguans understood that neither democracy nor gold could explain US power on the isthmus. Both the inheritors of the Somoza dynasty and its opponents in Nicaragua understood the multivalent nature of US power, and would spend the decade of development attempting to turn that power to their own ends.

The Alliance for Progress made Nicaragua a battleground over the relationship between political and economic development. In 1961, the government of Nicaragua was target of plans for democratization that US and Latin American leaders hoped would make the Alliance more than just an anti-communist counterrevolution.[5] Fusing US-centered designs for democratic development with Latin America's anticommunist democratic movement, the Alliance marshaled the energies of an antidictatorial coalition that had been at work in the Caribbean and Central America for decades.[6] Nicaragua also became an integral part of an economic experiment in regional development, the Central American Common Market (CACM), which combined the nation-building premises of modernization with transnational institutions that decentered state power. Devised by heterodox Latin American economists, the CACM would reshape the economies of Central America and make possible experiments in development aid that went beyond the nation-state. These impulses—democratization and regional economic development—combined with the shared anticommunism of both the Nicaraguan government and its political opposition, made Nicaragua a testing ground for development programs shaped by US officials and Nicaraguans in and out of power. The result spawned new techniques for organizing foreign aid that would become paramount in US foreign policy in decades to come.

Nicaragua became the confluence of impulses for democratization and regional development thanks to Latin American political and intellectual networks, repurposed through collaboration and contestation between Nicaraguans and US officials. This confluence would make Nicaragua one of the few economic success stories in the hemisphere by the end of the decade. It would also make possible the rise to power of the final member of the Somoza dynasty and create conditions for the final Latin American social revolution of the Cold War. An authoritarian disposition was certainly built into the Alliance for Progress, and tensions between ideology and strategy put democratization, socioeconomic transformation, and counterinsurgency at odds.[7] In Nicaragua, US aid harnessed the transformational ideals of the Alliance to make opposition forces the accomplices to authoritarianism. Both the Somoza dynasty and the country's opposition elite took part in cementing the dictatorship that came to dominate Nicaragua. This would turn members of that elite such as Cardenal and Coronel toward radicalism as the only escape from Nicaragua's position on the "doubtful strait."

Antidictatorial Coalition and the Alliance

The first draft of the Alliance for Progress was a product of Latin America ideas. When President John F. Kennedy announced the Alliance to the assembled Latin American diplomatic corps in the East Room of the White House on March 13, 1961, he famously invoked Brazilian president Juscelino Kubitschek's Operation Pan America as a precedent for the new ten-year plan to remake Latin America as a bulwark against communism in the same way the Marshall Plan had remade Europe a decade earlier. Kennedy also gave an inter-American cast to the announcement by invoking Simón Bolívar and José de San Martín, but for many listeners, especially those in Central America, several other ideas with Latin American roots stood out. Kennedy declared that an "alliance of free governments" must exclude Cuba and the Dominican Republic, foreshadowing US attempts to rally the nations of the hemisphere to joint intervention against pariah

governments of both the left and the right. In doing so, he elevated the antidictatorial campaign of Latin America's anticommunist democratic movement to
the center of US foreign policy in the region.[8]

Latin American political leaders such as José Figueres of Costa Rica heard
the speech as a call to arms against political despotism and an endorsement of
their decades-long antidictatorial struggles. Figueres had been a leader of the
celebrated Caribbean Legion, which in previous decades had gathered exiles
from around the region in often quixotic battles against Rafael Leonidas Trujillo, Anastasio Somoza García, and other regional despots.[9] The speech went
so far as to quote Figueres—"once dormant peoples are struggling upward
toward the sun, toward a better life"—indicating an alignment between the
modernizing goals of the Alliance and the antidictatorial mission with which
Figueres was openly affiliated. Many Latin American listeners heard in the
speech a declaration that political transformation was the precondition for
longer-term economic change, a belief that would amplify support for the Alliance throughout the region. In Nicaragua, Pedro Joaquín Chamorro, editor
of *La Prensa*, declared on March 14 that Kennedy had announced an "eradi-
cation of tyrannies" and suggested that Nicaragua's government, ruled by the
sons of Anastasio Somoza García, would be the next to fall after those of Cuba
and the Dominican Republic.[10]

Kennedy's announcement also contained another Latin American idea that
moved from South to North but would be repurposed by US power. Kennedy cited the Central American Common Market, initiated by the nations
of the isthmus a decade earlier, as a tool to end the "fragmentation of Latin
American economies," a "serious barrier to industrial growth." This regional
development program was the creation of the Economic Commission for Latin
America (ECLA), led by Argentinean economist Raúl Prebisch, and combined
Prebisch's concerns about primary commodity producers' declining terms of
trade with prescriptions for import substitution at the regional rather than national level.[11] Kennedy's endorsement of the heterodox economics of the
global South signaled that the Alliance would not simply re-create the free market prescriptions of the Eisenhower administration. Instead, the spiritual
power of the "Alianza" would be fused with the technocratic expertise of both
North and South to "transform the American continent into a vast crucible
of revolutionary ideas and efforts" fueling economic and political progress.

Adolf Berle was responsible for putting the Latin American antidictatorial
movement at the center of the Alliance. Though Berle would play a decisive
role in shaping administration policy only for a short time, his vision of US
imperial power built around an antidictatorial alliance against dictatorships of

the right and left was formative of the initial stages of the Alliance. Berle believed that after the imminent demise of dictators in Cuba and the Dominican Republic thanks to US-supported forces, Nicaragua's leadership should be the next to fall. As head of the Task Force on Latin America charged with shaping the incoming president's hemispheric policy, Berle sent recommendations for immediate action to the president-elect calling for the replacement of the current US ambassador in Nicaragua by someone able to negotiate the withdrawal of the Somoza family from power.[12] The current US ambassador, Thomas Whelan, was "widely believed to be in the pocket of the late dictator" and thus unfit to bring an end to the Somoza dynasty.

Berle was chosen by the incoming Kennedy administration as a bridge between the New Deal and the New Frontier.[13] As a member of the Roosevelt "brain trust," Berle had promoted a vision of economic reform predicated not on dismantling the structures of big business and capitalism, but on increasing governmental powers to regulate business in an effort to provide a counterweight to corporate power. He was closely involved with the formulation of Roosevelt's Good Neighbor policy of nonintervention in internal Latin American affairs, helping to shore up hemispheric alliances to combat the Great Depression and resist the encroachment of fascism.[14] After the Cuban revolution, Berle became one of the foremost proponents of overt use of US power in the hemisphere, believing that the threat of communist penetration was comparable to that of fascism two decades before.[15] He asserted that antidictatorial intervention should be carried out openly as a prerogative of US power and should be legitimated with the assistance of Latin America's democratic leadership. "Non-intervention," the foremost principle of hemispheric cooperation, "is not absolute but qualified," Berle argued, and political intervention could be justified by rallying networks of sympathetic democratic leaders for concerted action.[16]

The vision of the Alliance as antidictatorial coalition grew from Berle's contacts with activist political leaders and parties in the circum-Caribbean basin. After serving as assistant secretary of state for Latin America and ambassador to Brazil, Berle had also served as an adviser to the Puerto Rican government of Luis Muñoz Marín.[17] Berle began a close working relationship with the Puerto Rican creators of Operation Bootstrap, a program of economic development, building state capacity, and promoting private investment, from which the Alliance would take inspiration. In the Kennedy administration, Berle would be responsible for staffing Alliance programs and the State Department with Puerto Ricans such as Teodoro Moscoso and Arturo Morales Carrión, who provided Latin American voices in the creation of hemispheric policy and connections to the network of leaders Berle thought should be bearers of US power in the region.[18]

The Latin American leaders who shaped the early vision of the Alliance believed that politics should be at its center. Figucres rushed to associate the Alliance with the network of anticommunist democratic Latin American parties he had cultivated for decades, issuing a "Declaration of San José" signed by a roll call of party leaders in and out of power such as Víctor Raúl Haya de la Torre in Peru and Rómulo Betancourt in Venezuela.[19] The declaration included the names of Nicaraguan opposition leaders Fernando Agüero and Enrique Lacayo Farfán, closely associated with ongoing attempts at overthrowing Somoza rule in Nicaragua. "This is war!" Figueres wrote to President Kennedy, endorsing a muscular US interventionism guided by the personalistic network of political leaders such as himself and Berle.[20] Kennedy advisers such as Arthur Schlesinger encouraged the president to endorse these political leaders as part of a larger project to associate the Alliance with progressive political movements.[21] Kennedy would call Betancourt "all that we admire in a political leader" and rhetorically endorse his attempts at fostering anticommunist democracy in the region.[22]

The Bay of Pigs invasion and the assassination of Rafael Trujillo put the premises of antidictatorial US intervention into action. Berle lobbied Latin American leaders to support the exile invasion, counseling the president to "let 'er rip" when other advisers wavered.[23] The Bay of Pigs failure marked the end of Berle's influence in the White House. With his exit from power, the antidictatorial alliance would change in character, as State Department policy planners looked for ways to reinvent intervention following the debacle. Thanks to the assassination of Trujillo, the Dominican Republic would soon become an experiment in democratization by intervention supported by the remnants of the antidictatorial alliance.[24] Elsewhere the US government would continue its support for Latin American political movements, but such assistance began to be carried out covertly rather than as an explicit part of the Alliance for Progress.[25]

In contrast to the foreign policy morasses taking shape in both Cuba and the Dominican Republic, Nicaragua would soon become one of the few areas of promise for the Alliance in the Caribbean and Central America. The invading forces of the Bay of Pigs, seen off by President Luis Somoza at Puerto Cabezas in Nicaragua, made use of the infrastructure of the old US informal empire.[26] Standard Fruit Company provided the railroad that shipped men and munitions to the embarkation, built by the Central Intelligence Agency (CIA), and Nipco Pine repurposed its lumber facilities into troop barracks.[27] The old infrastructure of extractive capitalism would soon be replaced by new networks of technocratic modernization, and the Somoza family would take part in making the country the site of experiments in regional economic development and democratization by nonintervention.

Economic Integration and Democratic Transition

Dictatorships and modernization were incompatible. Or so at least affirmed Luis Somoza Debayle, named president of Nicaragua by his country's legislature after his father's assassination in 1956.[28] A decade before political theorists developed a science of "transitology" to understand and guide processes of democratization from southern Europe to Latin America, Luis Somoza contended that survival in the new political environment required innovation. In the years before the Alliance for Progress, authoritarian governments throughout the region were falling: Getúlio Vargas in Brazil, Juan Perón in Argentina, Manuel A. Odría in Peru, Gustavo Rojas Pinilla in Colombia, Marcos Pérez Jiménez in Venezuela.[29] Instead of following in his father's footsteps and cementing a strongman regime in the country where the Somoza family controlled so much of economic and political life, President Luis Somoza chose instead to declare his regime to be in "transition to democracy," implementing a constitutional reform to prevent his own or a family member's succession to the presidency and allowing political opponents to rally for the first time in decades.[30]

In Nicaragua, the Alliance turned antidictatorial intervention on its head, giving Luis Somoza a key role in political reform in collaboration with the new US ambassador, Aaron S. Brown. Nicaragua also became a pivotal part of the new regional economic infrastructure that would put Central America at the vanguard of economic development. The Central American Common Market was a fusion of the free trade ideology that many Latin Americans saw as a distasteful form of foreign intervention with the import substitution programs that ECLA pushed as a means of national industrial development.[31] The creators of the CACM imagined it as a means to provide the infant industries of Central America with a larger market in which to expand, removing trade barriers between countries and creating a common external tariff. The CACM would also compensate for the uneven industrial development between Central American economies, with Guatemala and El Salvador the most developed and Nicaragua and Honduras the least, by promoting "integration industries" within each country that would be protected from competition from other countries within the market.[32]

The US government had treated the CACM with disdain at its inception, until an about-face in the late 1950s amid fears of festering anti-Americanism after the attack on Richard Nixon's motorcade in Caracas in 1958.[33] Milton Eisenhower visited Central America and commented favorably on the burgeoning integration movement, and the Eisenhower administration took steps to turn the movement in a direction favorable to US foreign policy.[34] Given the influence of ECLA on Latin American thinking about development, a "matter of some concern," US officials sought to "supplant" the United Nations organization's guiding role in Central America.[35] Officials also understood the symbolic importance of putting Central America, widely considered the most economically and politically "backward" region of the hemisphere, at the vanguard of industrial and institutional development.

The decision by the Kennedy administration to embrace the CACM with "a bear hug," part of a "new look" for the US Agency for International Development (USAID) in Central America, came as officials sought to resolve the multiple contradictions in the administration's aid policy to the region after the Alliance's rocky beginnings.[36] Walt Rostow and his fellow social scientists at Harvard and MIT had helped to organize the growing consensus around the need for massive US economic assistance in Latin America as a means of staving off communist encroachment.[37] Their vision of technocratic modernization relied less on old-fashioned political networks and more on a belief that change could be guided through strategic planning and macroeconomic direction. Berle had scoffed at Rostow's position in the State Department's Policy Planning organization, likening the position to being "night watchman at Mount Washington."[38] Berle's Task Force on Latin America attended to the importance of the CACM, accounting for its inclusion in the earliest version of the Alliance, but Berle insisted that "technical matters" must be subservient to political action.[39] For Berle, allying with progressive democratic forces would allow US policy to overtly embrace imperial structures. He advocated for "one-way free trade" between Latin America and the United States, such as that maintained between European countries and their current or former colonies, as a form of imperial prerogative. After Berle's exit, Rostow used the Policy Planning organization to reconfigure the strategic goals of US foreign policy around technocratic planning.

According to the new ethos, aid structures would allow the United States to guide change in the region not by direct intervention, but by setting goals and fostering new regional institutions that would connect national, regional, and hemispheric development.[40] Policymakers saw the integration movement, giving Central Americans an economic stake in their neighbors' political stability, as a means of reducing the sorts of interference in the political life of neighboring states encouraged by the antidictatorial coalition. "Integration" would replace "intervention," maintaining political support for the Alliance while propelling the region toward economic takeoff.[41] The CACM provided a means to distance US policy from direct support of the oligarchic and militaristic governments of Central America while still promoting economic growth. The Regional Office for Central American Programs (ROCAP) distanced the US government from individual regimes and encouraged countries to plan for regional integration. New loans aimed at the regional level would be channeled through institutions such as the Central American Bank for Economic Integration (CABEI), funded by counterpart funds from the United States and the Central American countries.

Nicaragua had been a reluctant member of the early discussions of the CACM but signed the agreement in 1960. Nicaraguan elites were concerned that integration into a common market might be detrimental to the country's industries, given the superior level of industrialization of nearby El Salvador and Guatemala. As a means of allaying these fears, the other countries created a "gentleman's agreement," whereby a Nicaraguan would serve as head of CABEI and the institutions of integration would be distributed into the less developed countries.[42] The Central Bank would be located in Honduras, another of the region's least industrialized countries, while Nicaragua would become home to the Instituto Centroamericano de Administración de Empresas, or INCAE.[43] Created in association with the Harvard Business School, INCAE would train a new generation of business leaders in how to use government agencies and international institutions to drive industrial growth.[44]

As Nicaragua's 1963 elections approached, critics of US policy in Central America argued that policies that had ostensibly been designed to remove the Somozas from power were now serving to cement their control of national life by inscribing family rule onto the Nicaraguan landscape. The postponement of immediate political change in favor of economic development and integration served the Somozas well. The family was at the vanguard of regional integration given their monopoly of both air and sea freight through control of Marina Mercante Nicaragüense (MAMENIC) and Líneas Aéreas de Nicaragua (LANICA), the country's major shipping line and airline.[45] The Somozas had been at the forefront of industrialized agriculture in the country, using international funding to develop beef processing facilities to export cheap meat to serve a growing market for hamburgers in the United States. After the failed Bay of Pigs invasion, conspiracy and commerce would come together as Cuban exile leader Manuel Artime became the Somozas' business representative in Miami.[46]

According to Ralph C. Estrada, USAID administrator in Nicaragua, a future accounting of the Alliance would discover not that it had failed but that it had never been tried.[47] Even as the program for regional integration distanced the United States from individual regimes and depersonalized the modernization process, the US government worked closely with the Somoza family to design a program for national integration. US aid built an agricultural road on the volcanic island of Ometepe, half of which was owned by the Somoza family. The US government also provided emergency medical assistance to Miskito Indians on the Río Coco between Honduras and Nicaragua after a World Court decision shifted the international border. Luis Somoza had, according to Estrada, manufactured a national emergency by encouraging the Miskitos to emigrate from Honduras to Nicaragua to assuage opponents who criticized him for not contesting the tribunal's decision.[48] Finally, the United States endorsed the Nicaraguan government's military pretensions by helping to expand Las Mercedes International Airport, hub of the Somoza-owned national airline, to allow the use of jet aircraft. To Estrada, this sent a clear signal to local and regional leaders that economic modernization was merely a thin disguise for militarization and authoritarian power. He resigned.

The Opposition Confronts the Alliance

According to Carlos Cuadra Pasos, diplomat and aging intellectual leader of Nicaragua's historic Conservative Party, there were two types of countries under international law: the intervening and the intervened.[49] Nicaragua had once been an intervening country, especially during the dictatorship of José Santos Zelaya in the late nineteenth century, but had become in the twentieth century a "field of interventions." Given this precarious position, Cuadra Pasos believed Nicaragua must resist further intervention lest the political, economic, and cultural power of the United States upend the social order as it had during the Marine occupations of the early twentieth century. Pedro Joaquín Chamorro and other younger Conservatives who came of age under the Somoza dictatorship believed that, although US intervention had created many of their country's problems, US policies of nonintervention perpetuated them. Chamorro argued that US ambassadors practiced nonintervention in the same way that Pontius Pilate had, using the Somozas as local proxies to crucify the nation.[50] To bring about the right kind of intervention, the younger generation of Conservative activists would rally around a dynamic new leader, Fernando Agüero, and call on the United States and the Organization of American States to fulfill the antidictatorial promise of the Alliance for Progress.

The first major US interventions of the Alliance for Progress era did not go well. The botched Bay of Pigs invasion had caused a backlash of anti-interventionist sentiment among Latin American leaders who feared a revival of gunboat diplomacy. In the Dominican Republic, where the United States was using overt and covert means to bring about the country's first free elections in decades, policymakers resisted making the volatile transition there a "showcase" for the Alliance for Progress.[51] US intervention would help elect Juan Bosch, a leading member of the Caribbean antidictatorial network, in 1962, but Washington had little confidence in his government's ability to bring the stability needed to prevent the radical left from taking power.

Policy planners instead proposed Nicaragua as a test case for democratic transition, in hopes of demonstrating the antidictatorial bona fides of the Alliance without risking a collapse that might benefit the radical left.[52] Unlike in the Dominican Republic, in Nicaragua a stable transition could be virtually guaranteed because the democratization strategy was created by Luis Somoza in collaboration with US ambassador Aaron S. Brown. Embassy officials reconciled the idea of allowing the scion of the region's last dynastic dictatorship to choose his own successor, Nicaraguan foreign minister René Schick, by claiming that new foreign aid practices could be used to guarantee the new president's independence.[53]

The success of the democratization program depended on more than Somoza family cooperation. Though the Alliance for Progress was designed to prevent leftist insurrection, in Nicaragua the primary threat to stability came not from the left but from the Conservative opposition to the Somoza-controlled Liberal Party. Between 1956 and 1960, there were more than sixty attempted uprisings against the Somoza government, and in 1961 alone there were at least twenty-three.[54] Many of these uprisings were sponsored by members of the Conservative Party rooted in the country's landholding elite and headed by Emiliano Chamorro, great-uncle of Pedro Joaquín Chamorro. General Chamorro, often referred to as the "last caudillo" in the 1960s, had played a central role in the civil wars of the early twentieth century. Under his leadership, Conservative elites carried out coups and countercoups that frequently involved brief demonstrations of military heroism followed by negotiations with the United States and Liberal opponents, leading to "pacts" between the governing parties.[55] Insurrection, or even its threat, served as a means of gaining access to power in the absence of free elections under the Somoza regime.

Insurrection also served to maintain the vision of elite manhood that Conservatives believed justified their economic and social power.[56]

Nicaragua's Conservatives had long ties with the antidictatorial movement that helped inspire the Alliance for Progress. José Figueres had feuded over many years with Anastasio Somoza García as each leader sponsored invasions of the other's country. Shortly after the successful revolt against Fulgencio Batista in Cuba, Figueres helped sponsor an invasion of Nicaragua to overthrow Luis Somoza. In May of 1959, young members of the country's elite led by Enrique Lacayo Farfán of a dissident branch of the Liberal Party and Pedro Joaquín Chamorro of the Conservative Party flew into the rural *comarcas* Olama and Los Mollejones to instigate an expected national revolt.[57] The Cuban government had declined to support Chamorro's invasion, backing instead a group of invaders based in Honduras whom Che Guevara allegedly pledged to join should they form a beachhead within the country.[58] Chamorro's invading forces expected to be met by internal supporting auxiliaries and a nationwide strike, but the strike failed to materialize in large part because Nicaraguan workers refused participate.[59]

The invasion ended after two weeks as the invaders made a total surrender. The upper-class background of the invaders, who were from the country's most prominent families, prevented the government from killing them. It did not, however, prevent the use of torture as punishment, and Chamorro and other Conservatives broadcast their treatment as political prisoners in a form of elite *testimonio*.[60] His confrontations with the dictatorship generated authority for Chamorro within the Conservative movement, and descriptions of tortures committed on the bodies of members of the elite served as a synecdoche for the defilement of the national body. These descriptions also generated interest among networks connected to the antidictatorial movement such as the Inter-American Press Association and the Inter-American Association for Democracy and Freedom, groups that connected exile communities across the Americas and provided access to the US intelligence community.[61]

Having failed at insurrection, the younger generation of Conservatives looked to the Alliance for Progress as a possible bearer of social and economic reform. These young Conservatives, who founded the Unión Nacional de Acción Popular (UNAP) in the 1950s, helped bring the oratorically gifted ophthalmologist Fernando Agüero to power in the party as a new face of Conservative leadership.[62] They attempted to reconcile their party's roots in traditionalist Catholicism and feudal social structures with the growing clamor for social reform across Latin America, distancing themselves from the previous generation much as Luis Somoza attempted to distance his family from the stigma of dictatorship. Pedro Joaquín Chamorro worked with Reinaldo Téfel and Emilio Álvarez Montalván to alter the foundations of Conservative ideology to align it with the burgeoning Social Christian movements growing in popularity across Latin America, inspired by the encyclicals of Popes Leo XIII and Pius XI.[63] Like such movements in Chile and elsewhere, these movements often shared roots with the militant Catholicism of the Spanish Falange, which in Nicaragua had inspired the country's homegrown version of religious ultranationalism. Despite the wealth of many exponents, the communitarian ideals of Social Christians were often at odds with capitalism, leading Luis Somoza to dub them "little red fishes swimming in holy water."[64]

In the spirit of antibourgeois movements from the 1930s, younger Conservatives criticized the "plutocracy" of Grenada's Calle Atravesada, home to many of the wealthy landowners who funded anti-Somoza campaigns.[65] Members of the Conservative establishment accused the youth of pushing for reform out of a "guilt complex" over their families' roles in bringing about US intervention in the early twentieth century.[66] Even as young Conservatives distanced themselves from their party's reactionary past, they struggled to reconcile the growing demand for social change with their traditionalist values. Conservatives welcomed the Alliance for Progress's emphasis on governmental reform but worried that tax reform would allow the government to channel Conservative wealth to the Liberal Party. Chamorro and *La Prensa* found in Alliance doctrines of "self-help" a way to endorse their ideal of elite-guided social reform while bypassing the central government.[67] The Conservative landed oligarchy vehemently resisted comprehensive land reform, so *La Prensa* gave favorable press to the piecemeal reforms of large proprietors, as when the Wheelock family gave several hundred acres of land to their workers while maintaining their estates intact.[68] *La Prensa*'s management also touted their own voluntary measures to provide worker benefits without the need for labor agitation.[69]

"We want democracy, not dollars," Agüero told growing crowds of supporters who gathered to hear his speeches in towns all over the country, stoking dissatisfaction with the US emphasis on economic over political development in Nicaragua.[70] Without outside intervention, Agüero believed, a truly free election was impossible given the level of political and economic control the Somoza family exercised. Agüero echoed Latin American leaders of the democratic left who called for limiting Organization of American States (OAS) membership to democratic states and supported collective action to ensure free elections. Rómulo Betancourt, José Figueres, and others led a movement to demand a more robust form of hemispheric intervention that acceded to US wishes for an anticommunist crusade on condition of a wider pro-democracy campaign.[71] The United States joined with the majority of Latin American governments in 1959 to dismiss these proposals, although the OAS put in place a means to allow election observers when invited by local regimes.[72] It also created the Inter-American Commission on Human Rights, though with a limited mandate for investigation.[73]

The younger generation of Nicaragua's opposition agitated for a united front among the Conservative elite in favor of pro-democratic intervention. They searched the pronouncements of the US State Department for signs of antidictatorial disposition, interpreting US equivocations as signs of interventionist intent. Emilio Álvarez Montalván asserted that it was anti-interventionist sentiment on the part of Latin American oligarchs and military leaders, rather than US opposition, that prevented support for Betancourt's 1959 initiative to reconstruct the OAS around human rights and democracy.[74] Conservative elders Emiliano Chamorro and Carlos Cuadra Pasos admonished the younger generation that tearing down the "wall of non-intervention" could open an interventionist floodgate, once again inundating the "field of sovereignty, economy, and culture" with the influence of the United States.[75]

A submission to the Inter-American Human Rights Commission drafted by the younger Conservatives claimed that the electoral struggle in Nicaragua made it the site of the decisive battle in the hemisphere against tyranny.[76] The exposition quoted Kennedy's preelection proclamations of support for inter-American human rights and democracy, as well as his condemnations of the "co-dictatorship" of the Somoza brothers in Nicaragua. The submission also documented 150 cases of human rights abuses by the Guardia Nacional, including the murder of students and campesinos and the use of violent force to break up opposition political demonstrations. The submission proclaimed that the same means of US-led democratic intervention that had freed the "erstwhile enslaved Dominican Republic" could also free Nicaragua.[77]

In his frequent visits with the US ambassador, Agüero warned of a "blood bath" should the United States not take action to ensure free elections.[78] Upon expressions of US unwillingness to intervene in "internal issues," Agüero and the Conservatives attempted to call on the support of the antidictatorial coalition. Though Berle was no longer in the State Department, the presence of his associates, such as Teodoro Moscoso, gave Conservatives hope that the department might be willing to intervene on their behalf. In a private meeting with opposition members in El Salvador in June 1962, Conservatives claimed that Moscoso had compared the Somoza family to the Trujillos in the Dominican Republic and asserted that the Somozas' political backwardness was the country's chief obstacle to progress.[79] In August, Moscoso proclaimed in a magazine interview that US funding through the Alliance for Progress would be channeled through the political opposition rather than the central government.[80] Luis Somoza called this an "incitement to assassination," and the US embassy privately disavowed Moscoso's comments.[81]

In the absence of overt intervention against the Somozas, Agüero and his associates held out hope that the United States might still intervene covertly. Adolf Berle, though out of power in Washington, used his contacts with intelligence agencies and Latin American leaders to encourage the Nicaraguan opposition to believe that an anti-Somoza intervention might still be possible. Agüero traveled in 1962 to New York, where Berle mediated a discussion between Agüero and Luis Manuel Debayle, uncle of the Nicaraguan president.[82] Agüero had been encouraged to travel to the United States by Sacha Volman of the CIA-associated Institute for International Labor Research, who was at the time attempting to guide Juan Bosch in the Dominican Republic through a post-Trujillo democratic transition.[83] When word of this meeting reached the State Department, officials worked to assure the Somoza family and Agüero himself that Agüero was not the "chosen instrument" of US foreign policy.[84] Even while encouraging Agüero's hopes that the US government might force the ouster of the Somozas, Berle tried to dissuade him from setting his sights too high. There did not seem to be any great public call for a "conservative restoration," and even should the Somozas fall it could take some time after the deposition of a dictator to restore functioning democracy.[85]

Once it became clear that the US government would not support Agüero's accession to power as it had supported Bosch, the Conservatives attempted to force the United States to take action. Perceiving the importance US officials placed on a consensual transfer of power in Nicaragua, Agüero and his associates hoped to discredit the democratic transition by urging their supporters to boycott the election and abstain from voting.[86] Accompanying this abstention strategy was a warning to the US embassy that dissident factions would "take to the streets" and force a US intervention similar to that of 1927, which had sparked the Sandino rebellion.[87] The Conservative announcement of an election boycott convinced President Luis Somoza to allow a handful of OAS election observers the day of voting, but the United States took no further action.[88] To maintain his leadership in the face of the failure of this international gambit, on the day of the election in January 1963, Agüero, with a pistol tucked into his belt, led a small group into downtown Managua.[89] After allegedly taking refuge in a beauty salon, Agüero and his supporters were promptly arrested by the Guardia Nacional.

The election of René Schick to office marked the end of the antidictatorial alliance in Nicaragua. The members of the Conservative Party outside of power did not rise in rebellion as Agüero had promised. Instead, they took part in a transformation of the Alliance for Progress into a program of elite consensus-building that fused public and private sectors. In doing so, the Alliance successfully defused the threat of elite insurrection and built a broad coalition of support for US foreign policy and the Schick government around the goals of democratic modernization. The Alliance also created a path to power for the third and final Somoza president, Anastasio Somoza Debayle.

Integrating the Conservatives

The abstention of the Conservative opposition from the 1963 election put Nicaragua's status as democratic showcase in peril. By this time, critics were pointing out that the Alliance for Progress was not in fact encouraging a flowering of democracy in Latin America but might be encouraging a return of military authoritarianism.[90] To bolster the semblance of democratic government in Nicaragua, State Department planners and US embassy officials turned to Nicaragua's position on the Central American isthmus, Ernesto Cardenal's "doubtful strait," and the country's position within the burgeoning Central American Common Market as a means to salvage the idea that Nicaragua was engaged in a transition to democracy.

To build support for the Schick government, embassy officials used the structures of the CACM to depoliticize Nicaragua's economy and build consensus around the new president. In the same way the aid program had supported the presidency of Luis Somoza, the program would now be used to give the new president "backbone" to act independently.[91] As the Alliance was premised on intergovernmental support, US officials rejected the plan supported by Berle and Moscoso to overtly disburse aid directly to political groups.[92] Redefining political outsiders as the "private sector" and using the institutions of the Common Market, however, made possible a broadening of the Alliance by encouraging economic power-sharing among the feuding Liberal and Conservative factions. Despite the official practice of providing development funds exclusively to the public sector, US officials encouraged CABEI to channel loans for industrialization to the Corporación Nicaragüense de Inversiones, a private institution managed by Liberals and Conservatives with some independence from the Somozas.[93] INCAE, the business school created as part of the regional integration movement, was the first institution to be funded directly by the US government rather than through the Nicaraguan government.[94]

To broaden support for the Alliance for Progress, the US embassy began a series of programs to "strengthen grassroots democracy" and "'go behind the Somozas' to strengthen the will and ability of the citizenry to carry on in the difficult period up to and following the 1963 elections."[95] Though couched in the language of community development, the new programs that took shape distinguished themselves from earlier community development programs by putting politics at the center of aid. Unlike previous visions of community development as a form of bottom-up nation-building as exemplified in programs in Mexico and India, the new policy placed political elites at the center of a nexus of aid distribution.[96] Though the embassy acknowledged that so-called grassroots groups were themselves members of a "landed gentry," they were essential for national stability.[97] These programs thrived in Nicaragua because the political opposition actively sought the support of the US government, while the United States sought to increase stability by decentralizing Alliance programs. If antidictatorial political intervention was no longer an option, opposition forces still held on to the belief that the US government could be turned to their own benefit in distributing other forms of economic and social power.

US officials encouraged the cooperation of the different political factions in the disbursement of aid and allotted access to scholarships and small community development grants to organizations independently of the central government. The Instituto Nicaragüense de Desarrollo (INDE) was the first of many nongovernmental organizations that would act as intermediary between the US government and the people of Nicaragua, organized around INDE's identity as representative of the "private sector" rather than a political faction.[98] In practice, the group consisted of members of the Liberal Party who maintained some independence from the Somoza family. The embassy brought dissident Conservatives into the Alliance by creating nationwide committees for social development, naming Conservative Party members with ties to the Social Christian movement such as Emilio Álvarez Montalván to important positions.[99]

The result of these programs for democratization illustrate the new definition of democracy that was taking shape in State Department practice. Even US officials recognized that elections were corrupt and rigged against opposition parties. Democratization could nonetheless be achieved by bringing regime opponents into the political system by encouraging their cooperation not directly with the government, which opposition movements shunned as under the control of the Somozas, but with intermediary organizations with international ties. The US embassy encouraged the use of scholarships and training programs as a form of patronage, distributing prestigious grants based directly on political affiliation. Grant recipients then provided a network that the embassy used to disseminate news of the Alliance in Nicaragua.[100]

After the election of Schick, the Conservative Party's elder statesmen came out in opposition to the party's long-held traditions of antigovernment insurrection. To cool insurrectionary impulses, the Schick government announced a general amnesty for anti-Somoza rebels.[101] Emiliano Chamorro, the nonagenarian Conservative leader who had led dozens of antigovernment rebellions during his lifetime, joined Carlos Cuadra Pasos in declaring that the time for street fighting was over. Agüero's farcical display of revolutionary zeal in downtown Managua had only gained ridicule for the party.[102] According to reports received by the embassy, the Conservative establishment had not joined in Agüero's "simulacrum" of rebellion because the party elite wanted to wait until the cotton crop was picked.[103]

Thanks to the easy credit of the Alliance, Central American economies were growing at an astonishing pace, as trade in the Common Market increased more than 300 percent in five years.[104] Nicaragua not only outshone its neighbors but even attained the highest growth rate in the hemisphere in 1965. This boom caused a "veritable euphoria" for economic expansion and industrialization, and the new power-sharing premises of the Alliance assured the distribution of credit among elite factions.[105] Though premised on building national autonomy through agricultural and industrial diversification, much of the Alliance-sponsored credit went toward expanding production of the "white gold" of cotton instead of new crops and industries.

The various factions of the Conservative Party looked to the CACM as a potential panacea. Social Christian leaders believed that the CACM could help implement the Social Christian plan for a humanized capitalism.[106] Wealthy cotton grower Joaquín Zavala tried to transform his magazine *Revista Conservadora* from a mouthpiece for Conservative Party ideology into a regional force, changing its name to *Revista Conservadora del Pensamiento Centroamericano*. Its editorials and forums promoted economic integration as both a political and an economic project. Zavala earned praise as a moderating force among the Conservatives and solicited assistance from the US embassy when the magazine ran into economic difficulties.[107] *La Prensa* too welcomed the new economic horizons, arguing that as political caudillos were dying off, so too the "patron" of the past must give way to the "businessman" of the future for the economic good of the nation.[108] The paper used funds approved by the US embassy from CABEI to update its printing presses and began a weekly socioeconomic page to disseminate information about industrial development.[109]

The newspaper hewed to a firm anti-Somoza stance while looking hopefully toward signs that the Schick government might be independent of Somoza control.

The economic boom was made possible by ample credit from CACM institutions. The boom was also fueled by sheer imagination, as when State Department officials proposed that the prospect of a new transoceanic canal be used as a way of propping up the Schick government. Thanks to anti-American protests in Panama, the United States considered creating a second "nuclear" canal, using atomic energy for excavation. Nicaragua was prominent on the list of possible sites, which included Mexico, Panama, and Colombia. Though as embassy officials acknowledged, "no responsible Nicaraguan" believed that a canal would ever materialize, the mere possibility helped fuel among the country's economic elite a nationalist fervor and avidity at the prospect of the project, estimated at one hundred million dollars.[110] Of Conservative elites questioned by *Revista Conservadora*, only Pedro Joaquín Chamorro came out against the canal as an imperialist boondoggle.[111]

The administration of President Lyndon Baines Johnson made explicit the turn against democratic interventionism begun in the Kennedy administration. In the Dominican Republic, the Bosch government produced by the antidictatorial alliance came to an ignominious end with a coup, and the Johnson administration intervened militarily in 1965 to prevent Bosch's return. Nicaragua provided a 164-man rifle company as part of the occupying Inter-American Force. Conservative Party members, once avid for a Dominican-style intervention within Nicaragua, supported the US action in a declaration they shared with the US ambassador before making it public.[112]

Under the Schick government, the Alliance for Progress bought peace among elite factions who agreed to substitute economic competition for political rivalry, turning the antidictatorial alliance and regional development into programs that bolstered the central government by distributing aid largesse through civil society. US officials praised the CACM as virtually the only success story in the Alliance, and the US ambassador called Nicaragua "the most promising Central American Republic."[113] When the Johnson administration sought to revitalize the Alliance in South America, Rostow proposed a regional development plan that applied Central America's model of integration to all of Latin America.[114] Programs that openly funded civil society as in Nicaragua would become important throughout Latin America after it became public knowledge in the late 1960s that the CIA was funding political parties and civil society organizations worldwide. The congressional creators of Title IX of the Foreign Assistance Act would look to Central America as a site of innovative programs to rebuild US foreign aid around new doctrines of participatory development.[115] Yet the programs that made possible Nicaragua's fragile peace and prosperity would allow the ascension of Anastasio Somoza Debayle to the presidency and convince many Nicaraguans that insurrection was the only avenue of escape.

Public Space and Utopian Space

Even in the late 1960s, the Alliance for Progress still held radical potential. In 1966, on the archipelago of Solentiname at the southern end of Lake Nicaragua, poet, priest, and soon-to-be revolutionary Ernesto Cardenal founded a utopian community. Cardenal had developed the idea for a lay religious community in collaboration with poet and Trappist monk Thomas Merton and Cardenal's cousin, coeditor of La Prensa, Pablo Antonio Cuadra.[116] While their relatives in the Conservative Party took part in political combat and economic production, Cuadra and Cardenal attempted to place Nicaragua at the vanguard of Latin American culture by reviving the country's religious and poetic traditions.

Solentiname became a focal point for Conservative elite hopes for regenerating the spiritual life of the nation as prospects for political change dwindled. José Coronel Urtecho wrote that "progress has left [the archipelago] completely uncontaminated and outside its routes," making it the perfect site to regenerate Conservative values.[117] As the country's landed elite embraced the mechanized agriculture fueling the cotton boom and the industrial consumerism fostered by the CACM, Solentiname provided a site to renew the foundations of Conservative nationalism.[118] Believing their authority to govern grew from a rapport between themselves and the country's poor campesino majority, Conservatives worried that this connection was diminishing because of the economic boom, to the detriment of both campesino and elite.[119]

The country's most prosperous Conservative families donated money to what soon became an experiment in both religious and economic transformation. Taking advantage of growing emphasis on technical development for local agriculture under the Alliance for Progress, Cardenal turned Solentiname into an experiment in cooperative farming.[120] He brought technical advisers from US and Nicaraguan government and nongovernmental organizations like the American Institute for Free Labor Development (AIFLD), INDE, and the Instituto de Fomento Nacional (INFONAC) to train the campesinos of the islands in production for the market. Cardenal took advantage of the easy credit encouraged by the CACM institutions to take out bank loans to build a pier to serve his community.[121] The produce of the commune was then shipped from the archipelago to the nearby city of San Carlos on the launch christened *Alianza para el Progreso*, bought with funds from the US government.[122]

In January 1967, a few weeks before Nicaragua's scheduled election, Aaron Brown wrote to Washington to allay fears of unrest. Nicaragua was the "most promising Central American Republic," and Central America was widely believed to be the most promising region in what was left of the Alliance for Progress.[123] Since the election of Schick, head of the Guardia Nacional Anastasio Somoza Debayle ("Tacho") had made no secret of his desire to become president of Nicaragua. Embassy officials expressed their dismay: "How could he be so stupid," they wondered, as to want to be president as his family's businesses prospered and the United States continued to pour money into Military Assistance Programs for the Guardia?[124] Combining military and market imperatives, Somoza used advisers from INCAE to give his election campaign a technocratic style, promising to reform the CACM and turn the Guardia Nacional toward civic action and development.

Conservatives rallied around Fernando Agüero once again, bringing in other opposition parties to create the Unión Nacional Opositora (UNO). They pressured the embassy to "do something" about Tacho's candidacy, garnering only reiterated professions of US nonintervention in internal politics. As in 1963, Agüero warned of bloodshed should the United States not take action to prevent another Somoza in the presidency.[125] Ambassador Brown bemusedly noted that Conservatives continued to chase the "human rights will o' the wisp" just as they had during the previous election, and with just as little result.[126] Conservatives apprised the embassy of the plots and counterplots within the elite: one member told the ambassador that a relative had tried and failed to buy arms in Costa Rica. Others warned that communists were trying to use the election campaign to stoke violence in the country.[127]

Brown expressed disbelief that Conservatives would risk their economic position in a revolutionary venture, while also recognizing that politics was reaching an impasse. "Maybe Nicaragua needs to pass through the ordeal by fire," he wrote; "the catharsis could be healthy." Schick died in office of a heart attack in August 1966, further reducing the possibility of an independent election process. UNO members argued that the voter registration process had been corrupted by a Liberal Party machine that padded rolls with the names of dead, underage, and fictitious voters. The US embassy recognized that fraud was rampant but also that Tacho's victory was assured given the effectiveness of the Liberal Party patronage machine. Agüero asserted that given the depth of corruption, election-day observers would be insufficient, and the election itself should be postponed.

On January 22, 1967, supporters of Agüero rallied in downtown Managua. Before the election, street violence had been on the rise. Somoza proponents used retired Guardia soldiers to intimidate the opposition.[128] Conservatives formed their own street-action group, CIVES, that brought together young partisans of the FSLN with Agüero's forces. There were rumors that Agüero was using contacts with the US embassy to foster a military coup and that there were Social Christian sympathizers among the Guardia. Some hoped Agüero might even have the backing of General Gustavo Montiel, head of the Guardia now that Tacho had stepped down to run for president.[129] Agüero and *La Prensa* attempted to entice a restive Guardia with promised salary reforms for the rank and file to share the wealth monopolized by the corrupt brass.[130] In the streets of Managua, the popular campaign song "Con Agüero Muero" played while Conservative protesters and leftist student groups incongruously shouted "Viva la Guardia Nacional."

Tensions rose as the campaign rally stretched past its government-imposed curfew. According to later reports, Agüero was awaiting action by the Guardia, which he believed was going to take power and postpone the election, a move to be ratified by a Conservative march up Avenida Roosevelt to the presidential palace. When Guardia support failed to materialize, someone in the crowd shot at the surrounding troops, who responded by opening fire. The Guardia response was quick and concerted thanks to the distribution of radios through the US Military Assistance Program only days earlier.[131] The leaders of the opposition took refuge in the nearby Gran Hotel, which was primarily occupied by American tourists visiting the country for the celebration of the centenary of poet Rubén Darío. After a tense standoff, the US embassy acted as intermediary assuring the safe passage of Conservative leadership to their homes, though several them were later arrested. The embassy reported an estimated death toll of only sixteen but received reports of trucks full of bodies being hauled away from downtown.[132]

Anastasio Somoza Debayle won the election on February 5, 1967. US embassy officials met with opposition forces in the months following to try to assure social peace. When Conservative representatives who had received seats in the National Assembly despite what they claimed was a fraudulent election consulted with the US ambassador over whether to occupy their places, he reported telling them that "parliamentary opposition is essential to all democracies." He then added, "They agreed."[133] Fernando Agüero, mocked by Conservatives and embassy officials alike for his cowardice in hiding behind hostages during the Gran Hotel affair, soon began negotiations leading to a final pact with the Somoza government.

On the archipelago of Solentiname, Ernesto Cardenal's utopian community was failing as an agricultural cooperative. As the easy credit of the CACM boom dried up, the commune supported itself by selling primitivist artwork created by Solentiname's inhabitants.[134] After the election debacle of 1967, Cardenal would accept invitations to travel to Cuba, after which he began to formulate a fusion of Marxism and liberation theology that would provide an important ideological underpinning for the Sandinista rebellion. The community at Solentiname became a gathering point for young members of the opposition disillusioned with the failure of political solutions to their country's problems. Many of them, such as Carlos Agüero, nephew of the failed presidential candidate, would radicalize in the coming years. Within a decade, Solentiname would become a launching point for insurrection against the Somoza dictatorship.

The massacre of 1967 and the collapse of the commune at Solentiname marked the end of the Alliance for Progress in Nicaragua. Over the course of less than a decade, the antidictatorial coalition and economic integration movement at the heart of the Alliance were reshaped. This process succeeded in creating a social peace by giving both Liberal and Conservative elites a stake in the promise of shared economic growth. The Conservatives, who had long used civil war and insurrection to gain access to state power, instead took part in the benefits of the Alliance to gain access to economic and social capital brought by US-sponsored programs. In accepting the practices of the Alliance for Progress, the Conservatives gave up the use of partisan warfare and exile invasion, the tools of the Caribbean Legion, as means of negotiating with the Somoza dictatorship. Instead the Conservatives came to rely on the hope that the US government might still be interested in undermining dictatorship and dynastic power in the region. This hope was unfounded, shown by US support for the accession of Anastasio Somoza Debayle to power in 1967 thanks to a highly managed election process. With the demise of this hope and the pact with Somoza by Fernando Agüero, the Conservative Party ended as a political force in Nicaragua. Erstwhile Conservatives such as Pedro Joaquín Chamorro would continue to attempt to form a civic opposition within Nicaragua, while the FSLN would come to monopolize the path of insurrection. Conservative youth, disaffected members of the middle class, and restive campesinos who had once taken part in the innumerable antistate insurrections sponsored by Conservative elites would now be left with the FSLN as the only option. The Alliance for Progress succeeded as counterinsurgency in defusing the threat of insurrection from Nicaragua's traditional elites. But in transforming Nicaragua's internal power struggles into Cold War struggles, the Alliance would make leftist insurrection the only viable option for political change.

Chapter 2

Decentering Managua

In Sergio Ramírez's short story "De las propiedades del sueño (I)," written before 1972, the political opposition of a small Latin American country experiments with "collective dreaming."[1] Should enough people concentrate their dreams on a single object, such as that "the tyrant be overthrown and the people take power," their dream could be realized. The only catch: the object of their dream must doze as well, but "tyrants never sleep." In "De las propiedades del sueño (II)," written after 1972, the tyrant in question leans on the balustrade of his palace atop the fortified hill overlooking his capital city.[2] He fantasizes that "North American sages" have invented an earthquake machine that could raze the city's buildings and streets, allowing "S.E.," Su Excelencia the dictator, to use "millions of dollars of donations and soft loans" to line his pockets, maintain martial law to keep his political opponents in jails buried under rubble, and rebuild the capital into the "rich and flourishing urban center" of which he had always dreamed. As he nods in reverie, a "ferocious roar . . . from the center of the earth" awakens him. This roar is the sound of the dictator's dream coming true, as Managua was shaken and destroyed by a massive earthquake on the night of December 23, 1972. The roar is also, for Ramírez, the sound of a people awakening to complete their own collective ambition to overthrow the power of a tyrant and his allies.

According to the scenario created by Ramírez, who went from exiled novelist to Sandinista militant to his country's vice president over the span of a decade, the 1972 earthquake and the reconstruction of Managua are central to the story of the Nicaraguan revolution. As with the Alliance for Progress a decade before, critics of the reconstruction attributed its inadequacy to lack of will in execution rather than inherent flaws in conception. For many observers afterward, the center of the story has been the corruption and misuse of foreign aid that opened the eyes of the country's population to the dictator's malfeasance.[3] What Ramírez's stories capture is the way that many Nicaraguans perceived the destruction and reconstruction of their capital city in relation to their own recent experience. To Nicaraguans, the dictator Anastasio Somoza Debayle, who dreamed of rebuilding a city in his own image, was himself a product of the decade of development promoted by the United States as a liberal alternative to communist revolution. The plans for reconstruction that re-created Managua were not a departure from the theories and practices of the prior decade, but their culmination.

The new city that grew out of the failed reconstruction process has been likened to a "deformed octopus," product of failed planning and notable for its fragmentation compared with the old urban center.[4] Despite appearances, Managua *was* rebuilt after the earthquake according to a design. The earthquake devastated the old Managua of crowded streets and small businesses, where people of different economic strata lived in close if sometimes tense proximity. The permanent destruction of the old city was, however, man-made. The new Managua that took the place of the old city was the product of the latest in urban and administrative theory. The old downtown was fenced off to prevent redevelopment, and a new city was encouraged to radiate out from the previous center. This new city, planners believed, would encourage more rational urban development than was possible in the old congested and dangerous city center. They also hoped that more modern urban development would resolve the central problem of authoritarian rule in Nicaragua. In the name of safety, economic efficiency, social harmony, and—most of all—deeply contradictory ideas of modernization, the Somoza regime, US and international planners, and private enterprise rebuilt Managua in a way that did not ease social tensions but augmented them and helped bring about the last major social revolution of the Cold War.

Planners and politicians in the United States and Latin America built their cooperative vision of hemispheric growth around an ideal of a modern, orderly urban environment whose structure would encourage economic growth and political participation. Despite critiques leveled against development practice from the right and left after the failures of US foreign aid policy in the 1960s, these ideals continued to be implemented during the presidency of Richard Nixon, though with important changes. Thanks to new US policies of overtly embracing illiberal regimes, Nicaragua became object of new itera-

tions of development policy after the 1972 earthquake. The planners who re-
designed Managua made it a site for design experiments seeking to overcome
the central tensions manifest during the previous decade of development and
counterinsurgency in Asia, Latin America, and US cities: the tensions between
wealth and poverty, the rural and the urban, and dictatorship and democracy.[5]
The planners remade the urban fabric of Managua on a grand scale, and fostered popular discontent and urban rebellion on an even grander scale, much
as in the United States.[6]

The new Managua that took shape following the earthquake conformed in
many ways to the planners' design. The city was safer from natural disaster,
spread out away from the old city center. The city was also more conducive to
planning and development, divided by class and economic function in the fash-
ion of North American cities. The new Managua did not, however, limit the
power of the dictatorship, but rather augmented it and inscribed it into the
structure of the city itself. The collective rejection of this new city would create
an unlikely alliance of the Nicaraguan Conservative elite, the radical left, and
Managua's poor against the Somoza dynasty and its US backers. This alliance
began to unite around a rejection of both the dictatorship and the new, modernized Managua that the dictatorship had built. The beginnings of a revolutionary alliance of the right and left coalesced around an alternative vision of
urban space as the place where national identity and class harmony resided.[7]
Their efforts would bring about the 1979 Nicaraguan revolution and center a
revived Cold War in Managua, where the dissonance between the promise and
reality of modernization led to revolt against the new city and the geopolitical
order that brought it about.

Space and Development before the Earthquake

The vision of hemispheric integration begun under the Alliance for Progress was
unraveling by the end of the 1960s, undone partly by its own success. The Central American Common Market, a key experiment in regional integration
and transnational institution-building, was successful in encouraging the free
movement of goods and money across the region, increasing intraregional
trade threefold in half a decade.[8] As money moved, so moved people, and migration between Central American countries was on the rise. Planners saw increased
migration as a hopeful sign: Nicaragua was predicted to soon require imported
laborers thanks to industrial takeoff, as the combination of low population density and high economic growth would attract workers from overconcentrated

areas such as El Salvador.[9] Instead of spurring further integration, the increase of migrant workers between El Salvador and Honduras triggered an explosion. The two countries went to war in the 1969 Hundred-Hour War, undoing in days the decades-long work of regional integration.[10]

The same economic forces driving international migration also fueled urbanization, as CACM-led export growth and international credit helped mechanized export agriculture penetrate rural areas. The policies of US and Latin American governments had long used urban space to resolve the contradictions of uneven development. Both US-trained social scientists and Latin American thinkers shared the belief that urban space was the preeminent site for creating states and citizens with capabilities and worldviews necessary for living in the modern world.[11] In the imagination of many Latin American elites, the distinction between the rural and the urban underwrote a dichotomy between civilization and barbarism that reached back to the European conquest of the Americas. During the 1960s, Latin American social scientists in Chile and elsewhere, often sponsored by US funding, began to assert that urban space was no longer resolving conflict, as "marginal" populations in crowded slums served as tinder for revolution.[12] Cities were becoming sites of crime and terrorism. Not only did the United States and allied governments fear the revolt of the global South against the metropolitan urban North touted at Cuba's Tricontinental Conference, but guerrilla movements once based in rural areas now allegedly thrived in urban space.[13]

Nicaragua's capital was—like Washington, D.C., before the US Civil War—a symbolic center of compromise between antagonistic factions. Managua was chosen as capital in the nineteenth century as neutral ground between the warring oligarchies of the cities of León and Granada. Originally a fishing village, Managua was destroyed by an earthquake in 1931 and reconstructed along the Spanish colonial model: a grid of streets centered on a cathedral and plaza.[14] The rebuilding of the city corresponded to the rise of Anastasio Somoza García, who built his power in the 1930s first as head of the US–created Guardia Nacional and then as president of Nicaragua, artfully cultivating and manipulating the traditional landed elite, Nicaragua's workers, and the US government. The power of the city and the Somoza dynasty grew in tandem, and their symbiosis embodied both the promise and peril of the modernization process that US and Latin American elites propagated as a pan-American ideal.[15]

In the 1950s, thanks to a booming agro-industry in the countryside geared toward cotton export, Managua's population expanded rapidly, growing from forty thousand in 1920 to four hundred thousand in 1972 and from a quarter to half the country's urban population.[16] Consolidation of land in the countryside combined with growth in small urban industry brought by Nicaragua's new wealth caused peasants to migrate in large numbers to cities. Though Nicaragua's smaller cities experienced some growth, the largest economic expansion took place in the capital, home to most of the nation's industrial development. In the boom years of the 1950s and 1960s the downtown area's tightly packed streets became the site of burgeoning commerce and consumption by a small but growing middle class.[17]

After the bloody 1967 election, Nicaraguan elites and the US government accepted that Anastasio "Tacho" Somoza Debayle's rule in Nicaragua was based on force. Ambassador Aaron Brown stepped down after the election, replaced by more overtly pro-Somoza figures who urged strengthening US military and economic aid. Policymakers celebrated the fact that despite Latin America's rising wave of nationalism and anti-*yanquismo*, Nicaragua remained the US government's "best friend in the hemisphere." They claimed that the recent unrest was the exception to the rule, as Tacho had created a system in which he could "command instant obedience and execution."[18] In an attempt to improve the military's image, USAID sponsored a program in the 1960s to rebrand the Guardia as an urban civilian police force instead of a praetorian guard. USAID provided uniforms and small arms to distinguish the police from the army and thus ameliorate the appearance of Managua as a city under military occupation. The police nevertheless remained part of the Guardia and under the control of Somoza. On USAID's advice Somoza gave them new functions such as enforcing traffic laws, also creating a unit composed solely of women to help mitigate the dictatorship's brutal image.[19]

The deterioration of the Alliance for Progress and the collapse of Latin American integration suited the Nixon administration's approach to hemispheric affairs. Administration officials were critical of US domestic programs confronting racism and urban poverty, as well as the rhetoric of the global Great Society.[20] Under Nixon, domestic and international aid programs were reconstructed around the principles of federalism, devolving authority over shrinking social welfare budgets to local governments while increasing direct support for the apparatuses of "law and order."[21] Nixon expressed animosity to State Department attempts at promoting liberalization of authoritarian regimes.[22] He also personally opposed US funding for housing programs, which had been central to Kennedy and Johnson administration efforts to build alliances with Latin America's anticommunist democratic left around urban reform.[23]

Nicaragua exemplified the Nixon administration's desire to reduce US commitments abroad by devolving power to authoritarian governments. Nixon and Somoza expressed personal admiration for each other while providing mutual assistance.[24] Nixon's choice for ambassador to Nicaragua, Turner Shelton, was known less for his diplomatic savvy than for his closeness to Nixon's inner circle and his ties to shadowy businessmen like Howard Hughes. A former low-level State Department official, Shelton brought himself to Nixon's attention by sending a letter to Henry Kissinger decrying the "strong emotional ties to former Presidents," "professional elitism," "lack of responsiveness," "conformity," and "inbred" nature of the State Department, with an attached list of names of the worst offenders.[25] Kissinger forwarded the memo to the president with a long note suggesting Shelton be given a position from which to keep an eye on the department. A few months later, over State Department objections, Shelton was appointed ambassador to Nicaragua. He became renowned for his obsequious behavior toward Somoza, prompting complaints that he behaved more like a courtier than an ambassador.[26] With Shelton's assistance, the US president gave personal attention to Nicaraguan trade concerns, while Nicaragua provided one of the only unstinting pro-US voices in global forums amid a rising tide of North-South confrontation.

According to Nicaragua's anti-Somoza elite, preearthquake Managua expressed in disguised form the contradictions of power that had fueled the city's wealth.[27] While Managua's center thrived with supermarkets, theaters, and skyscrapers, it was surrounded by ever-growing slums whose inhabitants had been denied the promise of a better life that had attracted them to the city. The Conservative elite took economic advantage of the boom, while the elite's cultural vanguard at La Prensa looked askance at the "attractive and repulsive" qualities of urban growth.[28] With the benefits of commerce came materialism, manifest inequality, and dictatorship, all made possible through collusion between Liberal and Conservative elites. For Pedro Joaquín Chamorro, while the city contained the country's greatest prosperity, it also contained impoverished communities such as Acahualinca—an informal community constructed around the city's waste dump a few blocks from the commercial center—in conditions worse than any rural area.[29] Inspired by a newly reform-minded Catholic church and a global student movement, many middle- and upper-class Nicaraguans began in the late 1960s to abandon hopes of political reform and turn instead to ameliorating the conditions of poverty in their midst.[30] Just as this movement was beginning to build momentum, natural calamity transfigured the urban landscape, and with it the political future of the country.

Reconstruction and Decentralization of *Managua terremoteada*

The earthquake that struck Managua the night of December 23, 1972, measured 6.2 on the Richter scale, relatively small for such a destructive event. Nonetheless, an estimated 10,000 Managuans lost their lives; 20,000 were seriously injured; and 250,000 were left homeless.[31] The earthquake laid waste to the city's commercial, governmental, and residential core. The earthquake had special destructive force because it took place very close to the surface and in the center of Managua's concentrated downtown area, under which lay three major fault lines. The homes of the poor and middle classes that were concentrated in the city center and constructed of *taquezal*, structures of wood and mud, fell immediately. Many government and commercial buildings made of steel and concrete cracked and collapsed in on themselves. Only a handful of buildings of recent construction remained standing. After the shaking subsided, the closely packed buildings provided fodder for a fire that lasted for days. The city's fire trucks lay under rubble.[32]

Aid poured into Nicaragua from all over the world in response to news of a destroyed city that observers compared to Hiroshima or Nagasaki in 1945.[33] The Nicaraguan government was powerless to deal with the situation, as the Guardia dissolved spontaneously and its troops began to help family members flee or participate in the widespread looting. Order was restored by the declaration of martial law and the assistance of US troops from the Canal Zone. The Guardia took control over distribution of relief aid, and rumors began to spread of misappropriation by the regime.[34] The US Embassy recognized that some aid had been misused, but held that this was the result of the unusual circumstances of chaos as opposed to the inherent corruption of the regime.[35] As Managua's residents fled either to the city's outskirts or to other nearby towns, General Somoza ordered the downtown evacuated and surrounded it with barbed wire.

Given the near-total destruction of downtown Managua, as depicted in figure 2.1, rebuilding the city gave planners and politicians the opportunity to design a new urban space. And as Managua was universally perceived as the vital center of Nicaragua, to reimagine Managua was to open the possibility of a reimagined Nicaragua. The most fundamental and obvious fact about life in Nicaragua—that its political and economic life was dominated by one man— was also the most difficult to address. After the earthquake, Somoza declared himself the head of the Emergency Reconstruction Committee and made little attempt to disguise his near-total power. For US policymakers, the problem of what to do with Somoza was pivotal, but the delicate political situation deterred

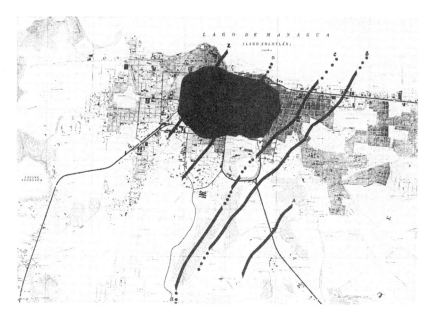

Figure 2.1. A graphic illustration of the totality of the downtown's destruction, showing the city's numerous fault lines (Kates et al., "Human Impact of the Managua Earthquake," 984). Courtesy of the American Association for the Advancement of Science.

openly debating a solution. Ambassador Shelton and President Nixon never wavered in their support for Somoza.[36]

The week after the earthquake, President Nixon devised a plan to use the disaster as an opportunity to advertise US generosity and support for Nicaragua by flying in person to the ruined city to deliver an aid check and bring supplies.[37] His advisers warned him that such a stunt could backfire, and not just because there were still decaying bodies and possibly remaining survivors under the rubble. The advisers thought that images of the president in the middle of a destroyed city might remind Americans of the war in Vietnam, as Operation Linebacker II accelerated the US bombing of Hanoi. The images might likewise remind Americans of their country's own urban crisis and lead them to ask, "Why are you worried about Nicaragua and you're not worried about our inner cities here?" Nixon sent a special envoy instead.[38]

Though America's conflict-ridden cities in the 1970s might seem to have offered little worth emulating, they were nonetheless taken as models by the planners who worked to reconceive Managua. A group of experts who came to Managua to conduct a comparative study of postdisaster development looked for precedent to the 1906 earthquake that devastated San Francisco. Ignoring the different circumstances in Managua and San Francisco, the experts took San Francisco's recovery and subsequent development into one of the continent's wealthiest cities as "the normal evolutionary model of urban growth in the wake of disaster."[39] In their report, which would be cited repeatedly in decades to come, these specialists argued that the segregation of urban commercial space from residential space and the segregation of the rich from the poor were inevitable processes that the earthquake had simply sped up. This evolutionary assumption that Nicaragua would, with the help of benevolent professionals, recapitulate the history of the United States from an earlier era underlay the consensus about planning.[40]

Because US aid programs had been designed around a liberal vision of Nicaragua's future modeled after the United States, many planners and State Department officials were less comfortable than Nixon and Shelton with giving Somoza uncritical support in reconstructing the city. In cables to the State Department, Ambassador Shelton lauded the consummate skill showed by Tacho after the quake, calling him the "indispensable man." The State Department and aid agencies were less comfortable acknowledging the total power of Somoza and referred to him alternatively as "the general," "the president," or most euphemistically "President of the National Emergency Committee."[41] This labeling presented the impression that these offices could be held by different individuals rather than a single "indispensable man."

The Nicaraguan elite was also critical of Somoza, but their compromises with the regime made it difficult to act. After the 1967 massacre and election, the opposition Conservative Party created a "pact" of alliance with the general brokered by the US embassy, guaranteeing their representation in the rubber-stamp legislature in exchange for cooperation. To bypass constitutional limits on succeeding himself as president, Somoza installed a junta including two Liberal Party members and Conservative Fernando Agüero, who had abandoned his insurrectionary stances from the prior decade—leading to a final break between Pedro Joaquín Chamorro and Agüero.[42] In his acerbic editorials in the opposition paper *La Prensa*, Chamorro lampooned Somoza as the "man with a thousand titles." Chamorro sardonically referred to Somoza as "the national hero" or, more ominously, the "man in the black limousine," whom Managuans saw from a distance as he drove past their shantytowns on the roads that international aid was constructing.[43] Chamorro even fused Somoza with the city's landscape, dubbing him "Loma de Tiscapa," the hill from which the presidential palace and prison overlooked the rubble of old Managua.[44]

All agreed that Managua had to be reconstructed, but the US government and Nicaraguan opposition first had to reconcile the problem of dictatorship with the promise of liberal development. The many different interested parties in the development of postearthquake Nicaragua reached an accord on how the city and country could be reconstructed while maintaining the appearance that US aid supported democracy. That accord was built around the idea of "deconcentration" or "decentralization" of the city of Managua, and of Managua itself within the life of the country. The politicians and planners involved came to agree that the city of Managua would be safer and more economically viable if rebuilt in a more dispersed manner, instead of allowing the unstable center to once again serve as the heart and nerve center of the city's life.[45] They also agreed that in lieu of focusing development solely on Managua, the city could be made safer and the country more prosperous by encouraging development in Nicaragua's other cities as well as in the countryside.

Where the participants to this consensus disagreed was in assessing the effects of decentralized development. Though "deconcentration" or "decentralization" were often used interchangeably, the two terms had very different implications. For planners and US officials wary of Somoza's ability to reconstruct a viable city, decentralizing development would promote a dispersal of power in the country and validate modernization theory's claim that modern economic growth undermined dictatorial control. For those who saw Somoza as "indispensable" for the continued stability of the country, this deconcentration of power would actually increase the dictator's control by creating more modern and efficient tools of government that would remain indefinitely in one man's hands. Not coincidentally, it was Ambassador Shelton, Somoza's most fervent supporter, who articulated most vocally the impersonal power of development aid, which, he claimed, "will in and of itself bring about the type of constructive and positive changes which are consistent with US policy and would serve to advance US policy objectives in Nicaragua."[46]

Nicaragua's catastrophe, and its government's close relationship with the United States, made it a proving ground for evolving ideas about modernization in urban environments. The problem of decentralization reflects the core issue of power under the modernization paradigm for development. In its classical conception, modernizers imagined societies developing as organic wholes in which economy and society are intimately linked. For theorists who took Western Europe and the United States as paragons of development, richer societies possessed institutions of government that worked in harmony with market forces to drive industrial and agricultural concentration and growth. The expansion of education and economic opportunity created an informed citizenry that held its government accountable to provide necessary services. Further, because excessive concentration of centralized power overtaxed bureaucratic capacity, the expansion of government power must be accompanied by the "devolution" of authority to local governments in the name of more efficient governance. Such devolution encouraged citizen participation. Local governments would be more accessible and encourage a mutual process of learning on the part of citizens and administrators.[47]

The plan to decentralize power in Nicaragua had three parts, which drew on the latest social scientific ideas on governance and development. First, "secondary cities" would be built up as alternative sites of development. The cities of Granada and León, old centers of power and wealth that had been supplanted by the growth of Managua, became home to tens of thousands of refugees after the earthquake. Foreign aid and investment would be directed there both by the government and international agencies to foster growth and provide incentive to keep refugees from returning to Managua.[48] Second, an agricultural credit program to aid small farmers would mitigate the concentration of land and wealth brought by agro-export-driven modernization. This program would also build the allegiance of campesinos to the government instead of to insurgents.[49] Finally, cooperatives and community development organizations would help the Nicaraguan people construct local political structures that would foster economic cooperation and enable them to express their needs and grievances to the government.[50]

In the early 1970s, many US policymakers still believed that the creation of well-functioning central planning systems was essential to reconciling the contradictions of US foreign aid. The US Congress since the mid-1960s had worked to develop new techniques and instruments to save a foreign aid program many believed was fostering inequality and autocracy in the Third World. Community development doctrine that had been created in places like India and Mexico was reformulated in the 1960s for application in the War on Poverty, as the Economic Opportunity Act called for the "maximum feasible participation" of the poor in poverty programs.[51] Amid the escalating war in Vietnam and the manifest failings of the Alliance for Progress, Congress took this revision of community development and applied it internationally. The writing of "participation" into development legislation with Title IX of the Foreign Assistance Act also served the counterinsurgency aims of the US government in both Southeast Asia and Latin America and became a tool to increase the involvement of poor populations in programs sponsored by the United States and US-supported governments. Under new directives, aid administrators would self-consciously encourage politicization of populations in aid-receiving countries, not to promote political participation as an end in itself, but as a way to manage both governments and people at a distance at both the national and local level.[52] Title IX was limited in its impact on the foreign aid bureaucracy, so Congress continued to push for institutional innovation. The same reformers also created the Inter-American Foundation, a new type of development institution that for the first time began to explicitly incorporate indigenous people into development practice. And in the early 1970s, liberal reformers would write a "basic human needs" mandate into foreign aid legislation, requiring that aid be directed toward the "poorest of the poor."[53]

In the minds of Somoza and his political allies, the process of dispersing power carried out by programs of decentralization and community development would not weaken the dictator. On the contrary, building governmental powers of planning and institutions of development not just in Managua but also throughout Nicaragua would allow the center of government, in the hands of Somoza himself, to exert its control more rationally and effectively over the country's entire territory. In the 1960s, community development had provided a means to link non-Somocista political elites to the Liberal Party government and its US allies. Now that such forces had been politically neutralized, decentralized development could serve to consolidate central government power.

Restructuring the city meant reallocating its property and financial power. Much of the land in the old city center had been owned by members of the country's commercial elite still not totally beholden to Somoza. Redevelopment outside the center on land owned by regime insiders would increase the ties of the middle class to the general rather than to his political rivals.[54] Ambassador Shelton and General Somoza also worked together to plan the forced takeover of the bank Corporación Nicaragüense de Inversiones, created during the Alliance for Progress to guarantee economic power-sharing among elite factions, and run by the general's political opposition. In the face of calamity, the government claimed that the bank was in danger of bankruptcy and could endanger the nation's future ability to receive credit.[55] The government thus ensured that new private investment would be channeled through the dictator's institutions.

Some members of the US Embassy and the State Department were less sanguine than Ambassador Shelton about Somoza's ever-tightening grip on power. They argued that the leverage provided by increasing economic assistance after the earthquake should be used to encourage a democratic opening of the regime, rather than a tightening of the general's already firm hold on the country. James Cheek, Embassy political officer, wrote cables arguing that the earthquake had changed drastically the political and cultural situation in the country. Ignoring these forces, he warned, could endanger the nation's stability.[56]

One of the hallmarks of US aid policy after the decade of development was increased emphasis on multilateralization, as policymakers urged international financial institutions to take over development programs in lieu of costly direct US supervision.[57] The US relationship with Nicaragua illustrated how such a system could remain a vehicle for Washington's influence. The US government encouraged international organizations to play a visible role in the reconstruction process, even as US agencies helped Somoza to orchestrate the entire mechanism. USAID coordinated its work with the World Bank, the Inter-American Development Bank, the United Nations, and the Organization of American States, in addition to many countries and private aid associations. These organizations likewise offered funding and advice. Still, because of the close relationship between Somoza and the US government, USAID was at the center of these efforts. The agency was charged not just with providing aid and planning advice but also with building a planning apparatus within the Nicaraguan government itself.[58]

The US agencies that implemented Managua's reconstruction acted at the intersection of congressional mandates to increase citizen participation and an executive mandate to support authoritarian power. Decentralization provided a possible means to reconcile these contradictory imperatives. Government agencies would provide credit for small farmers or urban homeowners, which would give the government a stake in the well-being of the poor even as the credit generated stronger allegiance among the poor themselves. At a time when enthusiasm for foreign aid was waning, promoting planning apparatuses at the national level and community programs at the local level offered a way to create a virtuous cycle of checks and balances of central and local power with less direct expenditure. In planners' vision of the new Nicaragua, political power might evolve from a classic patrimonial and populist dictatorship to a more modern and efficient state like the institutionalized party apparatus that ruled Mexico or the bureaucratic authoritarianism of the most industrialized countries of South America.[59]

Defenders of a generous US foreign aid program had since its beginnings emphasized the concept of "self-help" whenever the philosophy and methodology of US foreign aid was under attack by the US Congress, the president, or the American people themselves.[60] This idea suggested that the purpose of aid should be oriented less toward creating projects conceived and run by the US government and more toward building the capacity of aid-receiving governments to carry out projects on their own. Such countries would as a result be instilled with the ethos of development and thus act autonomously but congruently with the US interest in stability and democracy, as would the citizens of those countries within their own society.

One of the first tasks set by USAID after the earthquake was to create an urban planning ministry, which had never existed as an autonomous government unit. The Vice Ministry of Urban Planning that US advisers helped to construct, tasked with supervising urban development throughout the country, answered directly to the Nicaraguan head of state, Somoza. US planners recognized that getting the Nicaraguan government to carry out the reconstruction in the desired manner would require a certain amount of disciplining.[61] In the case of the urban planning office, this meant tying the continuation of US development aid to the continual production by the government of "action plans." These plans measured development by stating concrete goals and monitoring their fulfillment. Though US advisers recognized that giving full authority over the reconstruction process to a new and inexperienced bureaucracy was risky, USAID was unwilling to provide funds for a fully functioning international staff. This delegation of authority to the Nicaraguan government was born of necessity but was seen as beneficial, forcing the ministry to gain experience through practice. US advisers would guide this process from a distance, evaluating plans and determining whether US assistance would continue.

USAID tasked urban planning specialists from Harvard and the University of California, Berkeley with providing advice on how to reconstruct not only the city, but also the government that would oversee the city's orderly growth.[62] Lawrence Mann and Wilhelm von Moltke of Harvard were prominent urban designers charged with helping coordinate development in Nicaragua. Von Moltke had been involved with an earlier landmark project to create a new city, Ciudad Guayana in Venezuela, that Nicaraguan urban experts lauded as an example of beneficent planning.[63] In their reports, US experts argued that Managua could be rebuilt in a more efficient manner should decision making devolve from a single authority to a wider spectrum of public opinion. More rational city planning, the experts explained, would result from less "authoritarian control."[64]

US planners worked with the technocratic elite at INCAE, who greeted the prospect of decentralization with carefully calibrated enthusiasm.[65] Once a key part of the Central America integration movement, INCAE's technocrats were shunned by Somoza shortly after adding legitimacy to his 1967 election with their imprimatur.[66] Rather than speaking openly of dethroning Somoza, these technocrats argued that the decentralization project would "remove power from central authority" and place it in the hands of competent administrators like themselves.[67] Given the fact that any decision to devolve authority must come from Somoza himself, their plans were couched in technical language and relied on the ideas of efficiency and productivity that were the hallmarks of technocratic modernization. Though INCAE and USAID's planners obliquely criticized Somoza's control of the planning process, they contributed to the programs and apparatus that would allow him to dominate the city's future development.

The first plan for reconstructing the "new" Managua was created by a team of urban designers from the Mexican ministry of public works, who had begun studying ways to modernize the old city's downtown before the earthquake.[68] Once the disaster struck, the designers hastily updated their plans to create a master plan for the city, though without incorporating into their revisions extensive on-site study or consultation with the Nicaraguans themselves. The new city the designers envisioned was modeled after Mexico City. The downtown area would be rebuilt with high-rise residential buildings, government offices, and green spaces, with a much lower population density but preserving the city center's old status as the axis around which the metropolis would grow. US advisers rejected this plan as unsuited to Nicaragua for financial and social reasons. The modernist high-rises in which Managuans were to live and work were too alien to the population's traditional experience to be socially acceptable, thought the advisers.[69] They urged the planners to keep their expectations low and remember that Managua "will always be a small and quite poor city." A danger in bringing in foreign contractors to design housing, the advisers feared, was that the contractors might not set their sights low enough for what was appropriate for Nicaragua.[70]

Mixed with this lowering of expectations by planners, however, was another tendency: to imagine Managua as a US-style urban metropolis. This model featured new highways intended to allow the population to spread out and enjoy great freedom of mobility. According to the International Panel on Reconstruction and Redevelopment, the new Managua "will be more modern in that it will reflect the tendency observable in all parts of the world toward greater expansion of urban area than in urban population. There should, however, be no loss of accessibility, specifically as good surface transportation is made a top priority and as vehicular ownership continues to grow—which is to be expected."[71] In keeping with US development policy's emphasis on infrastructure as a primary engine of development, and pushed by Nixon's own proclivities for building highways instead of housing, US postearthquake aid was poured into road construction.

According to Nicaragua's ministry of planning, the destruction of the old city's core was a blessing. The congested streets of the old downtown could now be replaced by wide boulevards, easing the flow of vehicular traffic and commerce.[72] US aid was put toward building a "By-Pass" around the old city center. Other highways linking Managua to nearby cities would both support the decentralized metropolitan area and provide locations for new development (figure 2.2).

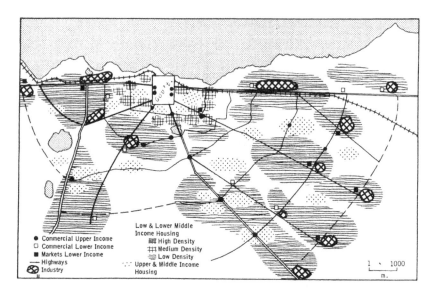

Figure 2.2. Planners' vision of a decentralized Managua, with an unspecified "government" at the center (Haas, *Reconstruction Following Disaster*, 241).

The new roads were constructed using labor-intensive *adoquines* (paving stones) and thus presented employment opportunities for earthquake victims.[73] The loan requests neglected to mention that the Somoza family was the primary producer of the paving stones for the new highways.[74] US aid agencies also overlooked the fact that individuals close to the government were using knowledge of development plans to buy land and reap enormous profits. Though many US officials were opposed to the expansion of Somoza's economic power, they rationalized that, given Somoza's expansive hold over the economy, it was impossible to plan the city in such a way that he would not benefit.[75] The status of the downtown area—an empty city center—illustrates the way US policies and Somoza's interests came together without the need for direct collusion. According to the US geological survey and the advice of architects and planners, rebuilding the downtown area to suitable seismic standards would be excessively expensive. They proposed that the country's development money could be better spent elsewhere. Somoza used their perspective to keep the downtown closed off for investment. He could therefore shift development plans and dollars toward areas beneficial to his interests. Planners might believe that they were creating an apolitical and well-designed urban system that undermined if not eliminated the general's authority. In practice, nevertheless, they contributed to the growth of his power.[76]

The way that planners synthesized the idea of a "small and poor" Managua with an automobile-friendly consumer metropolis was by essentially dividing Managua into several distinct cities, or self-sufficient "nuclei," which would then be tied together by the new roadways (figure 2.3). One of these cities would belong to the affluent rising middle class, who could aspire to owning a home on the outskirts of the city. Privately financed housing developments began to spring up after the earthquake, and planners expected their residents to use the new highways to commute to work and participate in Managua's new consumer boom.[77] New shopping centers designed to take advantage of the city's new infrastructure grew up around the periphery of the old city. Developers understood that many Managuans had lost their sense of community with the loss of the old downtown. Those responsible for the largest and most luxurious of the new shopping centers constructed around the new development "pole" in the southern part of the city advertised that they had re-created the streets of old Managua indoors. In practice this new Managua would belong primarily to the elite, as the shopping center could effectively be reached only by car, which remained a luxury in Nicaragua. Developers evoked the memory of the old Managua, designing a structure that would capture the vibrancy of the old city but indoors and accessible only by automobile. A new

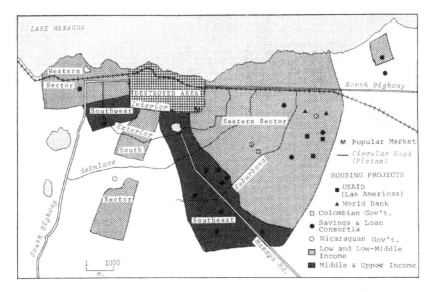

Figure 2.3. Illustration of post-earthquake Managua, showing the class structure of the emerging city. Housing projects were placed in areas marked as "low income" (Haas, *Reconstruction Following Disaster*, 133).

mall at Nejapa offered a "*casa-ciudad*," an indoor city, to customers. It would re-create the best the old city had to offer for a new middle class but also offer an escapist sensation that "you're not in Nicaragua."[78] The new Metrocentro mall directly south of the destroyed old city advertised itself, as seen in figure 2.4, as Managua's new "*eje*" or "axis."

¿POR QUE ANDAR POR LOS POLOS SI PUEDE ESTAR EN EL EJE?

Figure 2.4. Advertisement for Managua's Metrocentro Mall to the south of the destroyed city center echoed planners' language of "development poles": "Why go to the poles when you can be at the center?" (*La Prensa*, November 23, 1974).

The other city, isolated from the consumer capitalism of the motorized Managua, was the city of the working poor. The centerpiece of the US reconstruction effort and the heart of the "other" new Managua was the Las Américas housing project. USAID chose sites to the southeast of the old city center for the new project, conceived as a temporary shelter program to house the thousands of poor Managuans whose homes had been destroyed. Somoza's government rhetorically placed the new housing developments outside the new Managua, speaking glowingly of Nicaragua's new "third city": its population of seventy thousand was smaller only than León and Managua itself.[79] The sites for Las Américas 1, 2, 3 and 4 were chosen for their distance from seismic activity as well as their proximity to the city's industrial area, where residents would supposedly find employment.[80] The project, begun in February 1973 and completed by May, built eleven thousand shelters of wood and sheet metal. Each hut measured fifteen by fifteen feet and had a dirt floor. In response to criticism in the US press that aid money was merely creating slums, USAID spokespersons asserted that Las Américas was not a "housing" project but a "shelter" project, designed to accommodate displaced Managuans as quickly as possible.[81]

Because USAID purportedly did not have funds to adequately house Managua's poor, the project relied on a process of "self-help." The inhabitants of Las Américas would be given assistance in the form of tools and planning advice to improve their houses themselves, converting them from temporary shelters into comfortable homes. The housing projects, however, were beset by problems from the beginning. Managua's torrential rains during the winter season threatened to wash away the shelters, which had inadequate drainage systems. This rain notwithstanding, the government failed to provide potable water for its citizens. As part of its "civic action" training, the Guardia provided some assistance in improving local infrastructure but lost interest when the community's demands became too great. The Guardia remained a presence nonetheless, monitoring the activities of residents and trying to assure that they worked in industry or construction. The Guardia kept the poorest refugees from migrating there, which led to the creation of even larger illegal slums on the city's outskirts.[82] The government attempted to create community organizations for the residents but, rather than building a grassroots organization, used "food for work" programs to extract their labor.[83]

The promise of employment for the people of Las Américas failed to materialize. In the neighborhoods of old Managua, many lower-class people survived by providing goods and services for their wealthier neighbors. In Las Américas, however, the only neighbors were other people with low incomes.

This condition provided little opportunity for sustaining the small-scale commerce that was the lifeblood of mixed-class neighborhoods before the earthquake. Transportation proved insufficient to carry the residents of the housing project to more affluent parts of Managua where they might find employment.[84] The barrios lacked schools, health services, electricity, and proper sanitation.[85] Editorials in *La Prensa* lamented that deplorable conditions in Las Américas would bring about the moral as well as physical degradation of its inhabitants. The editorials pointed out that the only thriving commercial activity in the neighborhoods was vice.[86]

Receiving little assistance from authorized community organizations, the residents attempted to make their voices heard through committees to petition the government about the lack of reconstruction of their homes and the lack of services, but these complaints remained unanswered. All over the city, poor Managuans began to engage in spontaneous acts of violence to protest the government's deafness. Massive strikes of hospital and construction workers took place. In many cases the strikes resulted in significant gains in those sectors but left the majority of the poor untouched. The issue of water finally pushed the residents of Las Américas toward rebellion. Residents had long complained of the water stations interspersed throughout the neighborhoods. The stations functioned only from midnight until 6 a.m., causing residents to stand in long lines through the night (figure 2.5). In response to the residents' entreaties, the government announced that the public water services would be removed, and the residents would be charged to install taps in their homes. Riots broke out on the night of October 7, 1974. Residents destroyed the government-installed facilities.[87] Managua's poor were manifestly restive, unhappy with the attempts by their own and foreign governments to design better lives for them. Their concentration in working-class neighborhoods gave them a new opportunity to unite but also improved the government's capacity

Figure 2.5. "Dawn in Las Américas": Residents using water stations in the night ("Madrugada en Las Américas," *La Prensa*, August 24, 1974).

to supervise them. Given the fractured nature of the anti-Somoza opposition at the national level, would the decentralized Managua allow the poor to voice their grievances or simply relegate them to the periphery?

Managua and the Anti-Somoza Opposition

The new Managua that was emerging in the years following the earthquake was changing not just the old patterns of urban life but also the political life of the country. General Somoza succeeded in reshaping the city to augment both his personal wealth and political power but simultaneously helped unite the coalition of workers, peasants, radical leftists, and Conservative elites that would unseat him within the decade. One of the key explanations for the successful revolution in Nicaragua, as opposed to revolutionary failure in countries with equally brutal regimes such as El Salvador and Guatemala, is that the Nicaraguan elite turned against Somoza precisely because he overstepped the boundaries set by the agreement between the dynasty and the rest of the Nicaraguan elite, and attempted to garner too much power for himself.[88] What this interpretation overlooks is the role the shape of the new city itself played in forging a new revolutionary consciousness. Though Nicaraguans had long been critical of the disparities of wealth and poverty manifest in their country, especially in urban Managua, the new city disclosed these inequalities and the power relations that made them possible in a radically new way.

The nascent political opposition in Nicaragua objected to more than Somoza's heavy-handed attempts to use the reconstruction to garner wealth and power. Though members of the Nicaraguan opposition were perennially concerned about threats to their privilege, their businesses thrived after the earthquake. The private sector benefited from the explosion of construction and a rise in commodity prices, and economic analysts marveled at Nicaragua's swift economic recovery after such a disaster.[89] The postearthquake economic growth made the task of creating a unified anti-Somocista movement more difficult. Members of the private sector wished to enjoy the fruits of the economic expansion, but they also feared the growth of Somoza's power as a threat to their prerogatives.

The shape and structure of the "new" Managua itself became the object of the opposition's distaste, the city's very modernity seen as the source of social ills that must be resisted. The axes of revulsion toward Somoza were twofold, and each complemented and contradicted the other. On the one hand, Somoza displayed an atavistic appetite for acquiring power and wealth.[90] Members of the elite fretted that he gathered wealth not for its own sake, since the enterprises he owned before the earthquake had the potential to prosper if managed in a more efficient manner.[91] What disturbed them was that his "feudal" mentality meant that he gathered wealth not for profit but for personal control. On the other hand, the opposition argued, Somoza was too much in thrall to the "modern." He recklessly crisscrossed the city with new highways, creating an automobile-friendly city that separated rich from poor while destroying an invaluable sense of community, which for the patriarchal old elites was central to their conception of the nation.[92]

The tie that bound these two disparate visions of Somoza, the feudal baron and the ruthless modernizer, was the United States itself. Somoza was ridiculed by the opposition as shamefully subservient to the Americans, who were in turn seen, like Somoza himself, as possessed of both immense power and cultural barbarism.[93] Somoza was sometimes reputed to speak better English than Spanish. For this reason La Prensa's editors likened him to a "new Herod," more subservient to the Roman Empire than to the Hebrew people.[94] Somoza used the signing of aid contracts as photo opportunities, courted US officials who traveled to Nicaragua, and sought the privilege of personal meetings with President Nixon. After a meeting of the private sector, which used the occasion to criticize the dictator, Somoza held a rally in which he referred to the opposition as "arrechuras," a term connoting both sexual excitement and anger.[95] Somoza's use of colloquial turns of phrase provoked ridicule from the cultural elite, as did his fawning behavior toward US power. This elite disdain provoked by his behavior bolstered his populist credentials, as he offered himself to the country as the "indispensable man" linking Nicaragua to the prosperity symbolized by the United States.[96]

Members of the US embassy deprecated the Nicaraguan opposition as "rather a sorry lot."[97] They treated the opposition around the Somoza-dependent Conservative Party and Fernando Agüero as at best a useful token of Nicaragua's nominally democratic status and at worst feckless troublemakers. The embassy since the 1960s had ignored the cultural efflorescence that was taking place in the country, asserting that there was "meager cultural production apart from Rubén Darío," whose works were more than a half-century old. Embassy staff overlooked the growing stream of nationalist and revolutionary poetry filling both student publications and even revered traditionalist organs like La Prensa. Instead they believed that there was little cultural resentment of the decades-long Marine occupation of the country. They argued that the Somozas and the US-educated upper class constituted a firm bulwark against unrest.[98]

Some members of the US embassy, however, began to sense a shift in the national mood and conclude that the opposition and the private sector had developed a more constructive "self-consciousness" after the earthquake. This private sector appeared to be gravitating toward the perception that the general had overreached by expanding his private enterprise into areas such as the construction industry that were previously left to other sectors of the oligarchy. With the virtual collapse of the Central American Common Market, the institutions that the United States had used to encourage economic power-sharing were moribund. Somoza's use of government information about the future development of the city to garner lucrative land deals was also an unfair abuse of power. The awarding of construction contracts in favor of political patronage instead of economic efficiency rankled the elite, even though many of its constituents were still in agreement with the overall trend of modernization of the city. According to dissenting members of the US embassy staff, objections to Somoza's "feudalism" drove the elite away from him.[99]

The Nicaraguan private sector and nascent political opposition greeted the US vision of a modernized and decentralized Nicaragua with great hope. One of the pillars of the decentralization policy was the encouragement of healthy growth in other major cities of Nicaragua. The Conservative elite, whose base was in Granada, saw this prospect as a path to regaining some of their lost power and glory. Conservative intellectuals had since the 1960s called for a decentralization of population and industry from Managua.[100] A political conference gathering the most important voices of the private sector held out hope that reconstruction would foster both economic growth and the return of their traditional power. At the private-sector conference that drew Somoza's populist ire, attendees discussed the promise of decentralization as a promise of a more efficient and equitable Nicaragua.[101] Liberal and Conservative factions envisioned a future in which Somoza might retain political power and economic control but would return to the past practice of sharing economic largesse.

La Prensa editor Pedro Joaquín Chamorro welcomed the idea of a decentralized Nicaragua, although he criticized not just Somoza's avarice and subservience to the United States but also the private sector's eagerness to put their interests above those of the nation. In his political diary, published after his assassination, he ridiculed the vulgarity of members of his own family who belonged to the Conservative elite, whose only interest in life was the fine dining at Granada's "jockey club."[102] He referred to the Conservatives who participated in the "pact" with Somoza as *zancudos*, blood-sucking mosquitoes that drained the life from the country. Chamorro argued that the disastrous earthquake had caused, not just great physical and emotional harm to the Nicaraguan people, but also consequences that threatened the population's very identity. Chamorro compared the impact of the earthquake to that of the US Marine occupation earlier in the century, which had brought about the hated Somoza dynasty in the first place.[103]

The literary voice of the anti-Somoza opposition was Pablo Antonio Cuadra, who built his reputation on the exposition of a distinctly Nicaraguan nationhood. Cuadra portrayed Nicaraguan *mestizaje* as uniting the piety of Hispanic culture with the community spirit of pre-Hispanic indigenous culture. In his writings on "el nicaragüense," which dated to the 1940s, he described Nicaraguans as being culturally open to exchanges with foreigners. He interpreted this phenomenon as a mark of their curiosity about the world but also a cause of danger when such openness invited the foreign too deeply into the country's life.

To Cuadra, the postearthquake Managua designed by Somoza and the United States was not becoming "decentralized" but "de-centered." He compared the 1972 earthquake to the nineteenth-century invasion of reviled American filibuster William Walker.[104] Cuadra argued that Walker, who in the 1850s burned down Granada, the ancestral home of Conservative Nicaragua, had succeeded in unifying the Nicaraguan people by providing them with a common enemy.[105] The earthquake, though a tragedy of similar scale to the filibuster invasion, fractured them. The new, decentralized city was dividing Managuans along explosive class lines. The middle classes in their automobiles were succumbing to an extreme individualism, which disconnected them both from one another and from the lower classes. Conversely, packed inside their buses, Managua's poor were forming a new collective conscience, which threatened to explode into class warfare if not checked.[106] "A capital is a cathedral," Cuadra wrote. He warned ominously of the "monstrous politics" such a capital as Managua might engender.[107]

The trenchant critique of Somoza and the postearthquake reconstruction formulated in the pages of *La Prensa* gave ideological heft to a reinvigorated anti-Somocista opposition. Yet Chamorro's unwillingness to alienate the wealthy Conservative oligarchy prevented him from building a political platform that went beyond opposition to the dictator. For the 1974 election in which Somoza planned to reinstall himself as president, Chamorro started the "*No hay quien votar*" (There is no one to vote for) movement to encourage abstention. Unlike in the 1960s, Chamorro and his allies held out no hope that the US embassy might intervene in their favor. This movement had no discernible effect on the election's outcome, but the personal persecution it brought from Somoza buoyed Chamorro's image as leader of the anti-Somocista opposition. Somoza in fact had used the period after the earthquake to build his electoral

machine so that the US embassy worried only that Somoza might go over-
board and "win too big," further alienating the opposition.[108]

Members of the elite who had helped construct Nicaragua's developmental dictatorship turned against Somoza's vision. Francisco Laínez was one of
the most outspoken critics of the Somoza regime, publishing attacks in *La Prensa*
on a weekly basis. Having helped found the Nicaraguan Central Bank in 1961
and advised the Somozas throughout the decade, Laínez was intimate with
the economic and political structures governing Nicaragua. He critiqued
what he called the Nicaraguan "family-state" as engaging in a deliberate process of destruction of Nicaragua's identity and community in order to place
its people in a "concentration camp."[109] After welcoming the concept of decentralization, he described its implementation as a farce, a deliberate attempt
to wrest away the small gains of the country's labor movement.[110] The notion
of the reconstruction of Managua as a "national reconstruction" project was
a transparent attempt to justify the fact that the brunt of the sacrifice would
be borne by workers and peasants.[111] The foreign aid agencies that rushed into
Nicaragua made the problem worse, by increasing Nicaragua's indebtedness
and by propagating development plans alien to Nicaragua's needs.[112]

While the pages of *La Prensa* provided a forum for Conservative-rooted anti-
Somocismo, after the earthquake the paper also became the venue for a group of
young, educated Nicaraguans to express their more radical opposition to the regime. Journalists like William Ramírez, Rosario Murillo, and Bayardo Arce, all
of whom would become leaders in the coming Nicaraguan revolution, used the
paper to describe in detail the misery suffered by Nicaragua's poor. Whereas
Conservative critics such as Cuadra and Chamorro lamented the loss of community and national identity, the young militants described the formation of a
new sense of community among Managua's poor. Speaking for the poor residents of Las Américas and imagining a version of "self-help" independent of US
control, Murillo wrote: "Only we ourselves can solve our problems. Up to now
what Las Américas has obtained has been through struggles and efforts of we
who live here."[113] She and others in the FSLN saw in the spontaneous organization and acts of violence in Managua's poor neighborhoods hopeful signs of a
growing class consciousness. Instead of fearing this consciousness, as Pablo Antonio Cuadra did, the FSLN hoped to harness it to bring about a revolution.

An alternative design for the new Nicaragua was created by members of
the elite and the radical left, which manifested their shared distaste for the direction in which Nicaragua was moving. This also helped engender the common perspective that would forge the future alliance that would overthrow
Somoza. In 1974, Father Miguel d'Escoto, a member of the Maryknoll order,

founded the Fundación Nicaragüense para el Desarrollo de una Comunidad Integral (FUNDECI). D'Escoto had worked closely with the social reform movement in Chile associated with the Christian Democratic movement, which played a major role in US anticommunist efforts there during the Alliance for Progress.[114] FUNDECI brought together Nicaraguan and foreign architects and collected money from international organizations and from members of Nicaragua's elite to design and build a "model" community in the city of León, El Paraíso. It was funded by members of Nicaragua's elite who worked with the Somoza regime but also were beginning to seek alternatives.[115]

Designed by Chilean architect Jorge Gómez Ramos, El Paraíso was conceived as a model community for working-class Nicaraguans, whose design was based on close study of the needs of the poor (figure 2.6).[116] In contrast to the substandard housing projects in Managua, in the middle of this community would be a center, housing a church, market, school, and community meeting area. Chamorro asserted that such a community offered a semblance of middle-class living to the poor and could lead to the "reconstruction of *man* in Nicaragua."[117] Instead of living in a "barracks or anthill," as he asserted the poor often did in Managua, the members of this model community would have affordable but well-designed homes they could alter to their taste. The community was designed to account for both the "material" and "spiritual" needs of its inhabitants.

Managua's fractured image became a figurative battleground, over which a dictator and his opponents fought for the right to determine their nation's

Figure 2.6. Artist's rendering of the urban development El Paraíso (*La Prensa*, August 18, 1974).

future. The city would soon become a literal battleground, as avenues for peaceful protest closed down. After a successful Sandinista assault on the home of Somoza supporter "Chema" Castillo in December 1974, the dictator declared martial law, instituted press censorship, and initiated a campaign of harsh persecution of dissidents. Instead of turning to the dictator for protection, members of Nicaragua's elite began to actively collaborate with the leftist insurgents.[118] D'Escoto's plan for urban renewal around El Paraíso began to unite the radical and conservative wings of the anti-Somoza opposition. D'Escoto would soon play a key role in unifying the "Group of 12," bringing together the FSLN and the bourgeois opposition, and helping to forge an international consensus that Nicaragua's dictatorship must fall.[119] The first place the Group of 12 would meet on Nicaraguan soil was in the El Paraíso development in León.[120]

Even as the ideological power of modernization was crumbling elsewhere, the 1972 earthquake made Nicaragua a proving ground for the ideals of progress that still bound the United States and Latin America and held together the contradictory goals of US foreign policy. The special place of Nicaragua is illustrated by comparison with nearby Guatemala, which suffered an even more destructive earthquake in 1976. There, however, the destruction was confined to the indigenous and poor populations, and Guatemalan elites kept their distance from US aid. Though more lives were lost, US officials defined the Guatemala earthquake as an "economic disaster for the poor" that thus did not call for large-scale reconstruction.[121]

Managua's reconstruction process shows that in the early 1970s the premises of modernization were still alive in the Americas. The image of a bright industrial, automotive, and consumer future provided the sinews of a developmental ideal that tied together planners, the dictator, and oppositional forces. The reality of the new Managua, in which Sergio Ramírez and many others saw a dictator's dream and a nightmare for the poor, would provide the beginning of a new alternative alliance. Following the earthquake, both development practitioners and antidictatorial forces would begin to articulate themselves around new terms—"human rights," "basic human needs," and even "social revolution"—but the dream of reconfiguring political and economic development through a reorganized urban space would remain.

Chapter 3

Dis-integrating Rural Development

In his column on October 29, 1977, in the paper *La Prensa*, Pablo Antonio Cuadra told the story of a campesino who came to visit him in his office. The campesino asked for justice for a family that the Guardia Nacional had "disappeared" in the mountains around Matagalpa in northern Nicaragua.[1] For Cuadra, the campesino's use of the verb "disappeared" expressed the proliferation of "a new form of death: anonymous, negated, veiled," that corresponded to a new iteration of government power in the countryside. Cuadra asserted that the expression "to be disappeared," emblematic of human rights abuses throughout Latin America, had grown not out of the lexicon of an international human rights movement but organically out of the peasantry's experience of repression.

Even as government forces were attacking campesinos, Cuadra also noted that the language of the peasantry was making rural Nicaragua an object of international admiration "capable of conquering Spain itself," its former colonizer. Though the peasantry was threatened with destruction, rural culture was receiving more international attention than ever before. This was thanks to a revival of folk traditions by artists and revolutionaries who drew on the work of Conservative intellectuals such as Cuadra to make the Nicaraguan peasantry central to a global call for revolutionary justice, broadcasting their rendition of the voice of the campesino through poetry and song. This artistic revival complemented the work of activists in Nicaragua and the United States who brought the plight of campesinos to the attention of a growing international audience concerned with injustices in the dictatorships of Latin

America. These activists rendered the rural world threatened by military repression as both a repository of culture and an insurrectionary force.

The double image of the peasant as victim and revolutionary made Nicaragua's countryside in the 1970s contested territory, where tensions between political and economic development within liberal developmentalism were reconfigured in new techniques of Cold War counterinsurgency and international humanitarianism. The novelty Cuadra and others highlighted in the behavior of Nicaragua's government in the countryside was the product of a deliberate attempt by the US and Nicaraguan governments to repair breaches in the developmentalist consensus of the 1960s as revolutionary movements gained momentum across Central America. Debates over the relationship between political and economic development that had shaped the Alliance for Progress in the 1960s were revived in a new form as doctrines of human rights and basic human needs protection. These doctrines, though often at odds, were designed to rectify the political and economic abuses of developmentalist states, exemplified in Nicaragua by the wealth and power of the US-backed Somoza family. Human rights protection as implemented by the US government, especially under President Jimmy Carter, revived the idea that foreign aid could promote a more just though not necessarily democratic politics. A new doctrine of "basic human needs" protection, created by the US Congress and development agencies, renewed the idea that US foreign aid could promote equitable economic growth by mandating direct aid to the "poorest of the poor." In the context of Nicaragua's accelerating national revolt, basic human needs protection became part of a revised practice of developmental counterinsurgency, while human rights protection aimed to check the reach of state power.

Observers debating the causes of the Nicaraguan revolution, like so many others during the Cold War, swung between attributing the revolution to endogenous forces of national liberation and subversive external intervention.[2] The revolution in fact depended on the combined efforts of leftist insurgents, Nicaraguan nationalist elites, US politicians, and international human rights activists, among many others. The issue that brought this disparate coalition together was the image of Nicaragua's beleaguered campesino, brought about by the breakdown of the program for building a stable and prosperous Nicaragua through political and economic modernization that the United States had claimed to promote for more than forty years. As Nicaragua's anti-Somoza forces grew in strength over the 1970s, changes in US development practice revived the question of whether US policies served the interests of democracy or dictatorship. Nicaragua's political factions once again attempted to turn

US power to their own political ends, making Cold War developmentalism accessory to both revolution and counterrevolution.

The Sandino rebellion a half-century earlier had provoked an international outcry against US intervention, helping bring about the Good Neighbor policy and a policy of US hemispheric nonintervention honored as much in breach as in observance. During the 1930s, Nicaragua's Conservative elite had flirted with supporting agrarian rebellion but had missed its encounter with Sandino and instead backed the dictatorship of the first Somoza.[3] This lapse would not be repeated, and members of the anticommunist Conservative elite such as Cuadra helped provide essential ideological ammunition for an international effort to undermine their country's dictatorship. The US government attempted to harness this revolutionary conjuncture as well, turning as during the Alliance for Progress to promoting the private sector as nonpolitical force. The coalition of Conservatives, capitalists, and revolutionaries that took power when Somoza finally fell would try to convince the world that a new sort of revolutionary government might be possible, one that combined the models of liberal and social revolution and thus might transcend Cold War divides. The uncertain place of Nicaragua's rural population within this new order would haunt the new government as it embarked on its revolutionary venture.

Integrating Rural Nicaragua

In the first months of 1975, USAID mission director Bob Culbertson, who had recently served in the AID mission in Vietnam, traveled to the mountains of northern Nicaragua to evaluate the possibilities for what the agency billed as a revolutionary new development program. Just as postearthquake Managua was to be the site of a program to decentralize the urban population, a new government agency, the Instituto de Bienestar Campesino (Invierno), was to revolutionize the relationship between campesinos and their government as crisis escalated thanks to the growing success and popularity of the FSLN after the kidnapping of government officials in 1974.

Culbertson's "Letter from Matagalpa," designed to justify US development policy to skeptical Nicaraguans and discussed widely in the local press, described a region at a point of momentous transition. Like many development advocates before him, he invoked the immense promise of the land itself, with its "water resources plentitude which, related to the very fertile land resources, yield a very high growth potential." Despite apparent isolation and sparse population, the region was crisscrossed with lines of infrastructure and communication, a "radio-TV blanket over the entire region."[4] The world Culbertson described teetered on the brink of an epochal change. Thanks to the success of modernization "the world turns inward . . . communications proliferate . . . and the viable frontier begins to disappear," but "the campesino lives outside the modern economic system . . . a system not designed with his needs in mind—not really designed at all."[5]

The system had been designed by technocrats like Culbertson along with the dictatorial regime US agencies worked alongside. The situation he described was the direct result of the Alliance for Progress, which had promoted the synergy of an industrial and a frontier model of development. The campesinos around Matagalpa had struck out along roads built to serve a Nestlé milk factory that benefited from the agricultural industrialization promoted under the Central American Common Market. Peasants would clear and work land opened by new roads for a few years, until the land was bought up by large landowners served by the credit systems of the central government. Then the cycle would begin again as landless peasants or, in Culbertson's words, the "durable, creative . . . pioneering campesino," pushed onward. But the very success of that system in displacing campesinos and building the sinews of modern development was pushing the country to the brink of civil war.

The war in Vietnam, in which techniques tested in Latin America were transferred to Asia, had provided an important testing ground for the implementation of modernization programs in the name of counterinsurgency.[6] The strategic hamlet program was the centerpiece of the US strategy to "win hearts and minds" and recruit the Vietnamese peasantry into the nation-building program of President Ngo Dinh Diem.[7] Walt Rostow had famously argued that "Marx was a city boy" and that US agrarian policy was superior to that of the communists.[8] But as early as 1967 administrators like Culbertson had learned that US agrarian policy in Vietnam was failing, warning that "by the time we have won over the countryside, we will have lost the cities."[9] By 1975 the United States had lost both, but planners would once again try to solve the problem of the country and the city, this time with Nicaragua as testing ground.

After the 1972 earthquake and its stirring of cross-class rebellion, planners began to rethink development policy there in light of past failures. Managua had grown tremendously over the previous decades thanks to the process of technocratic innovation in the countryside that US development policies augmented. The cotton boom in the countryside financed by US credit had made Managua the prosperous center of a new Nicaragua for a small economic elite. Campesinos who were dispossessed of their land because of the consolidation promoted by modernization policies flocked to the city as economic opportunity in the countryside became scarce. These campesinos flooding into the metropolis crowded into poorly constructed housing that would be a hazard in a future earthquake. Their concentration in squalid conditions provided tinder for political unrest as well. Planners thus linked the process of development with a long-term program of counterinsurgency.[10]

Acknowledging that urbanization was causing problems in places like Nicaragua meant reworking the premises of development itself. The plan for a new Nicaragua devised by USAID and the new Nicaraguan planning apparatus did not abandon urbanization altogether. To discourage emigration from the countryside to the metropolis, planners tried to encourage the growth of Nicaragua's "secondary cities," primarily the old political centers of León and Granada that had been eclipsed by the growth of Managua.[11] Nicaragua's Conservative elite greeted this prospect with wary approval, imagining this might mean a gradual transfer of power away from Somoza.[12] Planners also wished to encourage the growth of rural municipalities, to provide markets for peasants to sell their goods and create political opportunities, giving peasants access to local authorities to whom they could appeal to address their grievances.[13]

The ultimate issue was the problem of land itself. The cotton boom of the 1950s and 60s had encouraged the consolidation of large farms and the industrialization of the production process.[14] The farm credit programs of the Alliance for Progress had encouraged this consolidation, granting credit for technological modernization that overwhelmingly benefited large producers. If peasants were to be kept from migrating to the city, then they would need some incentive to remain in place. Land reform was a perpetual promise of both radicals and reformers not just in Nicaragua but also throughout Latin America. Providing campesinos with their own land, duly titled by the government, might mitigate the disruptive processes of modernization and liberalization that had organized Central American elites' thinking about development since the nineteenth century. Reformists and populists, encouraged by the US government, offered campesinos land on which they could lay down roots and integrate into national life without becoming the rootless rural proletariat that so often drifted into cities in search of greater opportunity or provided tinder for rural rebellion.

One solution to this issue in Nicaragua, promoted by General Somoza himself, was colonization. Landless campesinos would be encouraged to migrate to Nicaragua's undeveloped "frontier," the region from the central highlands to the Caribbean coast with low population density, inhabited at its eastern end by non-Spanish-speaking Creoles and indigenous peoples. The flagship project was the Rigoberto Cabezas colony, begun in the 1960s and named for the nineteenth-century Nicaraguan general who united by force the east and west coasts of the country.[15] The same initiative shown by the urban migrant could be channeled to new, undeveloped areas. New communities could be built around more efficient modes of agriculture and social practice, integrating peasants into the life of the nation without bringing them to dangerously overcrowded urban slums. Planners recognized, however, that the ideal of colonization could not deal with all the pressures on Nicaragua's political reality in the late 1970s. Landless campesinos, unwilling or unable to further uproot themselves by moving to new colonies to the east, resorted to unauthorized land seizures and pressed the government to recognize their rights.[16] Though this process took place independently of the FSLN, revolutionaries linked their struggle with that of an independent and restive peasantry.

The Sandinista movement was itself divided over the problem of integration of countryside and city, as its members split over where to focus revolutionary struggle. In the early 1970s, the movement began to divide into three factions, each of which imagined a different vanguard for revolutionary development: peasants, workers, or the middle class. The Guerra Popular Prolongada faction argued that the conflict must take place in the mountains, winning the allegiance of the peasantry to carry out an extended struggle with the regime. The Proletario faction argued that urban Managua must be the locus of insurrection, galvanizing the urban trade union movement that had grown in the years after Managua's earthquake thanks to the construction boom. Finally, the Tercerista faction recognized the benefits of recruiting the national elite, which was becoming more and more alienated by the growth of Somoza's power after the 1972 earthquake. The factions representing the peasantry and the workers disagreed over where to locate the authentic revolutionary character of the Nicaraguan people, in the mountains or the cities. The Tercerista faction sidestepped this question, making the claim instead that the primary problem was political, and thus focused its energies on representing the Nicaraguan nation abroad. This recognition of the problem of representing Nicaragua's identity abroad gave the Tercerista faction better traction in recruiting allies in the international community, leading to eventual dominance over the other two factions.[17]

The US Congress was grappling with the problem of how to channel the revolutionary energies of Nicaragua's poor as well. As part of the disillusionment of Congress and the American people after the Vietnam War with the rhetoric and practice of modernization, there was a growing recognition that development as usually conceived did not lead to democracy. The countries of the southern cone—Chile, Argentina, and Uruguay—were by the mid-1970s growing economically but in the throes of "dirty wars" in which their military regimes used mass repression to inoculate their societies against leftist subversion. In Nicaragua, development experts acknowledged that, rather than reducing inequality and creating economic opportunity, large-scale projects such as those to build access roads deep into the hinterland and connect the east and west coasts of the country drove campesinos from their land.[18]

The congressional committees on international relations and appropriations, charged with overseeing foreign aid, began at this time to demand that aid be directed toward meeting the "basic human needs" of the poorest populations of recipient countries.[19] New aid appropriations were written with a specific injunction that economic aid whenever possible be directed toward a broadly conceived "poor" population, rather than toward large-scale infrastructure projects that tended to benefit dictators and elites. This imperative became salient in discussions of US aid to Nicaragua amid widespread allegations that Somoza had directed earthquake relief aid to his personal benefit, something the State Department had recognized as inevitable.[20] Congress began to demand innovative projects that would benefit those left out of the development process.

In response to changing visions of the purpose of foreign aid, planners at USAID began to rethink the foundations of the aid process.[21] According to the canon of modernization theory, a peasant was a peasant, whether in Afghanistan's Helmand Valley or Nicaragua's mountainous central highlands.[22] Critiques of planning methodology by the academic community and by those within the planning apparatus had begun in the late 1960s to point out that such simplistic equations were inadequate to deal with the complexities of local cultures. What was required, planners had begun to believe, was a government willing to grant officials who understood the nuances of their local situation the power and authority to adapt plans justly. Planners turned to the concept of "self-help" as the key to making plans work in local situations. Under the state-driven models of modernization, this concept of self-help vacillated between locating the impulse to action within the citizens themselves and their government. At times, self-help meant initiative on the part of local producers to improve their land, seek credit, and air their grievances to authorities. Simultaneously, self-help meant initiative on the part of the local Nicaraguan government to carry out development projects without the constant oversight and intervention of international planners, whose resources were inadequate to such continual supervision. Plans sometimes included assistance to private organizations, which could help organize producer cooperatives and serve as intermediaries between the populace and its government. Critics of the Alliance had since the 1960s called for greater channeling of aid through these organizations to circumvent the corrupt central power, but it was only the broader crisis in development practice that brought about substantive change.[23]

Responding to congressional pressure, US and Nicaraguan planners directed by Somoza and Ambassador Shelton tried to focus attention on the Instituto de Bienestar Campesino, or Invierno. Planners conceived Invierno in the early 1970s to deal with the issue of poverty and rural integration. Its designers described this program as encapsulating all the competing imperatives of development, linking national government with local initiative to provide long-sought egalitarian development. USAID officials called it a "truly revolutionary" program that would combine the imperatives of education, economic progress, and counterinsurgency in one efficient package. The program was, however, directed to only one portion of Nicaragua, the mountainous northern region and the area around Managua, to limit its scope. These were the regions in which the rural poor had least access to land.[24] They were not incidentally the two areas where the insurgency was most active and where the Somoza regime was least popular.[25] USAID officials sold Invierno to Congress as an experiment in rural development and counterinsurgency, in which Nicaragua's small size and the contained dimensions of the program would allow it to function as a "test tube" for development aid.[26] The program was to be a form of "benign counterinsurgency."[27]

Based on the new imperative of meeting the population's "basic human needs," planners sought new methods to "know" the peasants and their problems, which could redefine what it meant to be a peasant. Planners cooperated with the government to create a computerized database of all the credit needs of the peasants involved in Invierno's programs.[28] This database simplified the problem of distributing credit and reduced staff burdens by centralizing information on rural Nicaragua. Planners highlighted that the new computer system dealt with peasants as individuals, rather than groups, bypassing the traditional authority of local community leaders and putting government "extension agents" directly in touch with the population.[29] As with the program of postearthquake decentralization, the Somoza regime recognized the potential benefits of a program like Invierno. Rather than undermining the power of the regime, a program that collected information about the "basic needs" of the people of the countryside and created a class of peasants beholden to the government for land and credit would prove invaluable to a regime that wished to discourage peasants from assisting a growing insurgency.

Planners trying to sell these new development initiatives to Congress touted the Somoza regime's eagerness to participate. USAID emphasized that the American people could count on the Nicaraguan government's shared vision for development, in contrast to development projects in many other countries. The predicted overwhelming success of Invierno in Nicaragua, planners argued, might even make it a model to export to other troubled countries in the region and even around the world. When Congress questioned the Somoza regime's commitment to human rights, the State Department pointed to Invierno as a sign of the government's concerted efforts to better the lot of the poor.[30]

Key to the illusion of benign modernization propagated in congressional committees and USAID development plans was the division of US aid into military and civil programs. The distinction between military and civil society built into an idealized conception of rural development did not exist in Nicaragua.[31] Planners imagined a program like Invierno as embodying the ideal of "soft" counterinsurgency by ignoring the reality that the same government that enthusiastically carried out plans for rural development depended for its power on the brutal instruments of the Guardia Nacional. Although planners acknowledged campesino complaints that the recipients of aid by programs such as Invierno were often government informers, the planners could ignore this reality by invoking a development process that would reform both the campesino and the government over the long term, through institution-building and an idealized notion of political maturation.[32]

A signing ceremony in 1975 for an AID loan for Invierno brought the contradictions within the program to the fore. The ceremony took place in Matiguás, in the mountainous northern region near Matagalpa. Like other such ceremonies in the past, the event attended by Ambassador James Theberge was also a rally for Somoza's Liberal Party. According to AID mission director Robert Culbertson, Somoza's taking credit for rural development was equivalent to the US Democratic Party taking credit for the New Deal, an essential manifestation of democratic politics.[33] For the ambassador, Invierno was a clear sign to Somoza of continued US government support, and the ceremony in Matiguás, as "close as possible" to the guerrilla fighting, signaled the security of the regime and its continued close relation with small farmers.[34] Critics within the embassy contended that such collusion with the aims of the Somoza government put AID at risk of attack by guerrillas. These critics warned that trumpeting the revolutionary character of Invierno also created unrealistic expectations among the local population. Given the close congruence of the development program and the Somoza regime's aims, the economics officer asserted, "I think we have been had."[35]

If embassy officials had been taken in, it was by their own rhetoric. When pressed, State Department officials acknowledged that in practice the Guardia remained under a single command and that in rural areas there was no distinction between its military and civilian functions.[36] It had long been manifest that Somoza's Guardia Nacional united the imperatives of economic and military development in the name of personal power, not impersonal social development. The other side of the "benign counterinsurgency," obscured by the imagined divisibility of economic and political factors, was that the Guardia used torture and intimidation to discourage peasant support for insurgency. The US government was aware that the Somoza regime used corruption to maintain the Guardia's loyalty, as Guardia members appropriated the land of alleged insurgents.[37]

The link between the economic and military functions of the Guardia were present from its inception. Its creators believed that the Guardia's ability to foster economic and political modernization lay in the fact that it would displace the structures of *caudillismo*, the economic and military force of the oligarchy in rural Nicaragua.[38] The upward mobility provided by the Guardia, the fact that its officer corps and its rank and file were pulled from Nicaraguan campesinos rather than the old elite, might even provide the kernel for a middle class that would displace the old "unmodern" elite. Such a displacement of the elite in the countryside had in fact taken place, but the forces of the Guardia only bolstered the authoritarian dynasty to which the Guardia was beholden.

Within the authoritarian structure created around the Guardia, US planners had sought to solve the problem of development in Nicaragua by "integrating" the peasantry into national life while obscuring the military foundations of Nicaraguan governance. This effort was carried out by building the infrastructure that planners imagined was the key to creating a thriving national economy, crisscrossing the nation with highways and building expensive projects to bring electricity to distant parts of the country. The effort also involved studying and classifying the peasants in terms of their caloric intake, health problems, and level of education. Beneath the cold objectivity of social science statistics was another story. The integration of the campesino into the political life of the country was being carried out by violence while the instruments of violence were compartmentalized, and thereby explained away, by planners imagining Nicaragua's future. Under the pressure of the emerging international concern over human rights, the connection between military and economic development, and their mutual failures, would become too salient to ignore.

Finding the Campesino's Voice

While development bureaucracies gathered and disseminated depersonalized statistics to demonstrate how aid was helping the poor, activists in the United

States and Nicaragua began to try to narrate what life was like within "integrated rural development." Revulsion at the inhuman treatment of Nicaragua's peasantry brought together a diverse coalition of political, religious, and cultural movements that reached out to an international audience to alter the mixture of violence and development lacerating rural Nicaragua. Those wishing to speak for the peasant united around an image of a figure that was bound in tradition, a bearer of an archetypal national identity, but also something more. Peasants were the potential bearers of a revolutionary force powerful enough to overturn a brutal dictatorship and the imperial system that supported it.

The multiclass coalition united against the Somoza dictatorship around two ideas: revulsion at the corruption represented by Somoza's embrace of a twisted version of modernization, and a romantic vision of the Nicaraguan people victimized by this distorted modernity. The ideology of the Conservative elite and the radical FSLN, whose members often overlapped, found their most stable point of contact in the image of a peasantry that was simultaneously a victim of abuse but also a source of redemptive power.[39] The image of the Somoza dynasty as beholden to foreign powers and oppressing the native poor was pivotal to understanding the confluence of radicalism and conservatism that brought down the dynasty. Scholars have often credited the elite's turn against the dictatorship as driven by economic self-interest, especially after Somoza Debayle used the earthquake reconstruction to expand his economic empire.[40] Yet the concern with the cultural degradation of Nicaragua embodied in the plight of the campesino was essential to turning the elite not just against Somoza but toward the forces of revolution.

Nicaragua's Conservative oligarchy had in an earlier era cultivated an image of itself as having a uniquely close relationship to their country's poor, thanks to a cattle-raising culture that united elite and poor in a wholesome enterprise tied to the land.[41] This mythology arose as a direct reaction to US-imposed dollar diplomacy of the 1920s that undermined the oligarchy's economic power and caused Conservative elites to side first with the anti-American rebellion of Augusto Sandino and then with the authoritarian dictatorship of Anastasio Somoza García. In the 1970s, although Somoza Debayle was enriching himself through earthquake reconstruction, other elite families prospered too. The children of this elite, as in the generation of Sandino, disdained materialism and began to look to rural rebellion to rid the country of the foreign influence they believed was degrading their country. Unlike the earlier generation, many of these youths abandoned their comfortable lifestyles and joined in the revolutionary cause.[42] Perhaps more remarkably, they were joined in their utopian revolutionary hopes by an older generation that had been steeped in an ideology of authoritarian corporatism but became disillusioned by the US-driven modernization project's success in transforming their imagined national identity into the despotic caricature that was Anastasio Somoza Debayle.

Pablo Antonio Cuadra united the unstable impulses of reaction and revolution in Nicaragua. Over five decades of life as a public intellectual, he constructed what he acknowledged to be a romanticized image of the Nicaraguan campesino. He ascribed the Nicaraguan national genius to the legacy of a war-like Nahua culture and the artful rebelliousness of the Chorotega, which mixed with the blood of the conquistadors to create Nicaragua's unique *mestizaje*. He and fellow members of Nicaragua's intellectual elite cherished the mestizo avatars of Nicaraguan national culture such as Rubén Darío, who upset the hierarchy between Europe and the Americas by becoming the voice of literary modernism in the nineteenth century. In the search for a political ideal in the 1930s, members of this intellectual elite had embraced in quick succession the rebellion of Augusto Sandino and the reaction of Anastasio Somoza García. By the 1970s, Cuadra had become one of the Somoza dynasty's most vocal critics, and he and his fellow Conservatives began to embrace the spirit of rebellion.

The young scions of Granada's rich families who in the 1920s created a nationalist poetic vanguard had united in rejecting a "bourgeois spirit" that they saw emanating from the cultural influence of the United States. They were themselves steeped in US culture and lauded poets like Ezra Pound who aestheticized a disintegrative modernism. Like many other artistic elites in the interwar period, the Nicaraguans looked toward a quasi-fascist authoritarianism as a bulwark against fragmentation. Though Cuadra wrote some of the most influential texts on Nicaraguan national identity, his early work is concerned with what he saw as a "pan-hispanic" ideal, the possibility of reviving a Spanish American empire in the New World.[43] The work of Cuadra and José Coronel Urtecho was greeted warmly in Falangist Spain, though even these intellectuals thought this work's explicit imperialism too inflammatory for public consumption.[44]

In the 1960s, both Cuadra and Coronel Urtecho began to reconsider their nation's place in the international system. Cuadra and his colleague Pedro Joaquín Chamorro at *La Prensa* held on to the vanguardist critique of the bourgeoisie. Inverting the developmentalist vision of a national bourgeoisie as a lodestar of progress, Cuadra compared the members of his class to the perpetually underdeveloped Oscar from Günter Grass's post-Nazi work *The Tin Drum*: "Oscars of our cowardly middle class, Oscar-leaders with their booming voices that break window glass, but are venal and submissive; Oscar-priests, excellencies, titles from Harvard, white collars, Oscars-honoris causa. Oscars

all over [*hasta en la sopa*]."[45] Cuadra had, by the 1970s, rejected the antiliberal-
ism of his youth and instead embraced a liberal internationalism based on the
rule of law as the only protection for Nicaragua against both external and internal depredations.[46] Although he refused to embrace the Marxism that was radicalizing Nicaragua's youth, he acknowledged the usefulness of Marxist critiques
of ideologies of power.[47] He printed the radical poems of Sandinista youth in
La Prensa's prestigious cultural supplement and helped free from prison radicals
corralled by the Guardia.[48] Cuadra and Chamorro rejected outright, however,
the FSLN's strident critique of the bourgeoisie as a class; they upheld instead
the rural vision of the peasant small farmer and elite proprietor working in close
harmony as the essence of national identity. It was the cultural vulgarity of the
bourgeoisie, not its class status per se, that brought dishonor to the nation.

José Coronel Urtecho, on the other hand, disavowed his reactionary past
and embraced the goals of the FSLN despite having served the Somoza regime
for decades. In doing so, however, he tried to integrate the bourgeoisie into a
new vision of nationhood. Whereas Chamorro and Cuadra harangued the fellow members of their class for their immaturity, hampering Chamorro's attempt to form an alternative party outside the Liberal and Conservative nexus
controlled by Somoza, Coronel Urtecho set out to court the bourgeoisie.[49] In
1974, Coronel Urtecho, who had belonged with Cuadra to the vanguard generation of the 1930s, gave a series of speeches to the "private sector" at the
Universidad Centroamericana in Managua. Coronel Urtecho, like Cuadra, had
supported Somoza García in his youth and had been involved with the regime
through the late 1950s, when he retired from politics. He would return to political life in the early 1970s by recanting his early political errors and giving his
full support to the forces of the FSLN.[50] In his speeches to the private sector, he
formulated a blueprint for the coming cultural campaign against the Somoza
regime and enlisted the support of the capitalist elite. He gently mocked the
technocratic language of groups like the Instituto Centroamericano de Administración de Empresa (INCAE), which he said had, under the influence of the
United States, brought a "linguistic inflation" to Nicaragua and made private
enterprise unintelligible to the rest of the world.[51] More damningly, he suggested
that private enterprise was perpetuating a "colonial relationship" between the
United States and Nicaragua. He argued for the role of poets like himself in
repairing both this linguistic inflation and, by extension, the colonial relationship.[52] They could harness the beneficial influences of US culture, like its
modernist poetry, while resisting technocratic and consumer culture.

Coronel Urtecho appealed to the instinct for public relations of the entrepreneurial class, pointing out that revolutionary poet Ernesto Cardenal had filled a

stadium of fifteen thousand people in Caracas.[53] Inverting Cuadra's fears about the degradation of postearthquake Managua, Coronel pointed out that the beautiful murals inside the newly constructed malls showed the fruit of the marriage of capitalist and cultural development.[54] Politics in Managua was at a "dead end," but Coronel Urtecho suggested that an alliance of the cultural elite with the entrepreneurial class might bring about a renaissance. He also implied that the poetic vanguard's alliance with the political vanguard was not a threat to the country's economic well-being but might open still more economic opportunities.[55]

To corroborate the marketing potential of national culture, Nicaraguans could look proudly to the fact that the voice of the Nicaraguan peasantry was being heard in Europe, not in the form of tales of human rights abuses but in the songs of accordionist Carlos Mejía Godoy and his group Los de Palacagüina. Folk songs in campesino dialect like "Son tus perjúmenes mujer" became popular in Spain, bringing about a surprising "reconquest" of the former colonial country while also giving voice to the "anonymous" Nicaraguan peasant.[56] The song sold one hundred thousand copies, and Mejía Godoy used the attention he received in the Spanish press to publicize Somoza's abuses.[57] Thanks to this publicity, Spain would be one of the first countries to cut its military aid to the Somoza regime.[58]

As folk music became a vehicle for human rights activism, Ernesto Cardenal's idealized Christian community on the archipelago of Solentiname in Lake Nicaragua created a link between cultural appreciation of the peasantry and insurrection.[59] There he encouraged the campesinos to create art and poetry to express their distinct worldview. Rather than the high modernist style of Darío's poetry, which had provided the foundation for cultural nationalism, elite Nicaraguans began to take pride in the rough voice of the peasant, finding there an authenticity that economic modernization threatened to destroy. The radical intellectuals of the FSLN criticized previous attempts by the cultural elite to "co-opt" the voice of the poor in the numerous novels written in the vernacular language of rural Nicaragua.[60] The workshops of Cardenal instead attempted to allow the poor to speak for themselves, even as they were inculcated with Cardenal's own aesthetic practice.[61] It was in Solentiname that Mejía Godoy would find inspiration for his "Misa Campesina," or peasant mass, which linked liberation theology to Nicaragua's revolutionary struggle.[62] Many of Mejía Godoy's songs and Cardenal's social experiments carried a more radical program than simply rescuing the voice of the campesino. Mejía Godoy's song "Cristo de Palacagüina" imagines Christ being born in Nicaragua's interior; instead of following in the footsteps of his carpenter father, he states: "I want to be a guerrillero." In 1977, members of Cardenal's radical community on Solentiname launched raids against the Guardia, bringing harsh reprisals.

The FSLN drew on romantic visions of rural life to recruit the children of the oligarchy and the urban middle classes, asserting that armed struggle in "la montaña" could reconnect the fragments of national identity. In the mountains, FSLN cadres strove to shed their bourgeois backgrounds and get in touch with an authentic peasant consciousness.[63] Although the FSLN's attempts to recruit campesinos were often disappointing, the training of urban cadres in the mountains helped forge a long-term commitment to the struggle.[64]

As stories of human rights abuses began to gain international attention, the rhetoric of *La Prensa* took ever more radical turns as its editors flirted with the cause of revolutionaries and attempted to build a broad national alliance.[65] The editors downplayed the threat of communism, understanding that Somoza's staunch anticommunism was key to his grip over the imagination of those who controlled aid in Washington. The editors argued instead that the nationalism of Nicaragua's people would prevent the creation of a Cuban-style socialist state.[66] Social Christianity rooted in the simple piety of most Nicaraguans was the antidote to totalitarian takeover for Cuadra and Chamorro. They implicitly believed that the return to power of Nicaragua's culturally conservative oligarchy could best check the radical impulses of both an imperial modernity and a peasantry in rebellion (figure 3.1).

Pedro Joaquín Chamorro was the most prominent opposition figure in Nicaragua, and he made his newspaper the center of a nationwide and ultimately global campaign to discredit Somoza not only in Nicaragua but also internationally. In 1974 he began a campaign to mobilize public opinion to prosecute the accused rapists of Amada Pineda, a woman from the rural north who was arrested and tortured by the Guardia.[67] Though Pineda's husband was accused of being a communist, Chamorro and others claimed that her Nicaraguan womanhood trumped any political affiliation.[68] Thus Chamorro and others cultivated the "myth of rural sanctity," by which the purity of rural culture, particularly as cultivated and supervised by a cultural elite, could provide a bulwark against the depredations of both capitalist and communist modernity.[69]

In December 1974, the Somoza government declared a state of siege and instituted press censorship after the FSLN's successful attack on the home of Chema Castillo, who was holding a Christmas party for the US ambassador. When censorship was lifted in September 1977, owing to pressure from the US government, Chamorro reignited his campaign to delegitimize the Somoza regime. His target was the Centro Industrial de Hemoterapia, better known as Plasmaféresis. The company, reportedly owned by Cuban exiles connected with Somoza's financial empire, extracted the blood plasma of Managua's poorest

Aumentan los desaparecidos

OCOTAL (J. A. Sánchez). Visiblemente preocupados y con la caracterizada timidez que es habitual entre las personas sencillas, los campesinos Hipólito Rodríguez Colindres y su compañera Tomasa Lagos Maradiaga, originarios del lugar llamado Macuelizo, Depto. de Nueva Segovia, se presentaron ante mí con el fin de hacer del conocimiento público, por este medio de difusión lo que literalmente declararon para el mismo y que reza de la siguiente manera: "Señor periodista: venimos a decirle que nosotros queremos que

Pasa a la última página No. 5

Hipólito Rodríguez Colindres y Tomasa Lagos

Tal a como se veía venir, los doce nicaragüenses encausados por el gobierno por haber suscrito un documento pidiendo un diálogo nacional para encauzar al país por los caminos de la democracia, fueron fulminados con auto de prisión por la comisión de los delitos presuntos de:

—Asociación para delinquir; Institución para delinquir; Rebelión; Delito contra la Constitución Política del Estado y Apología del delito.

La sentencia fue dictada por el Juez 1º de lo Criminal de Distrito Dr. Guillermo Rivas Cuadra a los 23 días de haber-

Pasa a la última página No. 3

Valiente relato de campesino

Alejandro Aguirre Godoy.

Confirmada insolvencia del BAVINIC

OCOTAL (J. A. Sánchez). Sin andar con titubeos y con ánimo sereno, lo que es propio de quien dice la verdad, aunque en su contra se pudiera tomar cualquier represalia, el señor Alejandro Aguirre Godoy, de 32 años, quien dice ser nativo de Jalapa, Departamento de

Nueva Segovia y trabajador del Sr. René Paguaga Midence, en la finca de El Volcán, donde se desempeña como mandador de la misma, declara lo siguiente: "que el día lunes cinco de los corrientes, como a las diez de la mañana, cuando venía viajan-

Pasa a la última página No. 4

A solicitud del Sr. Fausto Zelaya, la AID, hizo una nueva carta afirmando que el faltante de cuatro millones de córdobas en el BAVINIC, se debe a que Nicaragua no ha enterado aún el dinero que tenía que depositar para el programa de viviendas.

Pasa a la última página No. 8

Figure 3.1. Two front-page images from *La Prensa*: The first story depicts the fearfulness of rural Nicaraguans, describing the "characteristic timidity habitual among simple people," while the second tells of the campesino's "valiant story" told "without hesitation and with serene spirit," demonstrating the peasantry's incipient aggressive defiance ("Aumentan los desaparecidos" and "Valiente relato de campesino," *La Prensa*, December 9, 1977).

citizens for export.[70] *La Prensa*'s campaign attacking Plasmaféresis, shown in figure 3.2, compared the "vampiric" extraction of the blood of poor Nicaraguans to genocide, and especially condemned its exploitation of women.[71]

Though conservative and radical groups relied on religious rhetoric to justify their stance against the government, the Catholic Church itself acted on its own imperatives. The decision of the Church hierarchy to turn against the Somoza regime marked a major shift in the weight of elite opinion against Somoza. During the early 1970s, Nicaraguan bishops condemned the Somoza regime for substituting force for legitimacy and came close to advocating open rebellion by insisting on a "duty of moral resistance."[72] Catholic missionaries were often in closest contact with rural Nicaragua, and, in 1976, a group of North American Capuchin priests working in rural Zelaya province began reporting the abuses of the Guardia to the US embassy and to the press.[73] By 1977, the Church leadership was openly defying the Somoza regime and calling for an end to the Guardia's abuses and corruption. The publication of Bishop Miguel Obando y Bravo's letters condemning the Somoza regime in congressional committees, Amnesty International human rights reports, and the international press added legitimacy to voices calling for Somoza's immediate removal.[74]

The lifting of the state of siege under US pressure allowed stories of large-scale massacres to circulate: forty-two peasants reported killed in the village of Kaskita, forty-four in Varillal.[75] The Guardia used torture to extract forced confessions or as reprisals for alleged collaboration with guerrillas. The land of

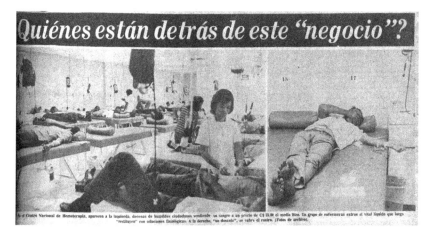

Figure 3.2. *La Prensa* illustration of the workings of Plasmaféresis ("Quienes están detrás este 'negocio'?," *La Prensa*, September 28, 1977).

dead, incarcerated, or missing peasants was confiscated by the Guardia and parceled out among soldiers and their informants.[76] The reports of atrocities in rural Nicaragua became symbolic of a universal struggle when picked up by new human rights–oriented NGOs in Washington. Groups such as the Washington Office on Latin America began to lobby for Congress to address the human rights violations, connecting abuses in Nicaragua to a greater moral failing in US foreign policy in the post–Vietnam War era. Though these groups took the plight of rural Nicaragua as the basis of their critique, they translated it into the language of human rights and thus erased the national particularity to which Nicaragua's elite opposition clung.

In response to lobbying, congressmen such as Ed Koch and Donald Fraser began to hold hearings to investigate the charges of human rights abuses in the Nicaraguan countryside. The hearings began in the House Committee on International Relations, to bring attention to the situation in Central America. They soon moved to the House Appropriations Committee, which was responsible for making concrete decisions about foreign aid. In an attempt at balance, the congressmen invited speakers in favor of and opposed to Somoza's continued rule. Somoza supporters invoked his faithful adherence to US anticommunist policies and warned of the dangers of a Cuban-backed insurgency. The congressmen invited Pedro Joaquín Chamorro to testify but the Somoza government revoked his passport because of a case against him pending in the Nicaraguan courts. In his stead, FSLN collaborator Fernando Cardenal, brother of Ernesto, gave a blistering testimony that accused the regime of genocide, creating concentration camps, and carrying out a total war in the countryside.[77] Chamorro was furious with what he believed were unsubstantiated exaggerations in Cardenal's testimony, straining his relationship with both radical members of his family and thus the FSLN itself.[78] Chamorro's rage might also have stemmed from recognition that he was losing control over the anti-Somoza movement. Though he privately suggested that if his own movement failed, he would go into exile and help the FSLN, he also began to predict his own martyrdom at hands of Somoza.[79] After receiving a series of menacing threats from Somoza cronies, he published a response in *La Prensa* that ended with the sentence "I await with tranquil conscience and peaceful soul the blow you have planned for me."[80]

Somoza's attempt to isolate Chamorro gave FSLN collaborators an opportunity to become the voice of the Nicaraguan opposition in Washington. This development would in turn contribute to the belief among Somoza supporters in Washington and radicalizing critics in Managua that the only choice for Nicaragua's future was between Somoza and the Sandinistas. Neither the FSLN nor Somoza objected to this belief, as both considered that in such a Manichean conflict their own side would be victorious.

Carter's Human Rights Policy

Human rights came to define public debate over Nicaragua thanks to the confluence of a growing lobby in the United States and the concerted efforts of Nicaragua's own anti-Somoza opposition. Though many other countries received US congressional and media scrutiny of their human rights practices, Nicaragua was salient because of the long US involvement there and its dictator's overt use of US support to bolster his power. As other countries like Guatemala and El Salvador rejected US aid with human rights conditions, Nicaragua became one of the few recipients that accepted and even embraced the public spectacle that the aid process was becoming.

US politicians and elite Nicaraguans opposed to Somoza agreed about two things: Somoza's security apparatus needed reform to better respect human rights, and Nicaragua needed US investment and aid to foster development. Given the profound entanglement between US military and development aid to Nicaragua, it would prove difficult to disengage political and military support for the Somoza regime while also continuing funding for development. These difficulties were exacerbated by the Carter administration's human rights policy, which attempted to combine the moral resonance of human rights with concrete policies for encouraging reform. The compromise that ensued, a turn toward channeling development aid away from government and toward the private sector, would nonetheless set the groundwork for a new paradigm in US foreign aid.

Far from carrying out a "crusade" based on ideological presuppositions, the Carter administration came only gradually to make human rights the center of its foreign policy.[81] The move was in reaction to the international and domestic clamor against abuses in places like Nicaragua, which forced the Carter administration to face the consequences of years of US modernization policies and support for undemocratic regimes like that of the Somozas.[82] The impetus for action came from the international publicity campaigns and from threats from Congress to cut foreign aid to allied governments if no action was taken to rectify abuses.[83] Although human rights is identified as the essential element of Carter's foreign policy, his administration's decision making in Latin America was often driven by concern to promote "nonintervention."[84] The centerpiece of Carter's policy in Latin America was turning over the Panama Canal to Panamanian sovereignty, a symbolic gesture to redress past interventions as well as a practical attempt to avoid an anti-American backlash that could disable the canal. This was meant to symbolize a larger return of sovereignty to Latin America as a whole.[85] It was hoped that this would restore a presumably lost sense of self-respect and self-determination to Latin Americans even as the move helped to reduce US entanglements that could lead to unpopular interventions such as in the Dominican Republic and Vietnam.

Carter and his appointees made numerous speeches touting the new turn in US foreign policy, vowing to "speak frankly about injustice, both at home and abroad."[86] Critics condemned this idealistic turn in foreign policy as a dangerous "missionary impulse" or "crusade" that threatened to entangle the United States government more deeply in foreign affairs. Away from the public eye, however, Carter spoke more often of a different sort of missionary impulse. He looked most favorably on intimate connections between the United States and poorer countries through "people to people" programs such as the Peace Corps or the actions of nongovernmental groups such as Christian missionaries. In a national security meeting, he mused about the good work done by a church group in Atlanta that sent thirty people into the mountains of Central America. Though publicly committed to a human rights agenda, he frequently expressed the belief that US–Latin American relations could be improved only on an interpersonal level. He thought sending congressmen to Central America in the style of the missionary-vacations of Christian charity groups provided "a good opportunity to exert our influence in an exciting and enjoyable way."[87]

The public face of Carter's human rights policy was the Bureau of Human Rights and Humanitarian Affairs in the State Department, led by civil rights activist Patricia Derian and her deputy Mark Schneider. This branch was engaged in putting human rights abuses in the public eye and thus pressuring repressive regimes to correct their abuses by condemning them in the tribunal of public opinion. The bureau's staff was opposed to the State Department tradition of "quiet diplomacy," which Derian and Schneider argued had long overlooked egregious abuses of human rights. Though Nicaragua was only one country among many in which US economic and military aid supported an illiberal regime, the long history of close cooperation between the two countries gave increased "symbolic value" to support for Somoza.[88] The tradition of quiet diplomacy continued alongside the new outspoken denunciation of abuses and helped cause the public impression that the Carter administration was vacillating in its commitment to human rights. For example, Undersecretary of State Terence Todman was dismissed for being too outspoken in his advocacy of the older tradition of diplomacy even while the administration itself took a more conservative turn.[89]

The State Department under Secretary Cyrus Vance organized a special committee to integrate the human rights issue with US foreign aid. Led by Deputy Secretary Warren Christopher, the Interagency Group on Human Rights and Foreign Assistance, or "Christopher Committee," attempted to debate policies in terms of "carrot and stick." This approach proved to be too blunt an instrument to carry out human rights initiatives, as the bureaucratic imperative to keep aid flowing on schedule made it difficult to signal both to the American public and Congress, as well as human rights violators, that aid was being cut off for specific definable reasons. Traditionalists argued that cutting off all aid would leave the US government with no leverage whatsoever and thus without recourse to influence friendly regimes.[90]

The "basic human needs" doctrine, like human rights protection, was pushed by the US Congress to disentangle development from the politics of authoritarianism in poor countries. As with Invierno, however, programs designed to benefit the poor of countries like Nicaragua remained complicit in the politics of dictatorship. After the increase of congressional scrutiny over aid programs, USAID put increased emphasis on two programs planners thought might satisfy "basic needs" criteria. Multimillion-dollar programs were designed to increase nutrition and reform Nicaragua's poorly funded public education system. The nutrition program, part of which was intended to encourage the iodization of salt to reduce thyroid disease, was tainted by the fact that the Somoza family owned one of the largest salt processors, and encouraging the expensive iodization process would drive smaller competitors out of business.[91] The neutrality of the education loan was undermined by the fact that the Nicaraguan ministry of education was used to gather government employees at Liberal Party rallies and to distribute party patronage. Politicized students often seized schools, seen as bastions of government support, to express their opposition to Somoza.[92]

Somoza had powerful allies in Washington who based their support on anticommunist principles but also marshaled the language of humanitarianism to keep aid flowing. Congressmen Charlie Wilson (Democrat of Texas) and John Murphy (Democrat of New York) were long-time advocates of Somoza as a staunch anticommunist ally. They held key positions on congressional committees that enabled them to threaten to interfere with the executive branch's global commitments if aid to Nicaragua was not continued. The congressmen argued that, thanks to the recasting of US aid to Nicaragua as nonpolitical and focused on "basic human needs," cutting aid would hurt ordinary Nicaraguans.[93] The Christopher Committee also proved susceptible to the developmentalist premises of an earlier era. The committee approved loans for continuing construction of a Rio Blanco–Siuna highway project, in the heart of the zone where the Guardia committed most of its abuses, asserting that the project would help poor "pioneer families" colonize "virgin territory."[94]

The National Security Council, headed by Zbigniew Brzezinski and advised on Latin American issues by Robert Pastor, tried to coordinate the contradictory impulses present in the State Department. Brzezinski and Pastor agreed with the prevailing critique of US policy in Latin America, arguing that its "paternalism" and "interventionism" had alienated Latin Americans. They believed that the old regional policy of the United States should be replaced by a more "modern" bilateral system, in which the United States would "get the most for our money" in Latin America.[95] While in favor of Carter's human rights policy as a public relations gesture to garner the praise of Latin Americans, Pastor and Brzezinski found the lack of a clear relationship between means and ends in US policy to be a hindrance to coherent policy. They preferred to deal with the crisis in Nicaragua and other Central American countries by intervening without appearing to—for example, by encouraging friendly Latin American states to mediate the conflict in Nicaragua.[96] Pastor argued that the correct way to overcome "paternalism" was to continue US aid but disconnect it from the now old-fashioned ideology of anticommunism. The cause of the paternalistic relationship, Pastor argued, was not just US attitudes but also Latin American expectations that the United States would intervene and decide political outcomes. He argued that US policy should be directed to encouraging Latin Americans to "develop a greater sense of responsibility and self-determination" even while trying to steer events in favorable directions.[97]

By the end of the 1970s, under pressure from the competing imperatives to meet the "basic human needs" of the peasantry while not supporting a repressive regime, a new practice of foreign aid was forming. Instead of giving money to corrupt governments, money would be given directly to Nicaraguan private organizations, which would then channel this money directly to the neediest populations.[98] The US government had long encouraged domestic private aid to foreign countries, especially after natural or man-made disasters. In the 1960s the US government disbursed aid to civil society primarily to build support for the central government. The deliberate cultivation of foreign private organizations as an alternative to unpopular governments was an outgrowth of the inability to resolve contradictions within the practice of development.[99]

To resolve the problems of foreign aid, US officials turned to organizations created during the Alliance for Progress as part of the program to build opposition support for the central government. To include opposition groups in aid distribution, USAID gave small grants to local nongovernmental organizations that dealt directly with the Nicaraguan people.[100] The Instituto Nicaragüense de

Desarrollo (INDE) brought together political forces not completely beholden to the Somozas and made them a part of the Alliance. When a decade later political pressure began to make aid to Somoza untenable, aid administrators sought to make these organizations an alternative to directly funding a dictatorship. An offshoot of INDE, the Fundación Nicaragüense de Desarrollo (FUNDE) had worked with USAID since its founding in 1969.[101] Their programs to provide credit, training, and support for peasant cooperatives provided an appealing alternative to state-led development.

Ambassador James Theberge noted that FUNDE "has helped to sensitize the private sector to its more altruistic responsibilities which has led it to denounce censorship and other arbitrary acts," and "involved us in delicate confrontations with the [government of Nicaragua] as it perceives the growth of potential rivals for power."[102] Support from aid agencies deepened the ties of the Nicaraguan private sector with the US government and gave planners hope that their programs could survive the crisis in foreign aid brought by the human rights agenda. The turn to such private organizations could be justified based on the perennial notion of "self-help," undermining "an excessive dependency of the poor on government and the existing oligarchical order" and establishing "a more pluralistic and self-help oriented system for meeting basic human needs."[103]

In response to the escalating crisis in Nicaragua and the broader crisis in development thinking, the idea was taking hold both in the United States and in Nicaragua that government funding of private sector groups did not constitute illegitimate intervention. Though the idea of directing foreign aid to the private sector would become in the 1980s the hallmark of President Ronald Reagan's attempt to revolutionize US foreign affairs, it was not at first an argument for free market principles that began driving US foreign aid policy toward privatization. It was instead a reaction to the crisis in development thinking produced by the realization that economic growth and modernization did not lead to democracy. The groups that served as intermediaries between the US government and the Nicaraguan people in the 1970s would provide the nucleus for a second attempt to unseat a Nicaraguan government, when the Reagan administration turned against the Sandinista government in the 1980s.

Human Rights and the Anti-Somoza Opposition

The projection of Nicaragua's campesinos onto an international screen opened political space in Nicaragua for debate about the country's future after the lifting of censorship. Though radio broadcasts remained under severe restriction, the elite mouthpiece of *La Prensa* became the most prominent voice of the opposition in Nicaragua and abroad. In trying to come to a consensus on what would come after Somoza, the elite displayed an ideological fragmentation that would prefigure the conflicts to come. This fragmentation was rooted in the contested relationship between force and development that had long shaped Nicaragua's history.

In 1977, the *Revista Conservadora del Pensamiento Centroamericano* polled one hundred members of the country's elite on their thoughts on the Carter administration's new human rights policies.[104] The survey asked respondents how they saw the human rights situation in Nicaragua, what they thought of Carter's human rights initiatives, and whether US human rights policy violated national "self-determination." Finally, the poll asked whether respondents supported the new move to channel US aid to nongovernmental forces. These businessmen, lawyers, and men of letters were the elite who would come to lead the loose collection of opposition groups known as the Frente Amplio Opositor (FAO). The FAO, while always unstable, came closest to enveloping Nicaragua's dissenting factions. It would also be charged with negotiating between the Somoza regime, the US government, and the political organizations that vied for the authority to speak for the Nicaraguan people.

Within this elite there were contradictory tendencies. Though agreeing that the human rights situation was dire, the elite split over deeper issues of what kind of change Nicaragua should undergo. On one side were those who called for a "bourgeois" revolution, grouped around the institutions of the "private sector" created in the 1960s as part of the Alliance for Progress. On the other side were those calling for more radical change but wishing to salvage the authority of the state. In between them was Pedro Joaquín Chamorro, who attempted to create an accord between divergent revolutionary impulses.

For those who spoke out in favor of reform rather than revolution, the channeling of aid through the "private sector" was the best solution to the problem of how to meet the development needs of Nicaragua's poorest population.[105] This approach marked a change from an earlier period, when the elite relied on the institutions of the Catholic Church to both validate the elite's authority and to dispense aid for social welfare.[106] With the spread of liberation theology, the Church had itself become an unreliable ally. Instead, the reformist elite expressed hope that the institutions of the "private sector," products of the Alliance for Progress like INDE and FUNDE, could preserve valuable links to the United States while undermining the untenable Somoza regime.

Other elite voices asserted that US policies needed reform but that the private sector could not solve the nation's problems. Most prominent among these voices was that of author Sergio Ramírez. Ramírez was a founding member of the opposition Grupo de los Doce, a group of prominent Nicaraguans who advocated Somoza's removal and negotiations with the FSLN. Ramírez was also clandestinely operating in cooperation with the FSLN's Tercerista faction. He stated that "the channels most apt for channeling aid from international cooperation . . . are States, which are supposed to have the mission of national development and the well-being of their citizens."[107] Edmundo Jarquín, who worked closely with Pedro Joaquín Chamorro but would embrace the goals of the FSLN, seconded Ramírez in this. Supporters of the FSLN desired the overthrow of the Somoza regime but also wished to retain the legitimacy of the state as the primary generator of development. The most radical projects of the FSLN would need the centralized planning capabilities of a state not unlike the one Somoza had tried to build. Pablo Antonio Cuadra gave the most enigmatic response to the question, sidestepping the idea of the private sector and stressing the need to "fortify natural communities . . . so that man can defend his interests and his dignity and his liberty."[108]

While the elite spoke openly about the problem of human rights and the need for reform of development practices, its members did not address the institution that linked these problems, the Guardia Nacional. The problem of what to do with the Guardia would come to divide the elite in the coming months of civil war and negotiation. The members of the elite with the deepest ties to Nicaragua's Conservative oligarchy worried most vocally about the Guardia.[109] The Conservative opposition relentlessly critiqued the abuses of the Guardia Nacional, but their fundamental objection was that Somoza had turned the Guardia into a "partisan force."[110] Pedro Joaquín Chamorro, in the midst of his most violent diatribes against the Somoza dynasty, distinguished between Somoza's "gangster accomplices" and those who "wear their stripes in the name of the country."[111] Though the "head" of the Guardia was corrupt, its body was composed of ordinary Nicaraguans with an innate sense of honor who were often disgusted with the infamy of their leaders. "The Guardia are our brothers," Chamorro argued.[112] Only the continued intervention of the United States had preserved it as an occupying army and thereby maintained its "unmodern" nature.[113]

The Conservative faction of the elite opposition would argue at the end of 1978 that the Guardia could be reformed, as its abuses stemmed entirely from Somoza. Salaries for members of the Guardia were low, and therefore its members attained their wealth by engaging in private activities for personal enrichment. Somoza granted the upper echelon of the Guardia lucrative government posts and land, which was then cultivated by campesinos under threat of Guardia reprisals. It was thus the Guardia's role in private enrichment that led to conflicts between them and the population. As part of a campaign to resuscitate the possibility of a nonpolitical Guardia, *La Prensa* would argue for the institution of a professionalized salary system. The rank and file of the Guardia, it argued, were in fact members of the campesino class and thus merited receiving lands. Only the elite members of the Guardia were engaged in despoiling the population. With Somoza's removal, the Guardia could finally fulfill its purpose as a neutral and apolitical national army.

Members of the anti-Somoza opposition more inclined to radical solutions, such as Father Miguel d'Escoto, argued that the Guardia, as a US-created and maintained military force, had been designed solely for control. For radicals, the US claim that Somoza's self-aggrandizement was a perversion of the original purpose was belied by the US government's continued support well after Somoza's intentions to continue in power became clear. What in the United States was often seen as an unfortunate necessity of Cold War geopolitics was to these Nicaraguans part of a grand design to undermine their sovereignty.[114]

The FSLN and its supporters were the only members of the anti-Somoza opposition who desired a total removal of US support for the regime but for Somoza to remain in power.[115] They understood that Somoza was dependent—economically and, more importantly, morally—on his ties with the United States. To achieve their plan to take power through military force, the FSLN needed Somoza to remain in power until their forces were strong enough to destroy the Guardia. Should an interim government take power without an FSLN victory, the prospects for their program to remake Nicaraguan society would be remote.[116]

The "bourgeois" opposition concerned itself least with the Guardia Nacional. It was this group that Robert Pastor called the "responsible opposition" because of its willingness to maintain the institutions of the Somoza government even if Somoza himself stepped down.[117] The bourgeois opposition was also the group most willing to seek the advice and intervention of the US government. The group's roots were in Alliance for Progress–era institutions that were conceived of as fundamentally separate from the state, even as they relied on both the Nicaraguan and US government for assistance and funding. It was this group that would also ally itself most completely with the US government after the overthrow of Somoza.

Between these fractious elites was Pedro Joaquín Chamorro. His family and business connections gave him ties to all sectors of the elite, and he attempted to synthesize their points of view in an anti-Somocista ideology that brought together the socialism of the left, the capitalism of the private sector, and the Christian corporatism of the Conservative oligarchy. His party, Unión Democrática de Liberación (UDEL), was an attempt to create an umbrella organization for the anti-Somoza opposition and a mass movement among Nicaragua's people. Chamorro's attempts to be everywhere at once made it impossible for him to satisfy the demands of the elite factions, though he provided a focus both for international attention and the dictator's ire.

Mediating the Revolution

On the morning of January 10, 1978, unknown assailants in the ruins of downtown Managua assassinated Pedro Joaquín Chamorro. When news of the assassination reached the public, spontaneous uprisings began to spread all over the country. After a memorial march in Managua commemorating Chamorro turned into a riot, the offices of Plasmaféresis were among the first to be burned.[118] Later, people in the countryside would loot and burn small businesses associated with Invierno as well.[119] The private sector called for a massive general strike, closing stores and factories.

The Nicaraguan populace, subjects of plans for modernization and subjected to human rights abuses, finally became the subjects of revolution that both Conservative and radical romantic nationalists predicted. The campesino had provided the image of an authentic nationalist body in jeopardy. Nevertheless, the revolt itself was in Nicaragua's cities rather than in the countryside. The city of Managua remained the stronghold of Somoza's power despite considerable unrest. The secondary cities of Masaya, León, Estelí, and Matagalpa, which planners targeted as alternate "poles of development," became lightning rods of rebellion.[120]

By September 1978, after the FSLN successfully took over the country's Palacio Nacional and as Somoza's Guardia responded by deepening its repression, the Carter administration decided that Somoza must go.[121] Yet the administration still faced difficulties in formulating a program of action. The philosophy of nonintervention prevented any overt attempt to unseat Somoza. Rather, policymakers preferred to engage in a mediation behind the scenes. US attempts to have Somoza install an apolitical leadership for the Guardia foundered because it became impossible to both choose politically acceptable candidates and preserve the appearance that these were not handpicked successors chosen by the United States. As a total FSLN victory began to seem unavoidable, members of the Carter administration openly considered military intervention. Brzezinski declared that the United States must maintain its position as the "decisive factor in determining political outcomes in Central America."[122] An attempt was made to garner support in the Organization of American States to create a "peace-keeping force" that could intercede between the Guardia and the FSLN, but the other Latin American states rejected it outright.

As the fall of Somoza approached, the FSLN proved willing to promise anything to preserve its alliance with the bourgeoisie and avoid armed intervention by the United States. The Frente declared its desire to adhere to a mixed economy and emphasized the national character of the revolution. The governing body, the Junta de Gobierno de Reconstrucción Nacional, made up of members of the radical and Conservative opposition, hearkened back to the failed post-earthquake reconstruction of Managua. It promised a broad interclass alliance to carry out the much greater task of rebuilding a nation after the prolonged liberation struggle.

Even as FSLN representatives maintained a conciliatory tone in the last days of the rebellion, knowing the future was theirs, it was the Conservative opposition that vehemently rejected US attempts at intervention. Up until the end, the Carter administration held on to idea that the Guardia was a legitimate representative of Nicaragua's population. When US officials proposed that the junta be widened to include moderates and possibly a member of the Guardia to make it "genuinely representative of the Nicaraguan people," it was Pedro Joaquín Chamorro's widow, Violeta Barrios de Chamorro, who most loudly denounced imperial intervention.[123] Chamorro's foremost political adviser at this time was Pablo Antonio Cuadra, who remembered the failure of a previous generation to ally itself with Sandino.[124] The Conservative elite believed that the Nicaraguan people had risen as one to overthrow Somoza, and they wished to avoid becoming beholden to foreign powers, whether those of Cuba or the United States. Though the moment of unity of a nation that had risen in arms to overthrow a tyrant would not last, radicals and Conservatives briefly embraced an idea of ideological pluralism that promised to transcend the divisions of the past.

Chapter 4

Pluralism, Development, and the Nicaraguan Revolution

A few months before he was gunned down by accomplices of the Somoza dictatorship in the rubble of downtown Managua in 1978, *La Prensa* editor Pedro Joaquín Chamorro published the story "El enigma de las Alemanas."[1] In it he describes the unsettling effects of a bus full of female German tourists "with blue eyes and very white skin" arriving in Totogalpa, the town in the Segovias that fifty years before had been the site of the US marine bombardment of Augusto Sandino's forces. The German tourists initially integrate with the community, until one day they strip naked and cavort in the town's fountain while singing a Schubert lied. The combination of northern European piety and sexual permissiveness rips the community apart, and the tourists are driven out "with fixed bayonets" by the Guardia Nacional.

Chamorro's wry parable encapsulated his hopes and fears as his country's revolution was beginning to unfold. As he wrote, Nicaragua's antidictatorial movement was uniting a heterogeneous network of international allies— European and Latin American social democrats, Caribbean radicals, and internationalist fellow travelers—promising to undo the damage decades of US-supported authoritarianism had inflicted. Chamorro, like many of his relatives from elite families who supported the revolution, believed that the legacy of US intervention had distorted political life and stunted economic development. Where this elite divided was over how they imagined the future to follow: Would bringing the world to Nicaragua—either in the form of rollicking tourists or revolutionary internationalists—overcome the legacy of authoritarianism? Or did the legacy of violence and intervention represented by the Guardia Nacional and the Somoza family run too deeply?

There was a third possibility. An unprecedented coalition of international forces supported the FSLN in overthrowing Anastasio Somoza Debayle's dictatorship. This revolutionary success set off a counterrevolution that had much in common with the military backlash that Chamorro had imagined, as the United States would in the decade to come support former members of the Guardia Nacional in waging a brutal war against Nicaragua's revolution. This counterrevolution was more than a recapitulation of older forms of US-supported anticommunism, however. As with the Cuban revolution two decades earlier, which had inspired a proliferation of modernization efforts by the US government and its allies, the Nicaraguan revolution engendered new forms of US intervention that proponents hoped would constitute a different sort of revolution.[2]

Events in Nicaragua took place at a moment when actors from the global South were pushing for a transformation of the world's political and economic order to promote economic redistribution and recognize the coexistence of capitalism and socialism.[3] The Reagan administration used the crisis in Central America to respond, making Nicaragua central to its own vision of economic and political development that reconfigured both the Cold War and the North-South divide.[4] Two new US programs, the Caribbean Basin Initiative (CBI) and Project Democracy, reimagined the process of international development whose failure many credited with a rising tide of revolution in Central America.[5] These programs were more than products of preexisting ideology waiting to be implemented: they were shaped by events in Central America to which they responded. In response to Nicaraguan revolutionaries' greatest success—the mobilization of international solidarity through revolutionary diplomacy—the Reagan administration propagated its own ideal of entrepreneurial internationalism to revolutionize political and economic development worldwide. In doing so, the administration reconfigured the insurgent ethos and the organizational forms of the alliance between socialism and social democracy that had made the Nicaraguan revolution possible, to bring about its demise.

Revolutionary Pluralism

The Junta de Gobierno de Reconstrucción Nacional (JGRN), which took power in Nicaragua in July 1979, was the product of a diplomatic revolution mediated by socialists, social democrats, and revolutionary nationalists who agreed that the Somoza dictatorship was an obstacle to progress. The US government attempt at moderating the dictatorship's abuses through human rights policies while repressing insurgency with basic human needs doctrine had failed, and a diverse coalition of global actors supplanted US influence. This diverse coalition represented a climax of cooperation between incongruous forces, some of whom believed that removing a patrimonial dictatorship would liberate the forces of capitalism, while others saw removing the dictator as opening a passage to socialism. For Nicaraguans trying to manage these global forces, the future of the revolution would depend on the future of foreign aid, as the developmental order promoted by the United States was in disarray and international actors jockeyed for influence over the emerging regime.

Designed to build broad international support, the JGRN represented a cross-section of the forces at work in Nicaragua, an internationalization of Latin American corporatism in a globalizing moment.[6] The five-person junta, depicted in figure 4.1, was divided along lines of international interests with a stake in the future of Nicaragua. Guerrilla leader Daniel Ortega represented the revolutionary tutelage of Cuba, which had given the FSLN training and support, if sometimes half-heartedly, for decades. Moisés Hassan, who was the child of Palestinian immigrants, had ties to national liberation forces in the nonaligned movement. Sergio Ramírez, internationally acclaimed novelist and key player in creating the multiclass coalition Los Doce, had worked in western Europe and Costa Rica and had ties to social democracy. Alfonso Robelo was an entrepreneur who represented the interests of Nicaragua's capitalist class and had worked closely with the US government during the anti-Somoza insurrection. Violeta Barrios de Chamorro, as the widow of the slain *La Prensa* editor, represented the cultural and political voice of Nicaraguan Conservative nationalism.[7] José Coronel Urtecho, who had helped frame the revolutionary efforts at alliance-building, congratulated Sergio Ramírez that the JGRN was a "work of art" in balancing so many disparate forces.[8]

Product of both diplomatic negotiation and the military initiative of the FSLN, the JGRN staked out common ground between radical socialist revolutionaries and their domestic and international fellow travelers by declaring adherence to what would become in the decade to come a formula: "nonalignment, a mixed economy, and pluralism." Each of these terms carried both local and international meanings during a moment when newly decolonized nations challenged global power structures in international fora while nationalist revolutions spread through Central America. Adherence to "nonalignment" placed Nicaragua outside East-West conflict and allied the country

Figure 4.1. Popular depiction of the five-person JGRN, with Violeta Chamorro at the center. Photograph by Susan Meiselas. Courtesy of Magnum Photos.

with nations calling for a New International Economic Order and global re-distribution. The JGRN's prescription for a "mixed economy" staked out a middle ground between free markets and state socialism, whose "principle constitutive elements" the junta promised "would be defined later on." Drawing from the lexicon of postcolonial internationalism, these slogans opened the possibility for links between Nicaragua and "all nations respectful of self-determination and mutually beneficial economic relations," a direct allusion to revolutionary critiques of US political and economic influence.[9] The creators of the JGRN program—most importantly Sergio Ramírez, the Grupo de Los Doce, and the Tercerista faction of the FSLN—emphasized the need for international assistance for reconstruction of a country wrecked by the Somoza counterinsurgency. The myriad abuses in the countryside and cities had been chronicled to the world as a product of US-supported counterinsurgency programs causing as much as $480 million in damages and $2 billion in production losses.[10]

The third term of the JGRN program, "pluralism," had only recently taken on new significance in the argot of international diplomacy thanks to the efforts of the Latin American left.[11] During the development decade of the 1960s, pluralism was touted by US modernizers as "the genius of American society," both a central goal of the modernization process and bulwark against its perverse socialist variant.[12] In the early 1970s, the Latin American left appropriated the concept of pluralism in its battles against US hegemony. When socialist Salvador Allende took power in Chile in 1970, he embraced international pluralism in a bid to encourage peaceful coexistence with potential antagonists in neighboring South American military regimes.[13] "Ideological pluralism" was soon picked up by Latin American and Caribbean leaders, such as Jamaica's Michael Manley, pushing both for an easing of sanctions against Cuba and greater US tolerance for self-determination in the hemisphere to include socialist forms of economic organization.[14]

This form of pluralism played an important role in Nicaraguan revolutionary alliance-building. During the growing crisis brought by escalating national revolt and international disapproval of the Somoza regime, Pedro Joaquín Chamorro and his allies played a key role in legitimizing the growing confluence of radical leftists and reformist elites. Chamorro's party, UDEL, was founded with the support of socialist and social Christian union organizations. The party defined its program of "ideological pluralism" around accepting socialist participation, despite its leaders' anticipation of US opposition.[15] The Tercerista faction of the Sandinistas, who made alliance with capitalist elites central to their insurrectionary strategy, had close ties with Chamorro's anti-

Somoza movement, even though Chamorro himself was wary of Cuban control of the revolutionary process. Cultural figures with Conservative backgrounds such as José Coronel Urtecho and Ernesto Cardenal used their literary authority to argue for a fundamental compatibility between social revolution and nationalist values. They also used their social networks as a conduit for money, arms, and conspiracy between clandestine struggle in Nicaragua and a far-flung international support network.[16]

Sergio Ramírez personally united Liberal and Conservative Nicaraguan antidictatorial factions while mediating the radical socialist and social democratic tendencies that would make the Nicaraguan revolution possible. Ramírez came from a Liberal background and was radicalized along with other students in the university city of León after a 1959 government massacre.[17] His literary work put him in contact with Conservative figures such as Coronel Urtecho and Pedro Joaquín Chamorro. He worked in Costa Rica as head of the publishing company EDUCA to propagate Central American educational literature as a counterweight to educational materials funded by the US government, and he spent time in the early 1970s in Berlin on a scholarship to write a novel about the failed Nicaraguan revolutions of previous decades.[18] Returning to Costa Rica, Ramírez created a solidarity network that broadcast human rights abuses and condemned the economic empire built by US support for the Somoza family.[19]

In 1978 Ramírez was contacted by former West German chancellor Willy Brandt through two German journalists traveling in Costa Rica.[20] Brandt was in the process of building a more assertive role for the Socialist International (SI) that he took over in 1976, shifting the organization of socialist parties from its European focus to an international posture.[21] This involved convening party congresses in Caracas and Lisbon that brought Latin American and European socialists and social democrats into contact. Brandt's SI gave special attention to Latin America's antidictatorial movements at a time when US economic and political hegemony was under attack in Central America. In creating international ties, Brandt worked to build the profile of both the SI and his own West German Social Democratic Party that was undergoing a global expansion. German party organizations made a case in the Third World for Germany's "desirability as a partner" in both politics and trade, and contrasted their own style of subdued anticommunist internationalism with the aggressive Cold War posture of the United States.[22] Brandt also used his connections with the German Social Democratic Party's Friedrich Ebert Stiftung (FES) to play a greater role in Latin American politics, promoting programs for political education that would build networks of party leaders.[23]

Brandt used his personal reputation to build bridges between European and Latin American politics, comparing the battle against Somoza to his own antifascist experiences during World War II.[24] The antidictatorial movement in Central America resonated with more recent European events, as socialists had played a key role in the postdictatorial moments in Spain and Portugal following the demise of Iberia's authoritarian regimes.[25] The SI had worked with the socialist leaders of these countries, Mario Soares and Felipe Gonzalez, to steer the emerging democratic governments away from communist control and build social democratic institutions. With Ramírez as intermediary, the German FES and Olof Palme's Swedish Social Democratic Party helped fund the regional diplomacy of the Grupo de Los Doce in coordinating Sandinista militants and non-Sandinista elites who worked to negotiate an end to Somoza.[26] The anti-Somoza struggle soon became a celebrated cause among European and Latin American social democrats thanks to the publicity campaign of Sandinista supporters such as Ernesto Cardenal, who was given a heroic welcome at the SI-sponsored "Conference on Processes of Democratization in the Iberian Peninsula and Latin America" outside Lisbon in 1978.[27]

The collaboration between Nicaraguan revolutionaries and socialist internationalists retraced many of the steps of the antidictatorial coalition of the early 1960s that had shaped the Alliance for Progress, now with European and Latin American backers in place of the United States.[28] The program of the JGRN was formed at FES-funded workshops outside San José at institutions once funded by the CIA.[29] European social democrats were also replacing the influence of the AFL-CIO in Latin American labor organizations, a key component of the US cultural Cold War during the 1960s.[30] Rather than alarming US officials, the role of European political foundations in mediating the Nicaraguan transition helped mollify US fears of Cuban influence. US officials reported that German training of leaders such as Los Doce coordinator Sergio Ramírez could help prevent revolutionaries from attempting to "duplicate the Cuban system in Nicaragua."[31]

Sandinista militants shaped their insurrectionary strategy around maintaining the allegiance of international social democracy to build economic support and forestall US intervention. They sought the assistance of the erstwhile associate of Alliance for Progress planner Adolf Berle, former Costa Rican president José Figueres, who provided weapons buried at his farm La Lucha to the Sandinista revolutionary army that used Costa Rica as base of operations.[32] Sergio Ramírez recruited avowed non-Marxist Edén Pastora to the revolutionary cause in order to convince social democratic leaders such as Venezuela's Carlos Andrés Pérez to support the revolution. Pastora had served as intermediary between the FSLN and Fernando Agüero's Conservatives during the failed 1967 uprising in Managua, but by the mid-1970s had retired as a revolutionary to focus on shark fishing in Costa Rica. After his recruitment to the Tercerista faction by Ramírez, his role in the 1978 assault on the Nicaraguan Palacio Nacional catapulted him to global prominence, and he became the face of the Sandinista revolution despite his ideological incongruence with other militants.

While the FSLN–social democracy connection worked to mitigate the image of Nicaragua's revolutionaries as Cuba-inspired vanguardists, many Europeans saw Nicaragua as helping to radicalize their own social commitments. The SI's general secretary argued that Nicaragua's fusion of radicals and reformists might "reconcile real freedom and far reaching socialist changes."[33] At the FES-sponsored "Seminario Internacional de Solidaridad con el Pueblo de Nicaragua," the socialist and social democratic parties of Europe and Latin America declared the Nicaraguan left's popular front strategy "worthy of imitation" in the face of "dependent capitalism," the "oligarchic state," and the "interventionist" tendencies of the United States.[34] Along with supporting the revolutionary efforts of the Frente Farabundo Martí para la Liberación Nacional (FMLN) in El Salvador, the social democratic representatives condemned US colonialism in Puerto Rico, claiming that the unincorporated US territory represented a model for colonialism in the hemisphere that they were combating.

The FSLN welcomed the support of anticommunist groups such as the Socialist International on the same principle of a tactical alliance with groups it saw as inherently "pro-imperialist" such as Nicaragua's national bourgeoisie.[35] The attitude toward national and international alliances reflected the influence of dependency theory on the FSLN's ideology, making the JGRN the first "dependentista and revolutionary government in Latin America" according to Jorge Castañeda.[36] In the hands of Sandinista thinkers, dependency theory was transformed from being primarily a theory of economic underdevelopment into a political praxis loosely based on economic theory. The JGRN, led by the dependency-influenced FSLN, put in practice a tactical concept of "diversified dependency" that attempted to turn the country's weakness into strength.[37] Revolutionary nationalist governments like that of Algeria in the 1970s first put forth this idea in recognition of their political and economic vulnerability in the international system.[38] Dependency theorists too argued that events of the 1970s had rendered economic autonomy unviable, necessitating a change in tactics.[39] By diversifying its domestic and international allies, the FSLN attempted to translate the international solidarity created by the anti-Somoza movement into both economic support and protection against imperial intervention.

When the JGRN took power in 1979, young Central American techno-crats such as Arturo Cruz Jr. looked hopefully to the Sandinista vanguard in hopes that Nicaragua might provide an alternative model to the stagnant military modernization that dominated the region.[40] The tactical coexistence of socialism and capitalism in the revolutionary moment led to the tentative acceptance of the revolution by institutions closely linked to US power in Central America. INCAE, the business school created during the Alliance for Progress, had since the 1960s trained Central American academics and business leaders in the use of transnational institutions such as the Central American Common Market to promote economic growth. INCAE's educators in the 1970s developed their own vision of ideological pluralism in light of the diversity of regimes in the region, from democratic Costa Rica to authoritarian Guatemala. The school trained business leaders in the idea of "political solvency," the ability for business administrators to work with diverse regime types to attain their economic goals.[41] With political transformation, they hoped, the Common Market might once again begin to function. Anti-Somoza business leaders believed that revolutionary pluralism might bring much-needed foreign aid that Somoza could no longer procure.[42] Some hoped Sandinista promises of a mixed economy might create a state capitalism that defused social tensions by redirecting economic surplus to promote social change, as earlier US-sponsored programs had purported but failed to do.[43]

The embrace of ideological pluralism by the JGRN blurred lines between capitalists and socialists in the name of "reconstruction," a term chosen for its broad appeal.[44] The states that based their support most firmly on revolutionary solidarity were the western hemisphere's two foremost revolutionary powers, Mexico and Cuba. Mexico's government under president José López Portillo supported the new Nicaragua as a revolutionary state-building project. Though Mexico accepted the FSLN as a vanguard party, it also sought to "foil an eventual complete Marxist take-over."[45] Fears of such a takeover were stoked by Cuba's role as intermediary between Nicaragua and the Soviet bloc in Eastern Europe. Though critics of the FSLN's social project claimed that the pluralist pretenses of the party were a mask for increasing dependence on international communism, the socialist bloc nations expressed wariness of the nascent revolution's intentions. Raúl Castro, for instance, attempted to convince the Soviet premier that the presence of priests at the highest levels of the FSLN was only for show, even though these priests played indispensable roles in the revolutionary project.[46]

The participation of social democrats in the revolutionary coalition helped convince the United States to support the new government. The JGRN asked the United States and western Europeans not for "help, but solidarity."[47] Instead, these countries conditioned their aid based on what became known as the "original program" of the revolution, the tripartite formula of "nonalignment, a mixed economy, and pluralism." The US Congress, with President Jimmy Carter's support, offered a $75 million aid package directed toward the private sector.[48] US aid to Nicaragua's revolutionary government was made possible by continuing the practice of detaching foreign aid from central governments begun during the Somoza dictatorship. When in the late 1970s the Carter administration had been forced by political pressure and its own avowed commitment to human rights to cut aid to the Somoza regime, aid continued in the form of assistance to promote the "basic human needs" of the population and to the private sector to cultivate nongovernmental allies. Because of the FSLN's ideology of internal and external diversification, aid to the private sector was compatible with the revolutionary project, and some expressed hope that they might even "finance a socialist project with North American imperial dollars."[49] US officials in turn believed that Nicaraguan dependence on both public and private US funds would lock the revolution into a relationship with the capitalist world and steer it on a "pragmatic, pluralist course."[50]

Thanks to both successful revolutionary diplomacy and outside intervention, Nicaragua was becoming a laboratory for experiments in transnational civil society funded overtly and covertly by para-state organizations with incongruous visions of the country's future. Along with its public aid to support pluralism, the Carter administration was also offering covert aid to "democratic elements" within the country.[51] Thanks to the diversification of foreign aid brought by European and Latin American governments, the US government would not be alone in this practice. Other nongovernmental political groups such as Costa Rica's Christian Democrats, supported by the German Konrad Adenauer Stiftung, supported their own "grass roots effort . . . bypassing the government" to steer Nicaragua toward "pluralistic development."[52] The newspaper *La Prensa*, which turned from celebration to critique of the new government soon after the revolution, received not just support from the US government but also nongovernmental groups in Scandinavia, allowing it to maintain an oppositional voice to the FSLN.[53] Internationalists also used funding from their own countries to support prorevolutionary organs such as the journal *Envío,* funded in part by the Canadian government, which became a major source for rallying anti-imperialist internationalist sentiment.[54]

As predicted in Pedro Joaquín Chamorro's novella, the world came to Nicaragua in 1979. The international support for Nicaraguan reconstruction and its manifestation in the development of Nicaraguan civil society gave a wide variety of governments and people around the world a stake in the direction the revolution would take. According to the FSLN's strategy of diversifying its dependencies, international pluralism would allow the country and the revolution to maintain its fragile autonomy. The careful balance of internal and external pluralism was not meant to last, however. The FSLN believed that revolutionary pluralism would give way to revolutionary solidarity.

Moral Conversion and Revolutionary Solidarity

For the revolution's vanguard, the successful overthrow of the Somoza family and installation of a revolutionary government was not an end but a beginning. The successful depiction of the Somoza family as a product of US military and financial subjection made possible two revolutionary events: the commitment of a significant portion of Nicaragua's population "from the most well-off to the most exploited" to the cause, and the cooperation of social democratic governments in overthrowing the regime.[55] Revolutionaries successfully exported an ethos of "moral conversion" that succeeded in recruiting international allies to their cause.[56] For the revolution to continue, this process of moral conversion through cultivating both internal and international solidarity had to continue as well.

The Sandinista ideal of "revolutionary subjectivity" combined elements of revolutionary militancy with the cultural vanguardism of Nicaragua's own Conservative elite. One facet of this revolutionary subjectivity was modeled on the Guevaran ethos in which guerrillas, often from wealthy backgrounds, sacrificed themselves for Latin America's peasant and working classes.[57] The other facet drew from Nicaragua's cultural vanguard, which had long sought to construct a robust national identity through artistic creation. With the revolutionary victory, the entire country was transformed into a utopian space modeled both on Ernesto Cardenal's Solentiname commune and the guerrilla ordeal in "la montaña."[58]

The literacy crusade was designed to continue the struggle for revolutionary solidarity by turning national reconstruction into transformation. Like the empty center of the capital city, the revolutionaries held that the poverty and illiteracy of the country's rural population was a legacy of subjugation and dependency on imperial power and international capitalism.[59] Designed around the pedagogy of Paulo Freire and on the model of the Cuban revolution's own literacy campaign, the crusade's organizers intended to both usher Nicaragua's campesinos into the modern world and inculcate them with revolutionary values.[60] The left had critiqued the Alliance for Progress for deliberately suppressing nationalism in its educational programs, so literacy materials fused nation and revolution by using the history of the Sandinista movement as pedagogy. "La revolución" provided the five vowels on which the foundation of revolutionary literacy would be built, and the crusade itself reenacted an idealized version of the revolutionary victory. During the decades-long militant struggle against the Somoza government, guerrilla activity in "la montaña," Nicaragua's sparsely populated hinterland, had served to forge the commitment of the often urban-born and well-educated young guerrilla fighters into committed revolutionaries.[61] Simultaneously, the revolutionary Christian movement in the cities had allowed young members of the elite and middle class to learn firsthand the plight of Nicaragua's poor. The literacy crusade re-created this revolutionary commitment for a new generation, often too young to have participated in combat, and thus attempted to integrate country and city.

Members of the government like Fernando Cardenal, Jesuit priest and brother of Ernesto Cardenal, were among the most vocal advocates of the multiclass nature of the revolution. They argued that the middle and upper classes played an essential role in the revolution and that the literacy crusade would serve to create such a commitment in a new generation. Fernando Cardenal had forged his commitment while serving the poor in the barrios of Colombia, while Ernesto Cardenal owed his own conversion to a visit to revolutionary Cuba after the failure of the Alliance for Progress–funded Solentiname project.[62] The Cardenals' conversion from privileged members of Nicaragua's upper class to the cause of the poor served as a model for the commitment of an entire revolutionary generation to come. Organized into *ejércitos, milicias, guerrilleros,* and *brigadas* named for revolutionary martyrs and dressed in the peasant *cotona* blouse popularized at Solentiname, urban Nicaraguans learned firsthand about the people, geography, and culture of their own country.[63] While educating the impoverished population, they would also collect information about little-known areas of the country, mining data about archaeological treasures, mineral wealth, and folklore. Sixty thousand young Nicaraguans were mobilized in this project, which was purported to cut Nicaragua's illiteracy from 50 percent to 10 percent in a year.[64]

Revolutionary commitment could also be marketed for international consumption. Inturismo, founded in 1979, linked education and pleasure with the commitment to a new revolutionary order.[65] Internally, the agency's mission was to provide Nicaragua's working classes with leisure activities once reserved for the elite. Inturismo refurbished Somoza-era resorts like Pochomil and Montelimar that had once served a small elite, giving workers places to enjoy the country's natural environment. Inturismo offered this image of a revolutionary paradise to the outside world as well, in brochures and advertisements appearing in leftist publications in North America and Europe that depicted Nicaragua's natural beauty and its revolution. Advertisements linked the rich cultural heritage of the nation to its utopian future.[66] In collaboration with the government, solidarity organizations began to create tour groups that offered sympathetic internationalists the opportunity to participate in the enjoyment of nature and cultural enlightenment, while getting to know the revolutionary process firsthand.

The FSLN used its party apparatus to cultivate internationalists who wished to express a deeper level of commitment to the revolutionary process. In collaboration with organizations like the Nicaragua Network in the United States, which had provided assistance during the revolutionary struggle, the FSLN organized workers in the style of Cuba's Venceremos Brigades to allow internationalists to participate in the harvesting of coffee and cotton.[67] Unlike the Cuban revolution, in which young people worked on state farms to harvest sugar cane, *brigadistas* from Nicaragua, Latin America, the United States, and Europe came and worked to harvest coffee and cotton on both state and private farms. Thanks to the revolutionary mixed economy that nationalized export but not production, harvesting crops by private growers earned much-needed foreign exchange for the government and thus assisted the revolutionary process.[68] Internationalists committed to social revolution also worked to strengthen the revolutionary public sector, offering expertise in education, agriculture, and technology to fulfill the revolution's promise of social justice.[69] Work, pleasure, and espionage could even be fused: when searching for an incentive to attract help in constructing a national intelligence apparatus, interior minister Tomás Borge suggested the East German Stasi use Nicaragua as a site for international training and a pleasant vacation destination.[70]

Alongside solidarity appeals to citizen diplomats, the JGRN invited heads of state to witness the revolution firsthand. Representatives of the Socialist International traveled to Managua as part of a "Committee for the Defense of the Revolution" in order to assess the viability of social democratic foreign aid. The earliest social democratic visitors expressed cautious approval of the steps the JGRN was taking to promote social revolution and political freedom. "We could see the coalition which brought down the old regime was extremely widely based," wrote one official, "and that this diversity was represented in the new government."[71] Amid the enthusiasm for the revolutionary cause, some social democrats expressed wariness of becoming "revolutionary tourists," seduced by the promises of a new order into ignoring its contradictions.[72] Nonetheless social democrats vowed political and economic support, eliciting undisguised joy from the revolution's vanguardist leadership. FSLN directorate member Bayardo Arce—dubbed the revolution's "sunny boy" by Europeans—was the designated liaison for international missions. European support was a "second 19th of July," effused Arce, a reaffirmation of revolutionary independence that would both bring essential foreign aid and security against US interference.[73]

This belief that new international ties could promote Nicaragua's independence manifested the FSLN's revolutionary ideologies of diversified dependence and moral solidarity. The reaction of social democratic representatives, who expressed alarm at the Nicaraguans' apparent belief that such aid had no strings attached, revealed the limits of this solidarity. Brandt wrote that "it cannot be acceptable for our friends from Nicaragua to claim sanction by way of our association for everything which they deem to be appropriate in their country."[74] Leaders in Spain, Portugal, and Venezuela especially expressed fear that the FSLN was using social democratic support as a cover for Leninist takeover, something social democrats in these countries had fought against during postauthoritarian transitions. As the revolution continued, social democrats made common cause with Nicaraguan dissidents who began reaching out to the world as well, creating their own form of solidarity around revolutionary disillusionment.

Class and Revolutionary Culture

The success of both the internal and international campaigns to foster solidarity helped the FSLN claim that the revolution fused nationalist and internationalist impulses. The commitment to maintaining the revolution's nationalist character was linked to the fact that the economic and cultural elite had participated in the revolution and had been crucial to obtaining international support. The pledge to allow an economic elite to maintain relative power in the country sat uneasily, however, with the rhetoric of Marxism and liberation theology that preached the evils of capitalism. Though many members of the elite pledged their solidarity, revolutionary internationalism failed to convert an important cohort. After the honeymoon period of revolutionary pluralism, this unconverted Conservative elite began to develop a critique that drew on the FSLN's own ideas about dependency. The dissolution of the revolutionary coalition was not foreordained but played out in a dispute over the relationship between class, nation, and Nicaragua's place in the international order.[75]

For the FSLN's leaders, the figure of Augusto Sandino reconciled revolutionary internationalism with national transformation. According to Sergio Ramírez in a speech to professionals training to become part of a revolutionary managerial class, Sandino's struggle a half-century before had been "the struggle of the people as a class" against the US marine occupation.[76] In making this appeal to a classless nation, Ramírez echoed the nationalist rhetoric of Nicaragua's Conservative elite, whose members had translated their opposition to Somocismo into revolutionary enthusiasm while remaining wary of Marxist ideas about class conflict. The revolutionary program depended on the allegiance of a technically trained and internationally connected cohort, and the Sandinista program of maintaining a "mixed economy" required reproducing moral commitment among its private capitalist producers. These technocrats and the "patriotic bourgeoisie" were necessary to produce and manage an economic surplus that could be turned to revolutionary ends. Government planners would use this surplus to build the "revolutionary public sector"—state farms and small producer cooperatives—while also fulfilling the promise of meeting the "basic human needs" of Nicaragua's poor.[77]

La Prensa was the traditional organ of this professional class. Since the 1960s Pedro Joaquín Chamorro's newspaper, comanaged with literary figure Pablo Antonio Cuadra, had attempted to reconcile its anticommunist and anti-Somoza commitments. With Chamorro's death, Cuadra became the paper's manager and took over as spokesman for the nationalism it represented. He also served as adviser to Violeta Chamorro, JGRN member and widow of Pedro Joaquín. In the first months after the revolution, Cuadra offered his support for the vision of revolutionary solidarity offered by the FSLN, praising his cousin Ernesto Cardenal's program for the democratization of culture through poetry workshops based on the experience of Solentiname. Cuadra saw the revolution as the flourishing of a "creative venture," unleashing energy suppressed by the Somoza regime.[78]

In April 1980, a power struggle took place in the JGRN between the representatives of the private sector, Robelo and Chamorro, and the members who supported the FSLN. Both Chamorro and Robelo resigned when the FSLN pushed to fill the Council of State with allied organizations. Simultaneously *La Prensa*'s staff and directorate split over the paper's allegedly "pro-imperialist" editorial positions. As a result, much of the paper's staff left and started a new, pro-FSLN paper, *El Nuevo Diario*, under the direction of Chamorro family member Xavier Chamorro.[79]

Remaining at a *La Prensa* now subsidized by US funds, Cuadra appropriated the dependency critique of Latin America's left to undermine the revolutionary government's nationalist credentials. Responding to plans for revitalizing the city center devastated by the 1972 earthquake, he expressed concern that Cuban advisers were imposing foreign models on Managua by means of "poorly digested foreign manuals," echoing his own earlier critique of the US reconstruction effort after the 1972 earthquake.[80] The same foreign influence was distorting culture: Cardenal's poetry workshops that had promised cultural democratization had been turned into a formula for proletcult-style revolutionary poetry. He asserted that FSLN organ *Barricada*'s reprinting of Castro's speech—"Within the revolution, everything"—indicated the onset of cultural "dirigismo."[81] Cuadra's critiques set off an internal debate that uncovered stark divisions over cultural policy.[82]

Cultural concerns overlapped with economic critiques. The Conservative nationalists at *La Prensa* were concerned that the FSLN's program would drive out the professional class, which had the expertise necessary to rebuild the country's economy.[83] Editorials exhorted the upper class to remain in Nicaragua rather than fleeing to Miami.[84] The FSLN was aware of this danger and offered incentives to nonparty professionals to remain and work in reconstruction.[85] Frequent attacks on "bourgeois culture" by the FSLN, and threats to elite property and status, caused many members of the elite to begin fleeing the country by 1980. The government mitigated the outflow by a continued influx of internationalists who offered their expertise to assist in the revolutionary project. This influx further stoked concern by Conservatives that the internationalizing influence was an affront to national culture.[86] To complete the developing charge that the FSLN was assuming the role of the Somoza dictatorship, *La Prensa* ran pieces charging the new state sector with "disloyal competition" for mistreating private producers, an accusation once aimed at the Somozas' use of economic power for political ends.[87]

La Prensa became an outlet for European and Latin American social democrats' critiques of the revolution, highlighting their calls for continued pluralism in the country and the conditionality of their countries' support on its maintenance.[88] While the FSLN broadcast its diplomatic missions to the world, representatives of the nascent opposition also traveled abroad seeking allies at the invitation of social democratic parties and European political foundations.[89] In the year after *La Prensa*'s open break with the FSLN's revolutionary vision, the newspaper's editorial page became a forum on global political economy. Serial features ran on socialist countries around the world and their experience under nonmarket economies. The paper ran frequent critiques of the Soviet Union and Cuba, contrasting the gray conformity of cultures built around socialist realism with the vibrancy of culture the revolutionary struggle had fostered. A series of features on Yugoslavia gave a tentatively positive slant to the possibility of socialism independent from the Eastern bloc.[90]

For Nicaraguan dissidents, European recognition was more important than approval at home.[91] Given Nicaragua's long semicolonial relationship with the United States, disaffected figures like Cuadra could not openly turn to that country for support without being branded as traitors. Therefore, the Conservative elite turned to western Europe for alternative models to the communism they feared was overtaking their country. In 1981, Cuadra traveled to West Germany at the invitation of one of its political foundations. He wrote a series of editorials locating the model upon which he wished to build Nicaragua's future. The first juxtaposed the high culture of Europe with that of Nicaragua, claiming that the revolution had put Nicaragua on equal footing with Europe. He extolled the "pure overflowing" waters of the Rhine as a fount of both culture and revolution that united with a revolutionary exuberance in Nicaragua. Citing the work of master folk artist Carlos Mejía Godoy, composer of both the "Misa Campesina" and Nicaragua's new national anthem, Cuadra asserted the parity of old world and new. Rather than asserting that Nicaragua had measured up to a foreign standard, he inverted the comparison, "with Indian eyes," dubbing the Germans the "Mayas of Europe." He stood Gothic cathedrals alongside the Mayan temples of Tikal, both fit for the metaphysical contemplations of Immanuel Kant or Ludwig van Beethoven.[92] Seeing in Germany's divided history the result of a quest for utopias, Cuadra claimed to have found along the Rhine a model for his own utopia, liberal democracy, and to have come to embrace the much-maligned designation "bourgeois."[93] Though the term "bourgeois" could signify a vapid desire for "a luxury automobile," he wrote, the desire for luxury could also manifest as a desire for cultural expression and constant critique and renovation. It is less a class than an attitude toward life: though Soviet culture attempted to rid itself of the bourgeoisie, it was only replaced with a grayer bureaucratic elite that fawned on cultural productions it could not reproduce.[94]

For the FSLN, Cuadra provided a troubling model of the failure of commitment. The party had foreseen that the "extreme right" would make campaigns like the literacy crusade an object of attack but had not anticipated that someone of Cuadra's cultural stature would remain outside the revolution.[95] In allying himself with counterrevolution, Cuadra lent cultural authority to the country's "private sector" that La Prensa had long disdained for its philistinism. European foundations held up Cuadra's dissent as the epitome of the kind of pluralism they wished to promote. The US government built on these affinities, subsidizing a publishing house in Costa Rica, Libro Libre, that issued reprints of Cuadra's most important collections of poems and essays while ex-cluding his earliest profascist writings.[96] It also disseminated the works of a growing cadre of disillusioned expatriates from the revolution.[97] The revival of the cultural Cold War around Nicaragua became a cooperative venture be-tween European, US, and Latin American social democrats and brought into the open the once covert funding of counterrevolutionary culture.[98] The Rea-gan administration would soon expand counterrevolution beyond culture, us-ing the kind of revolutionary disillusionment Cuadra embodied to underwrite the administration's own program for regional transformation.

Reagan and Enterprising Internationalism

As the struggle to conceive new relationships between political and economic development unfolded in Nicaragua, in October 1981 political leaders around the world gathered for the International Meeting on Cooperation and Devel-opment at Cancún, Mexico. The creators of the global forum sought to begin a program of "global negotiations" based on an economic program laid out in the *North-South* report created by former West German chancellor and leader of the Socialist International Willy Brandt. The Brandt report called for global financial restructuring, increased foreign aid from wealthy countries, and the strengthening of state-led development.[99] Nicaragua was not on the agenda, but many of the governments backing the program of "global Keynesianism" laid out there, such as Mexico's José López Portillo and France's François Mit-terand, used the occasion to press for a negotiated settlement in Central Amer-ica granting recognition of the revolutionary left as a political force.[100] Ronald Reagan in turn laid out the beginnings of what would become a global coun-terrevolution against the attempts of nonaligned and social democratic nations to reconfigure the structures of global trade and finance.

Reagan's speech took direct aim at efforts of proponents of a New Inter-national Economic Order who fought to overturn the economic structures cre-ated by the Bretton Woods Agreement. He argued for policies aimed at "stimulating international trade by opening up markets," "improving the cli-mate for private capital flows," and avoiding "misguided policies that restrain and interfere with the international marketplace." Over the next few years, Rea-gan would announce a series of programs that acted as counterproposals to the reforms proposed by European social democrats and Third World reformers. "Project Democracy," outlined at a speech at Westminster in London in 1982, and the Caribbean Basin Initiative, announced before the Organization of

American States, put into practice the rhetoric of democratic capitalist revolution promoted by Reagan. They also placed Nicaragua at the intersection of US reaction to both North-South and East-West conflict and put Central America in the crosshairs of a revived Cold War.

Mexican president José López Portillo, host of the Cancún forum, understood that the Cold War was a danger to the possibility of global negotiations, which he believed were imperative as Mexico faced an impending debt crisis. Though he discouraged open condemnations of "imperialism" to avoid antagonizing the United States, López Portillo used his speech at Cancún to encourage his listeners to "recognize the complexity and plurality of the world," and warned against "East-West conflict" undermining North-South cooperation.[101] He fought unsuccessfully to have Cuba's Fidel Castro included in the conference but did succeed in fostering a meeting between the US secretary of state and the Cuban foreign minister in an attempt to forestall US aggression against Cuba and intervention in Central America.[102] He also created with French president François Mitterand a peace plan for El Salvador that would involve recognition of the insurgent FMLN.

The leaders of revolutionary Nicaragua understood that the Reagan counterprogram—focusing on private sector development and a call to "create incentives for the investment of private enterprise in underdeveloped countries"—not only challenged the calls for a new "global Keynesianism" by western European social democrats but also played an essential part in the unfolding counterrevolution in Central America.[103] Nicaraguan diplomats saw Cancún as an indication of US antagonism to efforts to create global solidarity around the concept of social revolution. According to foreign minister and Maryknoll priest Miguel d'Escoto the "main obstacle to the development of the New International Economic Order" was the United States, which "has rejected all attempts at peaceful solutions to the problems of underdeveloped countries."[104]

The Reagan program begun at Cancún initiated the most far-reaching reconfiguration of US foreign aid policy since the announcement of the Alliance for Progress two decades earlier. The programs that would come to define US foreign policy in the western hemisphere—the creation of a "one-way" free trade program in the Caribbean Basin Initiative, the cultivation of entrepreneurs as a counterweight to socialism, and support for a global democratic crusade in the name of political pluralism—were not simply inversions of the policies pushed by the global South. They responded to the success of the process of coalition-building between Latin American and European socialists and social democrats that made the Sandinista-led Nicaraguan revolution possible and was threatening to overturn US-supported regimes in nearby El Salvador and Guatemala.

The Reagan administration's official attitude toward international development was shaped by critiques of previous administrations, especially their promotion of foreign aid and alleged tolerance for socialism as in Nicaragua. Intellectuals who would shape the counterrevolution in Central America argued that the idea of "ideological pluralism" had brought US acceptance of leftist regimes at the expense of authoritarian US allies. The authors of the "Santa Fe Report," who would take up positions in the National Security Council and serve as ambassadors to the region, argued that "ideological pluralism" was not a bad idea in itself but should include US acceptance of right-wing politics.[105] Jeane Kirkpatrick condemned the Carter administration's "full-blown philosophy of history" and "theory of social change" with its roots in modernization doctrines. She, like the Santa Fe Report's authors, argued that US policy should stop attacking authoritarian allies and turn to counterrevolution.[106]

Early attempts at shaping a new US policy in Central America were based on condemnation of Carter-era policies but quickly changed course. The Reagan transition team criticized the Carter administration for using "social engineering" to create a class of counterrevolutionary "middle income producers" through land reform in El Salvador.[107] After the insurrection led by the FMLN and supported by Nicaragua failed in 1981, analysts noted that the pivotal force in resisting the insurrection was a new capitalist class that did not support revolution as its counterpart had in Nicaragua.[108] Though El Salvador's oligarchs rejected both the radical politics of the left and the reformism of the United States, the administration hoped a new class of entrepreneur could openly ally itself with the United States in the name of private capitalist development. Surveys of the private sector in El Salvador revealed their envy of the international support for leftist insurgents and the government of José Napoléon Duarte. They too desired an "international," a new Truman Doctrine for Central America.[109] US officials hoped that creating mutual dependency between the private sector and the government would give the private sector a stake in stability. Such a stake was especially important in El Salvador, where the small economic elite adamantly opposed US economic interference and supported only military assistance in stamping out leftist armed rebellion.[110]

The Caribbean Basin Initiative was designed as a "logical follow-up to Cancún" and to promote counterrevolution in Central America.[111] At its heart was a proposal to allow free access for Caribbean countries to US markets for their goods. This opening of "one-way" free trade—advocated by Berle at the birth of the Alliance for Progress as an overtly imperial model—was meant to provide incentive for US investment in the region, stimulating the region's unstable economies. The proposal was also meant to encourage an entrepreneurial class within the region to expand its production and marketing to integrate itself into a much larger and more lucrative US market while also encouraging US investment.[112]

The administration set about revamping the entire US foreign aid apparatus around the cultivation of the "private sector" in Latin America.[113] Rather than erasing previous policies, the goals would change: no longer aiming to strengthen the power of central governments to plan and maintain order, foreign aid would instead aim at renewing the economic and military alliance of Latin American elites with the United States by stripping away commitments to alleviate poverty and reduce inequality. According to neoliberal critiques of prior US aid practices, encouragement of production for internal consumption or for small regional markets like the Central American Common Market had stunted capitalist growth within these countries.[114] Encouraging them to produce for the US market would build their capacity to eventually engage in the global market, and Caribbean countries that had once looked to Europe would begin to look to the United States.[115]

European social democrats at Cancún had proposed a "Marshall Plan" for the Third World, and elites all over the Caribbean region greeted the prospect of the Caribbean Basin Initiative as the fulfilment of this promise.[116] The idea of a "mini-Marshall Plan," as the program came to be described in national presses, offered the hope of a massive project modeled on the US support for European reconstruction after World War II. The idea that Central America might recapitulate the development of Europe, rather than the United States, gave some elites hope that the spiral of violence in the region could be checked by a commitment to economic growth while avoiding the unwholesome influence of American culture.[117] The FSLN expressed its willingness to be included in the new CBI, but the law expressly disallowed the participation of Nicaragua and Cuba. In addition to excluding Nicaragua, which the Nicaraguan private sector blamed on the FSLN, the administration also began crafting economic measures to further isolate the country.[118] The Reagan administration tried to undercut Central American visions of a new Marshall Plan, given its connotations of government planning and state-centric modernization, preferring instead to emphasize the cultivation of willing allies and the punishment of enemies.[119]

As part of its commitment to the private sector, the Reagan administration created a Private Enterprise Initiative within USAID. This was critiqued by many experts as a "development fad" and a superficial manifestation of ideology, given the initiative's small budget and inexperienced leadership. This super-ficiality concealed far-reaching changes in development practice, however.[120] A revamped USAID Latin American bureau under the direction of Otto Reich, who would soon come to head the Reagan administration's pro-Contra pro-paganda campaign, overturned the conventional wisdom in development of the past decade. The bureau asserted that focusing on poorest sectors was coun-terproductive and that emphasis on private sector growth would not weaken commitment to basic human needs or government institutions.[121] The turn from direct support for the poor was explicit: aid to the "poorest of the poor" was "a welfare not a development question."[122] This did not mean turning away from government assistance. By channeling funds such as export credits through the government to the private sector, the Reagan administration pro-vided a means for unstable regimes such as El Salvador's to cultivate support from a new entrepreneurial class less beholden to the old elite.[123] The new aid policy was to purchase the allegiance of already existing elites and call into be-ing a new entrepreneurial class through trade policy. Accompanying this shift in aid ideology was a change in aid administration. The US Agency for Inter-national Development had once been heavily engaged in a process of planning, trying to support economic projects while also helping build the capacity for government to create such plans on its own. The CBI increased funding for the region—promising $350 million in supplemental assistance—but did not significantly increase the planning apparatus of organizations like USAID. Rather, increased funding was to be given directly to governments to then dispense to the private sector, reshaping political relationships in countries such as Costa Rica where US-supported forces were mobilizing to destabilize the Nicaraguan government.[124]

The Caribbean Basin Initiative implemented the Reagan administration's response to the 1981 Cancún conference by turning the problem of poverty from a North-South issue into an East-West issue. The CBI also revived de-bates that had beset US development policy since the beginning of the Alliance for Progress: Was political development the precondition for economic trans-formation, as Latin America's antidictatorial movement supposed? Or would export-oriented economic growth promote political democratization? The Kennedy and Johnson administrations built their rhetorical edifices of mod-ernization on the latter proposition, allowing the Somoza family to thrive in Nicaragua and encouraging military authoritarianism throughout Latin America. Though the Reagan administration began by endorsing the Kirk-patrick doctrine and alliance with authoritarian governments, the struggle in Central America offered a way to construct US policy around more than just counterrevolution. The alliance between European and Latin American social democrats that helped the FSLN overturn the Somoza regime provided a blueprint for a revival of political development that became central to the Reagan revolution's revival of the Cold War.

Contra War and Project Democracy

The armed Nicaraguan counterrevolution began as an experiment in ideological pluralism. First in the fluid atmosphere of Miami and then in the mountains of Honduras, remnants of Somoza's Guardia Nacional came together with members of Nicaragua's Conservative opposition who had struggled against and compromised with the Somozas for decades and then moved north in a public performance of disillusionment with the revolution. Taking as blueprint a revision of the ideological pluralism that had legitimated Nicaragua's revolution in the eyes of the world, anti-Sandinista forces would attempt to reconcile their differences around a vision of protecting property and *patria* from encroaching communism. This ideological effort at branding the Contras as entrepreneurial freedom fighters was accompanied by an insurgency guided by Argentine and US advisers that had more in common with the willfully brutal repression practiced by the Somozas than with national liberation. Even as the Reagan administration purported to move beyond the outdated development doctrines of the 1960s, it used its own development ideology to bind together the democratic rhetoric and counterinsurgent violence on which US policy in Latin America was founded.

In 1982, the Reagan administration turned from counterrevolution to revolution, and in the process globalized Central America's political and economic struggles. Reagan delivered a speech before the British parliament that laid out the political component of the revised US foreign aid program. The "Project Democracy" speech proposed a program aimed to counteract decades of "covert political training and assistance to Marxist-Leninists" by the Soviet Union, suggesting that the United States and western Europeans engage in the "competition of ideas and values" with their communist adversaries. To do so, he promised to create a program "to foster the infrastructure of democracy, the system of a free press, unions, political parties, universities" based on cooperation between the Democratic and Republican Parties and representatives of American labor unions and business. The National Endowment for Democracy, created in 1983, was modeled explicitly on the German political foundations that were already at work in Central America. This new program was purported to allow the US government to openly promote programs for political development that had been primarily covert since the Alliance for Progress. Critics, especially in the US Congress, had long argued that covert political development was an oxymoron and pushed for robust support for political parties and institution-building.[125] While the Reagan administration's open avowal of political development was a departure from past US policy, political development became a complement to covert action rather than a replacement.

Two months before the Westminster speech, Edén Pastora announced the launch of his own revolutionary venture in Central America. Recruited by the FSLN for his non-Marxist credentials, he had sought US assistance in 1979 in a failed bid to take power and exclude his Cuban-backed comrades.[126] His guerrilla swagger had galvanized social democrats attracted to the romance of revolution who expressed awe at the "heady" experience of being near a fatigue-clad figure of an "actual living revolution."[127] Reputed to have an ego commensurate with his charisma, Pastora was unhappy with his secondary role in the new revolutionary state. In 1981 he wrote to Minister of Defense Humberto Ortega that he was leaving Nicaragua to "chase the scent of gunpowder," following the tradition of Che Guevara in continuing the revolutionary project in other countries.[128]

Unlike that of Guevara, Pastora's expatriation would soon be sponsored by the CIA.[129] As the CIA built its counterrevolutionary Contra forces in Honduras, planners recognized that the image of an army built around the remnants of Somoza's National Guard was detrimental to global public opinion. Pastora's exit was designed to deepen the schism between social democrats and the FSLN while promoting dissent within Nicaragua. Members of the Reagan administration had criticized what they called the "Havana-Mexico-Social Democracy Axis" in Central America.[130] Administration planners asked themselves how they could "use the Christian Democrat and Social Democrat international network the way the Soviets use their own fellow travelers? How do we undercut or modify the reach and outlook of the Socialist International?"[131] One answer was the recruitment of Pastora to fight with Contras in Costa Rica, seen as essential to the political if not the military aspect of the regional program. The CIA put such importance on both recruiting Pastora and maintaining his guerrilla credentials that it agreed to send weapons to antigovernment forces in Guatemala in order to gain his allegiance.[132]

With the defection of Pastora, the Reagan administration appropriated as its own the Socialist International's project for reforming the revolution in Nicaragua. Pastora would be accompanied in his defection by other figures, such as Alfonso Robelo and Arturo Cruz Jr. and Sr., who would play important

roles in the Reagan administration's anti-Sandinista campaign. While supporting counterrevolutionary armies on Nicaragua's borders, the Reagan administration disavowed attempting to bring the return of the despised Somoza
regime. Instead the administration claimed to be holding the Nicaraguans to
the promises of the true revolution, the program created in collaboration
between the revolutionaries and the Socialist International: "political pluralism,
a free, mixed-economy, and true non-alignment."[133]

The FSLN correctly predicted that the immediate fallout of Pastora's defection would be a drastic reshaping of the landscape of international solidarity.
Social democratic groups in Costa Rica, the Dominican Republic, and Venezuela would shift their support to Pastora as a potentially democratic alternative to
the FSLN. His disaffection would provoke "debility and doubts" among Europeans such as Felipe Gonzalez. The revolution's position with "friends" in the
US Congress would also be damaged, and Nicaraguan diplomats would have to
"carefully explain the situation" to allies in Sweden and West Germany. In Latin
America, only Mexico and Cuba were certain to remain faithful.[134]

Pastora traveled to western Europe, where he was welcomed by Socialist
International figures such as Gonzalez and Mario Soares, whom he convinced
to curtail their support for Nicaragua. Soares believed that Pastora's defection
"radically alter[ed] the situation" and required a shift in position to avoid "cov-
ering the objectives of the Eastern bloc."[135] Venezuela's Carlos Andrés Pérez
wrote to Willy Brandt expressing hope that Pastora would now serve as leverage for the SI and could be used to "provoke favorable reactions among the
Sandinista comandantes."[136]

The blow to FSLN support from the growing wave of defections did not
correspond to an outright Reagan victory, as the US Congress and US allies
continued to sharply criticize the Contra War. To counteract this criticism,
Nicaraguan Contra converts who became part of the Reagan program, such
as Arturo Cruz Jr. and Arturo Cruz Sr., took part in an expanded program to
shape political narratives in the United States. Arturo Cruz Sr. had taken part
in the anti-Somoza struggles of Nicaragua's Conservative faction in the 1950s
before becoming part of the international development system at the Inter-
American Development Bank.[137] After social democrats helped convince the
Nicaraguan government to hold elections in 1984, he would become the preferred US candidate before withdrawing under pressure from Oliver North.[138]

Contra publicists looked admiringly at the public diplomacy apparatus of
the FSLN and its supporters, who mobilized thousands of international visitors and cultivated both public and private support for the revolution.[139] Self-
described liberals who became public faces of the US Contra support network

used Nicaraguan defectors to legitimize their conversion to neoconservative foreign policy positions.[140] These operatives used connections to Nicaraguan dissidents to publicize their decisions to abandon a "liberal left" they believed had been duped by a successful Sandinista public diplomacy campaign. They argued that there was no "organized 'resistance support network'" in the United States or in Central America, and "the Sandinistas have shown how helpful such networks can be."[141] Such a network had been in operation since the Carter administration, but it had acted largely covertly. Converts to the Contra cause used their lobbying and public relations experience to reframe the image of the Contras away from that of a "peasant jacquerie led by an expropriated Coca-Cola salesman," branding them instead as the "Nicaraguan Resistance," the true heirs of the Nicaraguan revolution betrayed by the Sandinistas.[142] This reframing effort would inspire such statements as "democracy and free enterprise live only in the minds of the contras in the field, stubborn entrepreneurs who continue to seek a share of the marketplace."[143] Rebranding also underlay Reagan's declaration of admiration for what he called "the real Sandino."[144] The successful rebranding brought renewed congressional support for the Contras shortly before the Iran-Contra scandal became public.[145]

The program to reshape Central American politics around entrepreneurship and democratic revolution had far-reaching effects. The US propaganda campaign diminished intergovernmental support for Nicaragua outside the Soviet bloc, while growing anti-imperial sentiments strengthened the transnational solidarity network. European governments continued to encourage regional democracy, but social democrats would not reach consensus on whether the elections in Nicaragua and El Salvador met their standards. Meanwhile, Nicaraguan Contras and the semicovert network of US supporters engaged in an expanded notion of entrepreneurship, from drug trafficking to repurposing profits from missile sales, that destabilized political and social life on all sides of the Caribbean Basin.

When a young Arturo Cruz Jr. traveled to the United States for school in the 1970s, following the path of many other upper-class Nicaraguans, José Coronel Urtecho cautioned him to remember his roots, as "the Americans were always going to see [Cruz] as a foreigner." A decade later, as Cruz reconsidered his embroilment with the Nicaraguan revolution, US intelligence agencies, Oliver North, and the Iran-Contra scandal, he reflected on the sagacity of Coronel's warnings. "It was all in the family blood" and "a measure of Nicaraguan vulnerability," he feared, "this game of seeking outside antagonists and sponsors, finding strength through dependence on one great power or another, whether it be Castro, America, or Germany." Though he and his father had become icons of US foreign policy goals, disillusion with both US and Nicaraguan politics led Cruz to believe that the program for democratic revolution might only be perpetuating authoritarianism and dependency.[146]

Sergio Ramírez looked back on the Sandinista era in a different light. He would write that democracy had begun as a "tactic that adorned the surface" of FSLN strategy but became, through the globalized conflict of the 1980s, an essential part of the revolution.[147] The Reagan administration's democratization project also began as counterrevolutionary tactic, its rhetoric belied by overt violence and covert action that undermined democracy within the United States itself. In claiming the Contra War as the "true revolution" betrayed by the FSLN, members of the Reagan administration were doing more than "inverting rhetoric usually associated with the left."[148] They took networks, individuals, and ideas that Nicaraguans and their allies had used to make the revolution acceptable to international audiences and turned them to very different ends. The FSLN successfully galvanized thousands of supporters around the world, but mistook the level of commitment of key interlocutors, including domestic supporters and international social democratic leaders. The European and Latin American social democratic left, while never embracing the full extent of the Reagan program in Central America, did take part in shifting the international agenda from ideological pluralism that included recognition of socialism and the militant left, to democratic pluralism that made electoral democracy the endpoint of development.

Chapter 5

Retracing Imperial Paths on the Mosquito Coast

In 1969, a young geographer from the United States named Bernard Nietschmann and a Miskito Indian named Baldwin Garth retraced a path along Nicaragua's Caribbean shore described a century before by US diplomat and ethnographer Ephraim Squier.[1] Squier intended his work in Nicaragua and his writings about it to lay the groundwork for the eventual US replacement of British imperial power on Nicaragua's eastern shore in the interest of devising a trade route across the isthmus. Nietschmann's journey in 1969 was part of his study of the impact of market relations on indigenous turtle fishing practices.[2] Fourteen years later, Nietschmann would retrace his imperial route once again. In 1983, he traveled with members of the indigenous resistance group Misurasata bringing weapons and supplies to armed indigenous people fighting against Nicaragua's revolutionary Sandinista government. His aim was to document human rights abuses by the revolutionary government, but he would become part of a much larger movement to reshape the meaning of nationhood and the foundations of international development practice. Nietschmann believed Nicaragua's eastern shore was once again a site of imperial competition, now between the United States and the Soviet Union. The region would also become the setting for a struggle for indigenous autonomy that indigenous rights activists cast as the vanguard of a politically awakening Fourth World movement, a movement that they claimed challenged state power all over the world and transcended the parameters of the Cold War.

The indigenous uprising on Nicaragua's eastern shore was among the most contentious issues during the revolutionary 1980s.[3] The conflict between

Nicaragua's revolutionary government and ethnic groups on the east coast grew out of changes in international development practice after the 1960s and was sparked by the contest over revolutionary pluralism described in the previous chapter. The granting of special status to indigenous groups within foreign aid programs was the product of changes in development thinking after the Alliance for Progress that deemphasized state-led development and instead promoted participation, human rights, and basic needs. Thanks to its ideal of revolutionary pluralism, the Nicaraguan government encouraged international assistance under these new paradigms while simultaneously attempting to integrate the east coast into the revolution. The Miskitos and their allies would take this program of pluralism and turn it against the revolutionary state, in the process cultivating their own international alliances. These included a growing transnational indigenous rights movement, social democratic internationalists, and the Reagan administration's Contra forces.

The east coast conflict points beyond the Cold War to issues that would concern the international community in the 1990s and after. The late 1980s and 1990s saw the rise to global prominence of indigenous activism, especially in Latin America.[4] Scholarship on indigenous activism throughout Latin America makes clear that the antagonism between the Sandinistas and the Miskitos was not foreordained, as urban-based leftist movements in Latin America had long and productive relationships with indigenous activists.[5] The explosive nature of the Miskito struggle must be placed at the intersection of changing international paradigms, as indigenous activists drew on old imperial affinities and new discourses of international concern that combined the issues of cultural autonomy and ecological sustainability in a volatile mixture. The Miskitos and their allies translated their struggle into the language of sustainability and biodiversity that was changing the way development is practiced around the world. They also courted both imperial power and the international development community by making an explicit connection between armed indigenous people and ecology that exposed tensions within emergent postdevelopment thinking.[6] The international development apparatus has been called an "antipolitics machine," which substitutes international bureaucratic power for political action.[7] The Miskito struggle, however, shows that discourses of development when backed by imperial power could in fact foster new forms of political action and identification.

Caribbean Development under the Somozas

What is now Nicaragua's east coast was, during the time Ephraim Squier was plotting the routes of empire, a place apart. The Mosquito Coast, as the area from southern Nicaragua to Honduras was known, was from the seventeenth to the nineteenth century a foothold of the British Empire in Spanish America, and the Miskito people were allies of British power. The coast was annexed to the Nicaraguan state at the end of the nineteenth century and officially became part of Nicaragua's territory, its region named for President José Santos Zelaya, who unified the Pacific and the Caribbean coasts and fought to have a transisthmian canal built in Nicaragua. Though technically a part of Nicaragua, the eastern shore was more accessible by Caribbean sea lanes than over land and river from the west, and in the early twentieth century its economy became tied to the Caribbean basin, dominated by US power. Thus, among the Costeños, as residents were known, English and indigenous languages were more commonly spoken than Spanish, and Protestantism disseminated by Moravian missionaries was the dominant religion.[8]

In the 1920s, the US Marines used Miskito territorial knowledge in their counterinsurgency against Sandino.[9] After the general's murder, the Somoza dynasty, supported by the US government from 1936 to 1979, implemented two different forms of nation-building project to consolidate the dynasty's power over Nicaragua's fragmented landscape. One was a high modernist program of capital accumulation, centralization of authority, and ethnic assimilation. The other, a populist modernism, encouraged small farmers, limited decentralization of authority, and some degree of ethnic pluralism.[10] These two versions of modernization were complementary. They bolstered the personal power of the Somozas while serving the counterinsurgency goals of the US government. On the Pacific coast, this modernization created tensions that exacerbated political conflicts and brought about the 1979 revolution. On the Caribbean coast, however, capitalist enterprise coexisted with village-based subsistence practice and ethnic plurality. The revolution would come late to the east, with profound consequences.[11]

As seen from the Caribbean coast, the Alliance for Progress and the affiliation between the Somozas and the United States in the 1960s fused Latin American ideas of *mestizaje* with the US-promoted modernization ethos. The progressive vision of the Charter of Punta del Esta explicitly called for greater integration of the Indians of Latin America as part of the agrarian population that modernization theorists feared provided tinder for rural revolution. Agrarian reform, in addition to fostering a revitalized export agriculture, would

extend "the benefits of the land to those who work it, . . . ensuring in countries with Indian populations the integration of these populations into the economic, social, and culture processes of modern life."[12] Alliance advocate Arthur
Schlesinger absorbed the ideas of Latin American intellectuals such as Ger-
mán Arcienegas into the US-promoted vision of development. The Alliance
was to fuse the "two Americas," not North and South, but Indian and non-
Indian. The Alliance would bring about the "peaceful incorporation into
their national economic and political societies of a vast submerged population,
largely Indian, which has existed for centuries 'outside' both the money economy and party politics but which is now uneasily stirring with (and being
ruthlessly stirred by) new aspirations and expectations."[13] At the height of the
Alliance in the early 1960s, there were calls by planners and politicians to un-
dertake far-reaching programs to fuse the energies of governments in North
and South America in a project of "reincorporation" of Indians in Latin America, a project planners believed suited to the "missionary character" of North
Americans.[14]

Infrastructure programs designed to integrate the "inner frontiers" of Latin
American nations relied on the vision of *mestizaje* as peaceful commingling of
indigenous and European races. In lieu of comprehensive land reform, which
the Somoza family and their allies resisted, Nicaragua's government encouraged landless campesinos to move east and convert the tropical forest into cultivable land. These campesinos had often lost their land because of the
modernization policies on the west coast that subsidized technologically intensive cotton cultivation and thus land consolidation by larger enterprises.
General Anastasio Somoza Debayle considered as his "pet project" the Rigoberto Cabezas colony, the largest of these colonization projects, named for
the nineteenth-century general who unified the east and west coasts.[15] Another effect of the colonization of the east, besides "keeping the rabble out of
Managua," as one planner put it, would be the encouragement of the process
of *mestizaje*, the assimilation of indigenous people into the dominant Spanish-
speaking and capitalist-oriented national culture.[16] Proponents of the process
of modernization saw this as a beneficial by-product of economic and social
development and oriented programs toward this end.[17]

On the coast itself, economic growth and ethnic homogenization were
much less pronounced than in areas to the west. In exchange for a portion of
the profit from various resource-based industries, the Somoza family gave foreign companies concessions to carry out mining, fishing, and lumber extraction. Indigenous groups such as the Miskito, and to a lesser extent the Rama
and Mayangna (Sumu) people, participated in the wage economy and cash ex-

changes with foreign enterprises while maintaining ties to their village subsistence economies.[18] Indigenous activists, in collaboration with the Moravian church and development workers, created the Alliance for Progress for Miskito and Sumo (Alpromisu) in order to advocate for Indian rights and promote economic cooperation.[19] This organization would provide the basis for the group that opposed the Sandinista government in the 1980s. In the 1970s its members often worked in uneasy collaboration with the Somoza government. Under its auspices, indigenous intellectuals contacted an international community of like-minded activists, who encouraged the intellectuals to think broadly about self-determination and autonomy.[20]

For anti-Somoza Conservative nationalists like Pablo Antonio Cuadra, the east coast and its indigenous inhabitants represented the incompleteness of Nicaragua's nationhood. Scholars have critiqued Cuadra's mestizo nationalism as promoting a harmonious vision of race mixture that suppressed the violence of conquest.[21] In his writings in the 1930s, however, which received an interested audience throughout Latin America and in Falangist Spain, Cuadra blamed the liberalism of Bartolomé de las Casas for the lamentable fact that the east "was not conquered" and "still has not been."[22] For this reason, the Indians, ("*there* they are still Indians," in contrast to the purported *mestizaje* of the rest of the country) "wander in barbarism awaiting *hispanidad*."[23] Cuadra also looked to a prospective canal uniting the east and west coasts as "the imperial sign in the geographical" and lamented its absence as the failure of the imperial project of Spain, inhibited first by enlightenment liberalism and then by the influence of the United States.[24]

Although Cuadra disparaged the influence of the United States on Nicaragua's fragmented geography, US officials shared his deprecation of the "barbarism" of the east in the 1960s. The US government officially promoted development policies premised on *mestizaje*, while also treating the east and its inhabitants as a place and people apart. In 1967 the political officer of the US embassy visited the Caribbean port of Puerto Cabezas following a fire that devastated the city's downtown, the "biggest bit of excitement since the Bay of Pigs affair," which had been launched from there. He marveled at the indifference the local population showed toward the burning of the downtown area, whose stores had been controlled by Chinese immigrants and US traders. Lamenting that "the apathy and lethargy of the population assumes majestic proportions," he was perplexed as to why the Miskito population might be indifferent to such destruction, even as he described the concentration of wealth there in non-Miskito hands. He also described the devastation wrought on the urban and ecological landscape by a century of US-promoted economic exploitation, because of which "virtually every tree in a vast area accessible by train or truck was cut down," with no attention given to reforestation or erosion problems. The political officer then described the failure of reforestation programs, which often foundered because of the Miskito practice of burning the new plantings. He claimed this was a result of the Miskito vision of heaven as "a flat plain without a single tree." His resort to metaphysics ignored the fact that indigenous people used burning to replace nutrients in the denuded soil, express dissatisfaction with government policies, and sometimes even gain temporary employment in extinguishing the fires.[25]

Adopting the fatalistic resignation that he attributed to the Indians, the embassy officer sighed: "This is just one of those cases where nothing can be done this generation." Little over a decade later, the US embassy would abandon belief in the "majestic lethargy" of the local population and take intense interest in the political aspirations of the Miskito people. The east coast of Nicaragua changed from a place where observers predicted generations of stagnation to one of unpredictable ferment, and both the United States and the new revolutionary government in Managua would attempt to steer these political aspirations toward their own ends. The embassy official in 1967 joked that to promote development perhaps the Somoza government should "hire an anthropologist who can change the Indians' vision of heaven." Soon the coast would be rife with academics—anthropologists and others—hoping to foster a host of utopian visions.

The Revolution within the Revolution

In July 1979 the Somoza regime was overturned by a coalition of workers, peasants, and bourgeois reformers spearheaded by a vanguard party, the Frente Sandinista de Liberación Nacional. Thanks to the relative isolation of the Caribbean coast, the revolutionary movement in the west did not reach the east until after the downfall of the Somoza regime. The Junta de Gobierno de Reconstrucción Nacional, controlled by the Sandinistas, began to implement an ambitious program to integrate the east coast into the rest of the country through building economic and political ties between the two regions. The Sandinista government embraced high modernism in the form of centralized planning, while also encouraging its own version of grassroots development through radical programs for community betterment. In the west, this approach led to a broadly participatory form of popular revolutionary government, while in the east it gave rise to the first open insurrection in what would become an internationally supported civil war. Miskito insurgents and their international allies formulated a powerful critique of the government's programs, in which armed insurrection would play a key role.

Many of the new government's development programs borrowed heavily from the planning apparatus put together by the Somoza regime, the US government, and international development organizations in decades past.[26] These legacies of the era of the Alliance for Progress had lain dormant because of lack of political will on the part of the Somoza regime and the crises faced by the country beginning with the 1972 Managua earthquake. Though in the west, new forms of participatory democracy were taking root, the eastern revolution began as a top-down affair, much like the Alliance it echoed. The government declared that "the natural resources of our country are the property of the Nicaraguan people, represented by the Revolutionary State which is the only entity empowered to establish the rational and efficient tapping of those resources," and that "the Revolution recognizes the right of the indigenous communities to receive a quota from the exploitation of the timber resources in the region."[27] For indigenous communities experiencing a wave of nationalist consciousness, such "quotas" would not be enough.

The participatory elements of the revolution, when they came to the coast, also moved from west to east and top to bottom in ways that alienated Costeños. The literacy project was designed to mobilize the revolutionary energies of Nicaraguan youth to raise the educational level of the country's rural people and instill nationalist consciousness in the *brigadistas* who were to do the teaching. The program focused on the Spanish language as well as the revolutionary experience of the west, alienating the indigenous but bringing about the first negotiations between the revolution and Costeños.[28] Though the revolutionary government initially attempted to subsume the indigenous organization Alpromisu into its revolutionary mass organizations, it agreed to create a new organization, Misurasata, which would maintain its indigenous character while allying it with the Sandinista revolution.[29] The Sandinista literacy project was adapted to include indigenous languages, and Misurasata members participated in the program. The government pursued a dual approach, rejecting claims that it thought might lead to separatism while encouraging ethnic pluralism.[30]

Scholars like Luciano Baracco assert that it was the Sandinista's modernization policies that raised the ire of the Miskito people, policies adapted from those used by both the Alliance for Progress and the Cuban revolution since the 1960s. Charles R. Hale asserts instead that it was the covert influence of the US government that drove the Miskito rebellion, made possible by Miskito "Anglo-affinity" with US and British imperial forces. In fact, the revolutionary government's own vision of pluralist internationalism made possible the political alliance of the Miskito forces and the US government, not covertly, but with the full knowledge of the Nicaraguan government. The revolutionary government in its early years wished to maintain its economic relationship with the United States, while "diversifying its dependencies" and bringing in other sources of international aid. In the heady days after the revolutionary victory, the revolutionary government allowed the US government to openly fund nascent indigenous organizations, as figures such as Minister of Culture Ernesto Cardenal believed that the moral force of the revolution could be passed on to the Miskitos by the *brigadistas* who were spreading the revolutionary message all over Nicaragua.

In the immediate aftermath of the 1979 revolution, the US embassy began to support new forms of political organization that were only beginning to receive the attention of the international development community. In the 1970s, groups of indigenous people had begun to form transnational networks of activists who questioned the relationship between old models of ethnic assimilation and high modernist development practice. In 1971, a group of anthropologists funded by the World Council of Churches met at the University of the West Indies in Barbados to formalize an emerging understanding of the relationship between indigenous rights and state power. The Barbados declaration was one of the first documents promulgated by this emerging movement, and it demanded that governments recognize not only ethnic pluralism, by fostering education in indigenous languages, but also indigenous land rights, which had been suppressed by the expansion of market liberalism and state control of territory.[31]

New international organizations, often created by US and Western European academics and their indigenous contacts, began to lobby for new understandings of indigenous rights. Cultural Survival, founded by academics at Harvard University, was one such organization. Its members published descriptions of the often disastrous effects of large-scale development projects on indigenous peoples in the journal *Cultural Survival*. These academics lobbied the World Bank to take indigenous rights into account when planning and implementing the megaprojects that the World Bank promoted while ignoring the effects of such projects on indigenous people.[32] Members of Cultural Survival also solicited funds from the US Agency for International Development, arguing that highlighting indigenous rights was a key component of the "New Directions" policies on basic human needs that Congress had mandated the organization to consider since the early 1970s. While indigenist organizations working with the US government placed indigenous rights, specifically the right to land, squarely at the center of development policy, the organizations defused the revolutionary potential of indigenous sovereignty by proposing to assist indigenous groups in becoming "successful ethnic minorities."[33]

USAID programs supporting human rights in the late 1970s funded groups with the explicit aim of promoting indigenous rights through participation grounded in land rights in Latin America. Just as a decade earlier dissatisfaction with development policies had led to new programs fostering "civic and political development," the legislation of human rights protections into foreign assistance was aimed both at monitoring recipients of US foreign aid and reforming development practice. Cultural Survival used the language of community development from the 1960s. The group called for "maximum feasible Indian participation" in formulating and carrying out projects, but without an "unrealistic insistence that Indian groups should suddenly run their affairs according to the parliamentary procedures we know."[34]

Cultural Survival submitted its first grant proposal to USAID in July 1979, proposing a series of projects as "investigations and evaluations of alternative development strategies," to assist "native people . . . who are most disadvantageously affected by current development programs." The proposal touted the organization's connections in Brazil, where founder David Maybury-Lewis had long worked with the Akwĕ-Shavante people, as well as in Paraguay, Bolivia, Peru, Ecuador, Colombia, and Honduras. The proposal ranked the organization's priorities as land rights, fostering indigenous "coherence" as groups, legal assistance, education, and medical assistance.[35] Controverting critiques that the culture the group sought to preserve was romantic folklore, they asserted that their aim was preserving cultural adaptability through helping indigenous people obtain tangible benefits. Foremost among these tangible necessities was land.

In November 1980, Misurasata invited US embassy officials to attend its first anniversary celebration in the city of Waspam on the banks of the Río Coco. The official who attended noted the excitement of the participants gathered from all over the region, even as simultaneous celebrations took place in the other major cities of the east coast. Misurasata brought representatives not just from the east coast but also from the indigenous communities of Monimbo, Sutiava, and Sébaco, sites of important revolts during the insurrections that brought down the Somoza government. Indigenous representatives from Honduras and Costa Rica also attended. The head of the US delegation marveled at slogans on posters written in indigenous languages, while remarking that the socialist revolutionary rhetoric that pervaded Managua was scarce (neglecting to note how he managed to translate the numerous languages represented).

He also observed that FSLN supporters tried and failed to get the indigenous people to repeat their chants. Workers in the literacy campaign avoided the rally entirely.[36] While the head of the US delegation emphasized the independence of the indigenous movement from Managua, another official noted in private that "the themes were 'Indian Power,' the 'convivencia' of all ethnic groups, and allegiance to the objectives of the revolution for whom so many died." Even as workers at the US embassy cultivated their ties with the indigenous leadership, some staff members worried that a coming conflagration might upset the coexistence of indigenous demands and the revolutionary government's projects.[37]

Misurasata also lobbied the US embassy in Managua for funding and received appropriations to create offices in Managua as well as the major cities on the east coast where an indigenous political ferment was taking place. USAID worked with Misurasata leaders such as Steadman Fagoth to formulate development projects such as a program to revitalize production of tuno, a raw material in making chewing gum that had been bought from indigenous people by US companies like Wrigley but that had fallen into disuse. Misurasata leaders decided, however, that such development projects should come after what they saw as a more pressing issue: getting the revolutionary government to recognize their land rights. To this end, Miskito leaders solicited USAID to help Misurasata carry out a survey of indigenous land rights reaching back to the colonial period. The embassy recognized that direct funding of such projects involved the US government too closely with local politics, so the embassy solicited Cultural Survival to act as intermediary.[38] When Cultural Survival's representative Theodore Macdonald wrote to Minister of Culture Ernesto Cardenal notifying him of his plans to visit the Miskito, he mentioned his connections with Oxfam rather than USAID.[39] Nonetheless, US support for Misurasata was no secret.

The land demarcation project provided the spark that ignited conflict between Misurasata and the Sandinistas. In 1981 the government accused Misurasata's leadership of fomenting ethnic separatism and attempting to create an independent state. Large-scale rebellion began when the government arrested Misurasata's leadership. Miskito activists accused the government of widespread human rights abuses. The indigenous coalition fragmented, and leader Steadman Fagoth created a new organization, Misura, allied with the US-backed Contra army in Honduras. Misurasata leader Brooklyn Rivera maintained the organization's name but moved first to Honduras and then to Costa Rica, where he aligned his forces with a different counterrevolutionary group. In response to the military threat, the government moved large numbers of Miskitos into relocation camps away from the Honduran border and destroyed their villages. This relocation program galvanized international criticism of heavy-handed methods by both opponents and supporters of the revolution.[40]

Interpretations of the Costeño and specifically Miskito rejection of the Sandinista program differed over causes. As conflict unfolded, academics, activists, and policymakers in Latin America, the United States, and Europe involved themselves in the "Miskito question" throughout the 1980s in an attempt to steer international policy. The Reagan administration exploited the Sandinista treatment of indigenous people to lobby for Contra funding. Western European countries that provided Nicaragua with much-needed economic and technical assistance also expressed grave concern over the issue. They pressured the Sandinista government to reform its policies and check human rights abuses.

Both the Sandinistas and the Miskitos mobilized international academics and activist networks to defend and propagate each side's interpretation of events. Young internationalist academics attached themselves in solidarity with the revolution to government agencies attempting to understand the east coast. First the Centro de Investigación y Estudios de la Reforma Agraria (CIERA) and later the Centro de Investigaciones y Documentación de la Costa Atlántica (CIDCA) carried out studies of the Caribbean region.[41] A number of researchers argued that class exploitation and US imperialism were the ultimate causes of underdevelopment in the east. They argued for cultural autonomy for the Atlantic coast's people and warned that lack of respect for indigenous and Creole traditions would further alienate these people from the revolution.[42] Imagining a future in which social revolution would tear down Central America's old colonial borders, anthropologists Philippe Bourgois and Georg Grünberg argued that autonomy for Zelaya would "cement a firmer national unity" and help bring about a future "Union of Socialist States of Central America."[43] Bourgois would later be expelled from the country as the revolutionary government rejected calls for regional autonomy.[44]

Activist scholars held that the people of the east coast had developed a "colonized consciousness" that caused them to feel greater affinity for the United States than for the Nicaraguan government. Indigenous people customarily called anyone from the west "Spaniards," including government officials or revolutionary cadres, linking them to a long history of colonial abuses. These academics saw themselves as engaging in a process of "decolonizing" the Atlantic coast, by replacing the economic and social structures created first by British and then by US influence in the region. According to this interpretation, the Costeños' divided consciousness made them vulnerable to manipulation by

US government agents. Both the Sandinista government and its academic allies recognized that government policy toward the coast was imperfect. Observers recognized that the FSLN cadres who traveled to the east carried with them long-standing prejudices about the backwardness of the region. According to this interpretation, the source of the violent clash between Sandinistas and indigenous peoples was cultural misunderstanding and outside interference by the United States. The situation could be corrected by more conscientious and culturally respectful practices on the part of the revolutionary government and its cadres, and an end to US interference.[45]

A second group of activists and intellectuals took up the cause of the Miskito people in the name of indigenous rights and the larger Fourth World movement begun by indigenous activists in Canada who argued for greater cultural and territorial autonomy.[46] While recognizing the importance of cultural sensitivity, these groups focused more intently on the question of land rights, resource control, and indigenous culture as something distinct from that of the rest of the Nicaraguan nation. For Miskito activists and their international supporters, the "decolonization" of US influence the Sandinistas claimed to be carrying out was actually colonial penetration by a "foreign" government in Managua. The Miskito interpretation countering that of the Sandinista supporters held that the conflict on the east coast was the result of indigenous response to the contradiction between the Sandinista rhetoric of national self-determination and Costeño feelings of being colonized people within a larger, often hostile, national body. This interpretation was favored by indigenous movements and pan-indigenist organizations that allied themselves to the Costeño cause. According to this view, British imperial power had allowed indigenous people, specifically the Miskito, a great deal of autonomy and ability to resist the encroachment first by the Spanish empire and later the Spanish-speaking Nicaraguan government. This situation continued once the United States became the dominant power. Though US companies extracted profits from the region, their provision of wage labor and imported goods allowed the coast people to maintain their semi-subsistence culture while tying them to international markets.

The joint project to map indigenous lands by Misurasata, USAID, and Cultural Survival was the most salient manifestation of the indigenist approach. What began as a project to map community land claims around northeastern Nicaragua led to a territorial claim by Miskito activists to roughly one-third of the country's soil. Mapping of indigenous territory based on local knowledge had been fundamental to the creation of a Fourth World movement, begun by Canadian indigenous groups such as the Inuit, Cree, and Dené as a way of both gaining territorial autonomy and restraining government development projects.[47] In Nicaragua, such struggles would become linked to geopolitics, and new ways of imagining how indigenous groups might ground their claims would be born there.

For the Miskitos' indigenist allies, the struggle in Nicaragua, though potentially global in scope, was grounded in indigenous control of territory. Abstract recognition of land rights was not enough: many of these internationalist indigenists also advocated explicitly for armed insurrection. Though the issue divided indigenist organizations, prominent Native American activists offered to assist in the Miskitos' armed rebellion against the Nicaraguan government to defend this indigenous territory.[48] Anthropologist Charles Hale argues that the mapping project begun in 1980 uncovered the fact that most communities had only tenuous legal claims to their customary lands. This condition, he contends, led the communities to make a much broader territorial claim than justified by the legal titles that activists claimed existed. Misurasata's Plan 81 claimed the majority of the east coast territory for indigenous people. It was this expansive land claim, combined with rumors that Misurasata planned to proclaim independence and claim protection from an outside imperial power, that led the Nicaraguan government to arrest Misurasata's leadership.[49]

In reaction to the restiveness of the indigenous population, the Sandinista government mobilized the developmentalist assumptions that had underpinned government policies on the east coast since the 1960s. In 1981, Nicaraguan government planners warned that the villages along the Río Coco, the traditional heart of Miskito culture between Nicaragua and Honduras, were in a "disaster zone [*zona de desastre*]," subject to dangerous flooding that made traditional life there unsustainable. The planners suggested voluntary relocation of Miskitos to safer areas, offering government investment in projects like sawmills and agricultural processing plants to provide employment for people who chose to resettle.[50] Once fighting broke out between the government and indigenous people, the government implemented a large-scale relocation program, this time involuntary. It was premised on protecting Miskitos from another disaster, the Contra War, which was beginning to spread along the border between Nicaragua and Honduras. Thousands of Miskitos were relocated to an area called Tasba Pri, where they would be housed, employed, and supervised by the government. The program provoked an international outcry and deepened the armed conflict with the indigenous people.

Thanks to growing international attention, indigenous activists and their supporters who initially looked favorably on the Nicaraguan revolution began to criticize government policies on the east coast. Native American activist groups in the United States, like the International Indian Treaty Council (IITC) and American Indian Movement (AIM), split over the issue.[51] The Indian Law Resource Center, which lobbied for indigenous legal rights, hired Miskito activist Armstrong Wiggins and lobbied against Sandinista policies. Though these groups did not align themselves with the entirety of Reagan administration policies toward Nicaragua, FSLN supporters accused them of implicitly supporting a US administration that only cynically supported indigenous rights.

In helping move indigenous rights to the center of international aid in the 1980s, Cultural Survival and like-minded organizations promised a "reevaluation of the meaning of terms such as 'development,' 'progress,' and 'modernization.'"[52] In doing so they made their mission compatible with the counterinsurgency foundations of international development. Cultural Survival aroused the interest of US officials by warning that the "destructive effects" of modernization programs were causing grave instability in international hot spots such as Iran and Afghanistan, where lack of attention to ethnic minorities threatened "the stability of the polity itself."[53] The Nicaraguan revolutionary government encouraged such instability with development projects carried out in the name of revolution and war, incurring international condemnation. Simultaneously, the US government, in supporting the Contra War, used development aid to displace Miskito people in Honduras to build infrastructure improving that country's capacity as a military base.[54] Even as indigenous rights organizations tried to move beyond the flawed premises of mid-twentieth-century development policy, those allied with both the US government and revolutionary Nicaragua reinforced its counterinsurgent foundations.

Internationalism and Fourth World Revolution

The most prominent and controversial advocate of the indigenous armed struggle during the 1980s was Bernard Nietschmann, a professor of geography at the University of California, Berkeley. He conducted his fieldwork in the late 1960s and early 1970s in the Miskito village of Tasbapauni, where he studied the effects of the commercialization of turtle fishing in indigenous culture and ecology.[55] It was during this fieldwork that he and Baldwin Garth retraced Squier's route, as much out of bravado as of academic necessity. Though Nietschmann gained local prestige from the feat, Garth was shunned by the community for defying its norms and embroiling himself in the geographer's alien world. In his memoir of this period, Nietschmann expressed moral ambivalence that his academic work was bringing him prestige while bringing the

Miskitos little tangible benefit. Worse yet, his work had helped bring about fishing regulations by the Somoza government that helped conserve vulnerable turtle populations while hurting the Miskitos economically.[56] Nietschmann would overcome these feelings of guilt a few years later by throwing himself unambiguously into advocacy for indigenous armed struggle.

Nietschmann's academic work grew from the academic subfield of political ecology that was growing in importance in the 1970s. Its earliest progenitors, such as Carl O. Sauer, built the discipline of cultural geography around a critique of the emerging post–World War II development practice. In a report to the Rockefeller Foundation in the 1950s, Sauer critiqued programs to foster a green revolution begun in Mexico and later transplanted to Southeast Asia as a "crusade" that threatened to "destroy the ecological balance" of rural communities.[57] The foundation suppressed the report as inimical to its growing program for global developmentalism. In the 1960s, academics in geography, anthropology, and related disciplines began to combine an appreciation of the ecological sensibilities of peasant societies with recognition of the continued relevance of indigenous practices in Latin America despite official national ideologies of *mestizaje*. These academics would begin formulating a critique of development as practiced both by nation-states and international institutions, privileging local knowledges and practices over the global models propagated in the Cold War. Nietschmann would take part in this critique, adding to an appreciation of local ecological understandings a support for armed indigenous insurrection as the key to environmental sustainability.

Nietschmann traveled to post-revolutionary Nicaragua in 1980 at the invitation of the Instituto Nicaragüense de Recursos Naturales y del Ambiente (IRENA) to investigate the possibility of creating a national reserve in the Miskito Cays, a biologically rich group of islands and reefs off the country's eastern shore. Plans for this reserve were shelved as rebellion grew among the Miskito. He returned in 1983, this time without the permission of the government in Managua. He traveled with Misurasata leader Brooklyn Rivera from Costa Rica into Nicaragua to document alleged human rights abuses carried out by the Nicaraguan government against the coastal population. Nietschmann presented his findings in testimony before the Organization of American States Commission on Human Rights.[58]

Rivera and his allies turned to Nietschmann and other potential allies to rally support for their faction of the indigenous resistance movement, which was at odds with the organization led by Steadman Fagoth in Honduras. Nietschmann obliged them by becoming their advocate through numerous articles, op-eds, and testimonials, even carrying out a campaign to discredit Misurasata's opponents within the indigenous activist community.[59] He appeared on Pat Robertson's *700 Club* to appeal to the US conservative community, and his work was held up by Oliver North's public diplomacy network in support of US funding for the Contras.[60]

Instead of warning against British imperialism as Squier had more than a century earlier, Nietschmann claimed that the Soviet and Cuban governments were allied to build an overland canal route to supply what he described as an expansionist leftist government in Managua. Though he disclaimed support for the US-backed Contras in Honduras and attacked the US government for ignoring Indian rights, he lobbied for increased US support of the Miskito armed struggle. In 1984, he wrote to Senator Orrin Hatch (Republican of Utah), suggesting a broad reconception of the Reagan administration's justification of the Contra War with Sandinista Nicaragua. The premise that the purpose of the Contras was to interdict arms moving to El Salvador was thin, he wrote, so he proposed that instead the US government ally itself with the indigenous struggle and repurpose the war as one for indigenous liberation, as depicted in figure 5.1.[61]

Nietschmann's role in the Sandinista-Miskito conflict highlights the contested relationship between violence, autonomy, and development brought about by this "revolution within the revolution," and the role of development ideology in stoking conflict. Nietschmann's writings express the connection between cultural identity, land, and armed resistance, all of which he synthesized into what he termed an "ecopolitical" understanding of indigenous rights. His work received a wide hearing within communities of anthropologists, geographers, and ecologists.[62] Nietschmann continually encouraged the Miskito leadership to link their struggle to expansive claims for territorial control that ignored the nation-state's frontiers, as shown in figure 5.2. Misurasata activists needed little goading, as they based their claims to autonomy on land claims that reached back not just to the "reincorporation" of the Mosquitia by the Nicaraguan government in the nineteenth century, but to the Spanish conquest five centuries before. More than just a legal claim, the activists made a moral case that the central government was attempting to destroy the customary indigenous way of life.[63]

Nietschmann added to the moral case rooted in tradition a much broader ecological mandate to defend indigenous culture. The traditional practices of indigenous societies, he argued, helped protect the environment because indigenous people traditionally practiced sustainable methods of production.[64] He contrasted their methods of semisubsistence ecology with the state-led programs of growth of both the capitalist Somoza regime and the socialist Sandinistas. Though in his earlier work Nietschmann demonstrated the willingness

Figure 5.1. Cover of Bernard Nietschmann, "Fourth World Revolution: With Yapti Tasba Guerrillas Fighting the Sandinista Invasion." Courtesy of the Bancroft Library.

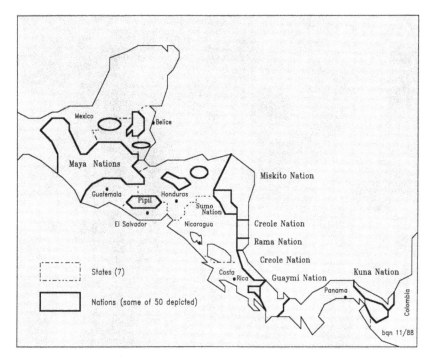

Figure 5.2. Nietschmann's depiction of the "States" and "Nations" of Central America, showing indigenous rights to control much of the region's territory and spanning state borders (Nietschmann, manuscript of "Fourth World Revolution," 540). Courtesy of the Bancroft Library.

of indigenous and Creole people to engage in the market economy to the detriment of the environment, his work as a publicist for indigenous autonomy encouraged an equation between indigenous identity and ecological practice that he believed could counterbalance the corrupting influence of market relations.[65] Moreover, he argued that the Miskito and other indigenous people offered a natural buffer against the expansionist tendencies of global communism.

Many academics and activists who supported liberation movements in Central America during the 1980s supported the use of armed struggle by local forces to defend themselves against depredations of military power guided by the United States. This support was usually couched in terms of "self-defense," and solidarity groups often rooted in pacifism wrestled with the question of how to ally themselves with armed struggle. Nietschmann distinguished himself by his willingness to openly advocate the use of violence, and he connected the use of violence with the larger problem of ecological sustainability.[66] Nietschmann asserted that a "warrior tradition" in Miskito culture, within which he readily inserted himself as shown in figure 5.3, accounted for their region's relatively sound ecological condition. The reason Miskito lands had not undergone the same ecologically unsound industrial agricultural development as the rest of the country was that Miskitos had defended their rights through arms, first against the Spanish empire and then the Nicaraguan government.[67] The same intimate connection with the landscape that made their ecological practices sustainable also made them undefeatable warriors when protecting their own territory.

Nietschmann attempted to link ecology and armed resistance to garner continued US support for the Miskito resistance, but he also sought to infuse Miskito consciousness with the memory of this warrior tradition. For Nietschmann, the Miskito struggle was only a single instance of a much wider global struggle between indigenous people and state powers. He believed that an inherent contradiction existed between state imperatives to control development and resources, and minority desire for self-determination and cultural autonomy. Though he condemned the US government as a state power that encroached upon its own indigenous peoples' lands, he supported it as an imperial power that could protect indigenous culture when it suited US interests.[68]

Figure 5.3. Frontispiece for Nietschmann's manuscript, depicting himself with the Indian rebels of "Yapti Tasba." Courtesy of the Bancroft Library.

By 1985 Nietschmann was heavily involved not just with documenting Sandinista abuses and publicizing the indigenous cause but also in assisting in
conceptualizing a much wider form of struggle. He worked with the branch
of the Miskito resistance allied with Contras based in Costa Rica that the CIA
had cultivated for the purpose of undermining the FSLN's international solidarity. This group, led by former Sandinista allies Edén Pastora and Alfonso
Robelo, coalesced as the Alianza Revolucionaria Democrática (ARDE) and
distinguished itself from Contra forces in Honduras by its advocacy of social
democratic principles. Nietschmann found an ideological ally in Hugo Spadafora, a Panamanian doctor who had fought with Amilcar Cabral in West Af-
rica and then on the southern front of the Sandinista war against Somoza.
Spadafora joined the Contra movement once Pastora took up arms against the
FSLN in the name of the betrayed revolution. Both Pastora and Spadafora cultivated public images as social democratic versions of Che Guevara. Though
Che had failed to revolutionize Bolivia's indigenous population, Nietschmann
believed he could help Spadafora avoid the same mistake.[69]

The relationship between Indians and the ARDE leadership was strained.
Nevertheless, Spadafora embraced the concept of indigenous rebellion and enlisted Nietschmann to help conceive a broader ideological strategy.[70] When
the US Congress mandated through the Boland Amendment that the US government cut all funding to the Contras, Spadafora became an important liaison between Oliver North's operation to continue illegally funding the
Contras and the Panamanian government of Manuel Noriega.[71] According
to Nietschmann, Spadafora conceived of using the funds provided by North
to create a "Brigada Simón Bolívar" that would depose dictatorships throughout Latin America, in the style of the Caribbean Legion of an earlier generation.[72] First they would depose the Sandinistas in Nicaragua, followed by
Noriega in Panama, and then Castro in Cuba, and continue from there.[73]
Spadafora and Nietschmann conceived of a natural alliance of campesinos
and indigenous people that they believed had been suppressed by the socialist
pretensions of previous revolutionary forces.

The Brigada Simón Bolívar was not to be, undone by the shadowy connections that made its conception possible. The same network that funneled
guns and money from the United States via Panama to the resistance fighters
in Nicaragua was also being used to traffic vast quantities of cocaine. Nietschmann describes Spadafora as being opposed to this practice as contrary
to his revolutionary principles. In taking a stand against this trafficking, he became a declared enemy of one of its prime movers, Panamanian dictator
Manuel Noriega. Spadafora allegedly attempted to alert the US government

to Noriega's drug-smuggling practices. When US officials rebuffed him, he traveled to Panama to attempt to document his allegations. Upon arrival, the Panamanian Defense Forces under command of Noriega apprehended, tortured, and killed him.[74]

According to Nietschmann, with the death of Spadafora the balance of power in Misurasata's leadership shifted from those who sought a military victory within Nicaragua itself to others, such as Brooklyn Rivera, who favored a political solution. Nietschmann in fact criticized Rivera for believing "more in political than in military confrontation."[75] Nietschmann's support for a military solution to the Miskito conflict arose out of his belief in the connection between ecology and armed struggle, which he would consistently support throughout the anti-Sandinista conflict and even after the Cold War.

Despite his disdain for politics, Nietschmann served as an adviser to Misurasata during peace talks in Mexico City, Bogotá, and Managua, where the Sandinista leadership accused him and other "foreign advisers" of discouraging Miskito rebels from agreeing to peace. The international advisers to Misurasata, Armstrong Wiggins and Steve Tullberg of the Indian Law Resource Center, Jim Anaya of the National Indian Youth Council, and Theodore Macdonald of Cultural Survival, backed Rivera's peace initiatives that were fostered by US Senator Ted Kennedy (Democrat of Massachusetts). Nietschmann supported these initiatives because he believed the waning of Contra aid necessitated a "time-out" for Miskito fighters to recuperate their forces. He also seemed to believe that his and Spadafora's fantasy of an international liberation brigade uniting the Third and Fourth World in revolution might bring about a new infusion of international support.

Negotiations between the Sandinistas and Miskito fighters began in 1984 and lasted until the end of the Contra War. After their early rejection of the indigenous movement as ally of imperialism, FSLN intellectuals such as Carlos Alemán Ocampo successfully urged their government to see the indigenous struggle as fundamentally different from the Contras, "a revolution, not a counterrevolution."[76] The government ultimately moderated its treatment of indigenous people, closing many of its relocation camps and helping the Miskito return to their villages along the border with Honduras. The government also worked to integrate into the new constitution enacted in 1987 regional autonomy for the east coast, officially recognizing its ethnically plural character.[77] This move was hailed by activists as a "revolutionary step for Latin America" that offered national relations based for the first time on "equity and autonomy."[78] The new constitution granted the east coast autonomy not in the name of indigenous territorial rights, however, as Miskito activists had conceived, but

rather in recognition of limited rights to self-determination of individual ethnic groups.[79]

In reaction to the perceived deprecation of indigenous nationhood, Misurasata leader Brooklyn Rivera famously stated, "Ethnic groups run restaurants.
We have an army. We are a people."[80] Such rhetoric played well with international indigenist allies, and Rivera and his group antagonized the Sandinista
government by bringing representatives inside the Nicaraguan war zone.[81]
Though Rivera's Misurasata was the first Miskito group to negotiate with the
government, his internationalist allies pushed him to advocate for armed struggle after other groups began to negotiate cease-fires and hand over their
arms.[82] Though boastful of the move toward autonomy gained by the Miskito
struggle, Nietschmann regretted that the struggle had finally been "reduced
to politics."[83] From his point of view, armed struggle was not simply an instrument to achieve recognition from the government; it was essential to maintain autonomy and the militant culture he romanticized. When the end of
civil war and the Cold War ultimately brought peace, the question of how to
justify such armed struggle would remain.[84]

Autonomy and Ecology after the Cold War

The 1987 Nicaraguan constitution divided the east coast's Zelaya province into
the Northern and Southern Autonomous Regions and made provisions for recognition of indigenous autonomy that indigenous activists considered a model
for other Latin American countries.[85] The recognition of indigenous rights to
control of resources, though limited, gave communities recourse both within
the country and in international venues to check development projects that
these communities believe detrimental to their interests.[86] On the other hand,
many indigenous groups in the autonomous regions continued to see the central government as an antagonist as much as an ally.[87] Activists maintained connections with a coalition of international aid groups in order to counterbalance
the central government, continuing coastal peoples' long tradition of seeking allies outside their country's borders.

Nietschmann's work with the Miskito people continued after the end of
both the Contra War and the Cold War. He continued to argue that the best
means to preserve indigenous self-determination was by linking ecology and
indigenous self-defense. Beginning in 1991 he once again participated in a
project to establish a protected area for the Miskito Cays, where he had first
traveled in 1969 with Baldwin Garth and later visited at the behest of the

revolutionary government. His project, funded by USAID and the Mac-Arthur Foundation, created an 800,000-hectare protected area that included the offshore Miskito Cays and twenty-three coastal communities that depended on fishing there. Funded as part of a $12 million USAID natural resources program, it was built around a community organization called Mikupia, made up of demobilized Miskito fighters, and a US-based NGO, the Caribbean Conservation Corporation (CCC).[88]

Nietschmann argued that the threat to Miskito subsistence practices and the threat to the ecosystem of the Miskito Cays were interdependent. Resource piracy by illegal commercial fishing operations was destroying the marine habitat. The rising incidence of drug smuggling also presented a security threat to indigenous people.[89] Nietschmann and others continued to argue that without self-defense capabilities on the part of indigenous people, autonomy rights would be meaningless. Rather than seeking redress from what he considered a corrupt central government, Nietschmann tried to get funding from the international community to help arm the Miskitos to protect their territory.[90] More than just a conservation plan, Nietschmann and his indigenous allies argued that the Cays project was part of a new "ecopolitical approach to demarcate and protect [the Miskito nation's] territory."[91] Nietschmann hoped through the creation of conservation spaces to link the Miskito people of Nicaragua with those in Honduras, whose territory he believed also to be occupied by an illegitimate nation-state.

The project foundered amid accusations of betrayal and mutual recrimination between Nietschmann, USAID, and the US NGOs charged with implementing the project. USAID for its part expressed reservations about Nietschmann's participation in the project. Administrators recognized that Nietschmann's participation in the autonomy struggle, especially his accompaniment of armed rebels into "the bush," had given him a great deal of authority with Miskito communities. One official even referred to him as a "founding father" of the autonomous region.[92] While touting the project as a product of postrevolutionary reconciliation, USAID downplayed the political content of the project, focusing instead on its potential to foster the development goals of the central government.[93]

Nietschmann in turn accused USAID of carrying out "colonial conservation" by bypassing community organizations and community understandings in implementing his project. Nietschmann and the Indian Law Resource Center presented evidence to the Miskito communities involved in the Cays project that AID and the CCC had mismanaged funds. Nietschmann wrote in 1996 that the Miskito communities had voted to "expel" both USAID and

CCC associates from their communities. They would instead take responsibility to police their own territory using their own community resources.[94] Once again the Miskito communities were at odds with their central government, but the imperial tides had turned, and the US government no longer saw its interest in indigenous autonomy.[95] The new post-Sandinista regime under Violeta Chamorro elected in 1990 showed a willingness to incorporate Miskito leaders into the government and named Brooklyn Rivera head of the newly created Ministry of Atlantic Coast Development. Minister of Government Antonio Lacayo expressed privately to US representatives that the coast needed less autonomy and more economic development.[96]

The controversy around the Miskito Cays presents in miniature many of the dilemmas that surround indigenous autonomy after the Cold War. Nietschmann's argument for indigenous self-defense proclaimed indigenous autonomy but also required collaboration with outside powers—those of Britain, the United States, or the international aid community—to check the encroachment of the nation-state's designs for development. Miskito autonomy advocates, with the help of Nietschmann, gained allies in the international NGO community by translating their political struggle into the new language of ecology and biodiversity. With the US government tentatively allied with Nicaragua's post-Sandinista government, however, the incentive to support indigenous autonomy was diminished, and indigenous peoples once again occupied a dangerous territory both within the state and apart. The Miskitos, other indigenous groups, and the organizations that try to speak for them internationally continue to navigate precarious terrain between state, empire, and global society.

Chapter 6

Institutionalized Precarity in Postwar Nicaragua

On the eve of Nicaragua's historic 1990 election, Pablo Antonio Cuadra lamented that the degradation of his country's natural environment was an "invisible cancer" threatening to deform the nation's "spiritual ecology."[1] The degradation of the country's lakes and forests boded catastrophe worse than that brought by the destruction of Managua's "syntax" in the 1972 earthquake. The Sandinista government, he argued, had failed in part because it attempted to replace one alien syntax, a corrupt vision of modernization that had created a grotesque Managua, with another, socialism inspired by Marxism and Leninism. In contrast, Sandinista authors like Sergio Ramírez argued that the revolution had attempted to complete the process of modernization by replacing the alienating influence of the United States with genuinely Nicaraguan characteristics, to "synthesize the struggle for identity and modernity to give us the definitive face of the Nicaraguan."[2] Despite their differences, revolutionary and counterrevolutionary agreed that national identity—inscribed on the land itself—was scarred by decades of conflict over the meaning of modernity.[3]

In February 1990, FSLN candidate Daniel Ortega lost an election to Violeta Barrios de Chamorro for the presidency of Nicaragua, ending the decade-long conflict between the revolution and the US-backed counterrevolution. Observers saw it as an augur of democratization and collapsing socialism around the world as the Cold War ended. For Nicaraguans, the process of reconstruction of the war-torn country would require a reconstruction of meaning, as the structures and concepts built around Cold War competition's development promises were exhausted. Planners in Washington attempted to build a new set of meanings by implementing a "blueprint for a neoliberal republic" that would dismantle the revolution's legacy and make Nicaragua a showcase of postsocialist transition.[4] Nicaraguans had their own ideas, generating conflict between international imperatives and local politics.

The new syntax of post–Cold War political order that took shape in Latin America in the early 1990s was built around concepts that assimilated neoliberal ideas through local forms of mediation.[5] *Concertación* named a process of elite negotiation that governments from Mexico to Chile used to reconcile changes in economic structure with the growing demand for democratization.[6] Like many other ideas in the age of development, *concertación* had its origins in Latin American political culture but took on new meaning in an international context. The process of "consensus-making" that it connoted undergirded a series of performances that were key to negotiating the drastic political and economic changes that shook the region. Nicaragua's new government acceded to US demands that it adjust to neoliberal ideas, but in using *concertación* to align the local and the international the government brought further impositions on its sovereignty.

While Nicaraguans were attempting to negotiate the terms of *concertación*, a second governing concept fused the environmental and international constraints the country faced. "Sustainable development," although part of the development lexicon for decades, emerged as a governing concept only in the late 1980s, just as the Washington consensus was taking hold. Instead of invoking the austerity associated with neoliberalism, sustainable development critiqued the past failures of development by emphasizing environmental conservation alongside economic constraint brought by massive debt, corruption, and endemic poverty. The international aid apparatus, including USAID, began to reconstitute itself around the new idea, as it had done before with pluralism, entrepreneurship, human rights, and modernization. Though the Alliance for Progress was long dead, it was resurrected in hollow echo by an Alliance for Sustainable Development in Central America.[7] The replacement of "progress" with "sustainable development" indicated that, by the 1990s, the era set off by the Cuban Revolution and the Alliance for Progress had come to an end.

In the absence of grand plans for modernization and takeoff offered by capitalist or socialist revolutions, Nicaraguan politics returned to a simple foundation: property. The distribution of property, most importantly land itself, was at the center of Nicaragua's conflicts in the age of development: the struggle between the Somoza family and the oligarchs over control of valuable farmland for industrial agriculture, the distribution of land in the reconstructed Managua, the opening of new agricultural territory in the east, and the conflict over peasant property that fueled the Contra War. What stability was achieved in the 1990s resulted from the right and left granting central importance to private property, a tenuous consensus that the revolution could survive in the form of redistributed land. Though this consensus conformed to neoliberal strictures, the fractious nature of US power brought new forms of intervention as dissident elements in the United States and Nicaragua rejected *concertación* and attempted to turn back the revolution. It was not neoliberalism alone, but conflict between competing forms of intervention that institutionalized the precariousness of Nicaraguan economic and political life in the post–Cold War era.

Post–Cold War Development

The element of surprise looms large in most accounts of the end of the Cold War. Politicians and experts failed to predict the fall of the Berlin Wall, the rapid collapse of the Soviet empire in Eastern Europe, and the ultimate dissolution of the Soviet Union itself. Surprise is also a key element in narratives of the end of Sandinista rule in Nicaragua. The Sandinistas themselves failed to foresee their election loss in February 1990. According to Julio Valle Castillo, it felt like "nature revolted" when the results of perhaps the most closely observed election in history made clear that Sandinista President Daniel Ortega had lost by a wide margin to Violeta Chamorro, widow of slain *La Prensa* editor Pedro Joaquín Chamorro.[8]

Opinions differ on whether the US government and the members of Chamorro's loose coalition of parties known as the Unión Nacional Opositora (UNO) had foreseen the election outcome.[9] Many polls predicted a solid victory for the Sandinistas, and the international media reported on the enthusiasm of crowds gathered for Ortega's election rallies.[10] On the one hand, supporters of the Sandinistas equated the victory of Violeta Chamorro with a victory of US military aggression against Nicaragua, asserting that it was war exhaustion rather than disillusion with the Sandinista revolutionary project that drove millions of Nicaraguans to choose Chamorro on election day. Supporters of the US-backed counterrevolution held that Nicaraguans voted against the tyranny of a socialist vanguard party and the scarcity that followed their economic policies.[11]

Though it is true that the US government supported the election of Doña Violeta against Daniel Ortega, the immediate aftermath of the election indicates that the US government had little control over the newly elected nationalist government. One of the first and most controversial decisions of the

Chamorro government, organized by her son-in-law and chief adviser Antonio Lacayo, was to leave intact the Sandinista army under Humberto Ortega, brother of Daniel, instead of replacing it with either a Contra army or an entirely new force. Many argue that this decision not only made possible a peaceful transition between the two governments but also indicated that the new government was not a puppet of the US government. The George H. W. Bush administration had little choice but to support the government that it had done so much to bring into power, even though the government was in practice far from its ideal, quickly proving willing to act independently of US wishes.[12] Despite reservations about the direction the Chamorro government was taking, the United States offered vast amounts of aid, making Nicaragua one of the largest per capita aid recipients in the world. When Doña Violeta visited Congress, she received a standing ovation, though many US politicians recognized her status as a figurehead and wondered where the real power in the government lay.[13]

Scholars are correct in saying that US policy in Nicaragua embodied neoliberal thinking, built around the principles of free market capitalism, private property, shrinking government, and entrepreneurship. Given the longer history of US involvement in Nicaragua, nevertheless, what is most striking about the US plan for a "neoliberal republic" was not the comprehensive nature of its plan for governance, but rather the absence of such a plan. US policy toward Nicaragua since the 1960s had been characterized by the United States' thoroughness in its efforts at building a comprehensive picture of the needs of the nation to stave off social revolution. Planners and politicians studied peasant agriculture, nutrition, education, and gender relations, modeling the feedback relation between each realm of life. Peasants shorn of indigeneity and forced to leave their farms would be integrated in the urban metropolis of Managua, where the seeds of industrial production were sprouting along new highways that led to the ultimate symbol of economic takeoff, a newly refurbished Las Mercedes international airport.[14] At the center of this humming mechanism was the military power of a US-trained National Guard, designed to oversee the gradual democratization of the country and engage in only a minimum of human rights abuses to preserve stability and prevent insurrection.

Unlike modernization theory's elaborate plans for reconstructive surgery that envisioned decades of labor, democratization theory as elaborated in the 1980s held that democracy could be delivered by relatively quick processes of elite negotiation rather than by the long and bloody process of modernization.[15] Theorists envisioned enlightened elites, guided by intellectuals like themselves, making possible much more rapid democratic transition. Nicaragua's transition from socialism to liberal democracy embodied this transformative power of elite negotiations, although democratization theorists were loath to take the transition as a paragon because of the distorting presence of US military and economic power.[16]

The 1990 Nicaraguan transition had all the marks of an elite-driven democratization process, and the new government cast aside many of the central symbols of power in the age of modernization: masculine prowess and technocratic efficiency. The Chamorro campaign highlighted her contrast with the strength and decisiveness of the Somoza-era's military modernization and the Ortega campaign's image of the guerrillero-turned-politician as a *gallo ennavajado* (armed fighting cock). Instead the campaign emphasized her frailness and vulnerability, a symbol of an injured nation after decades of war.[17] Chamorro's campaign also cast her as a mother figure who could unify a broken nation. She could unify the feuding nation as she did her feuding family—one son a leader of the Contras and another the head of the FSLN's official paper, *Barricada*—who nonetheless continued to gather for weekly family dinners.[18]

More than a campaign tactic however, the return to family ties among the elite served for the Chamorro-Lacayo administration as a principle on which to base what they imagined was the "detotalitarization" of Nicaragua.[19] According to the dominant interpretation of the Sandinista phenomenon on the right, the Sandinistas had been engaged in a process of converting Nicaragua into a bureaucratic socialist state along the lines of the dismal Eastern European satellites, replacing old networks of family and regional alliances with a new centralized state power that the Somoza government had never managed to create. Though this totalitarian fantasy was far from the reality of the Sandinista state, the Sandinistas had in fact placed important weight in converting members of the Conservative elite to their cause. By the end of the 1980s, however, the hopeful days of the literacy crusade, envisioned as bringing together the country's rich and poor in the name of the revolution, were long over. The revolutionary project lost the favor of much of the elite, many of whom embraced the Reagan administration's vision of entrepreneurial internationalism as an alternative to Sandinismo.[20]

The Chamorro-Lacayo government filled its ranks with members of the elite families in much the same way the Sandinistas did at the onset of their government in 1979.[21] Many observers noted the fact that the second-in-command of the Sandinista military belonged to the family network that came to power with Chamorro's election. US officials appreciated the usefulness of such family ties in making possible a smooth transition between governments, while also recognizing their own lack of control over such networks.[22] The fact that the new government was populated with prominent members of the old elite became a subject of controversy: on the left, the modus vivendi quickly reached by the FSLN and the new government was indicative of the revolution's failure. Scholars like Carlos Vilas, who had also served in academic institutes affiliated with the revolutionary government, blamed the incompleteness of the revolution on the unwillingness of the Sandinistas to embrace a radical project because of their ties to the old oligarchy.[23] The tactical compromises of political pluralism and a mixed economy to assuage international opinion were a betrayal of the goals of the revolution.[24]

The right, too, was struck more by the continuity than the change between the FSLN and Chamorro governments, and understood the new government not as a triumph but as a betrayal of the Contra struggle. Although supporters of the counterrevolutionaries continued to speak of the Contra forces as heroic freedom fighters, the legacy of the Iran-Contra scandal constrained the Bush administration's ability to treat the Contra forces as a victorious army. The Reagan administration had orchestrated an elaborate campaign to build the image of the Contras as peasants disaffected by socialism and entrepreneurs who wanted free markets. Because of congressional restrictions and skeptical public opinion, exacerbated by the revelation of the baroque mixture of blatant illegality and madcap hubris of the Iran-Contra affair, first the Reagan and then the George H. W. Bush administration turned to casting the Contras as helpless victims of totalitarianism. By asserting that Contra forces were primarily composed of refugees in Honduras and Costa Rica, the US government convinced Congress to continue funding the Contras as a form of humanitarian aid rather than as a counterrevolutionary army.[25] Though the Bush administration kept the Contras intact to exert pressure on the Sandinista government, the Contra leadership lost what traction it had in Washington.[26]

The Contra War definitively ended with the election of February 1990. The new government promised the demobilized forces land concentrated around "development poles," territories in the country's northern, southern, and eastern zones.[27] The decline in US support at the end of the 1980s had also helped bring about a crisis in leadership, as many Contra forces rejected a patchwork leadership of former members of Somoza's National Guard, the oligarchic elite, and renovating entrepreneurs. Supporters in both the United States and Nicaragua alleged a betrayal of the peasant roots of the insurrection by both the US and Nicaraguan governments.[28] These supporters pointed out that the rank and file was composed of campesinos with indigenous roots, led by the same pseudo-mestizo elite rooted in the Spanish conquest that governed in Managua.[29]

Pablo Antonio Cuadra, one of the principal intellectual architects of Nicaragua's "myth of *mestizaje*," played a pivotal role in shaping the narrative that resistance to the FSLN was rooted in the country's racial past. After the 1990 election, Cuadra served as an adviser to Violeta Chamorro, meeting regularly and authoring many of her speeches.[30] Critics asserted that Cuadra's nationalist emphasis on *mestizaje* envisioned a harmonious union of races while justifying the ultimate domination of the conquistador.[31] In discussing literature, Cuadra did emphasize the mutually reinforcing nature of indigeneity and *mestizaje*, incorporating indigenous symbols into what was ultimately a hispano-centric corpus. As was evident in his editorials in *La Prensa*, however, in politics he expressed a much darker vision of *mestizaje* as the product of an originary violation at the heart of Nicaraguan culture.[32] While the Chamorro-Lacayo government was attempting to foster a vision of familial reconciliation, Cuadra used his cultural influence as preeminent man of letters and editor of *La Prensa* to guide the paper away from being a mouthpiece of the new regime, even as Violeta Chamorro as president and Christina Chamorro, Violeta's daughter and wife of Antonio Lacayo, maintained a powerful influence at the paper.[33]

Though US officials never explicitly endorsed the myth of *mestizaje*, under the influence of modernization theory they often corroborated its importance to political and economic development during the 1960s and 1970s. Planners held that the "homogeneous" ethnic character of Nicaragua's majority Spanish-speaking population made carrying out the projects of industrialization and urbanization more practicable.[34] Planners also argued that the indigenous and Creole populations of the east coast, who spoke English and indigenous languages, would eventually be "hispanized" and integrated into the life of the nation. Planners supported the "colonization" projects in the country's less populated eastern region, which had been dear to Anastasio Somoza Debayle, to increase agricultural production, remove population pressure from a rapidly urbanizing Managua, and avoid the need for a comprehensive land reform dreaded by the country's elite.

By the 1980s, international institutions had turned away from *mestizaje* as a central pillar of development. The Sandinista government, with its roots in the Spanish-speaking west coast, carried out modernization projects on the east coast in the same spirit as the previous Somoza government. Though couched in the language of anti-imperialism rather than hispanization, these projects caused mass disaffection among the Creole and indigenous populations. Simultaneously, however, the international aid apparatus was beginning to support indigenous rights as an alternative to the state-led development advocated by modernization theory.[35] In addition to the political limits to the promise of eastward expansion, a newly forming environmental consciousness claimed that such expansion, rather than contributing to the wealth of the country, was destroying many of its most valuable resources.[36] People still spoke of an agricultural frontier, though reports warned that east coast land did not in fact offer new soil for cultivation.[37]

The United States in the 1990s no longer supported the ethnic and territorial integration of Latin American countries that the United States had promoted since the 1960s. An aid memorandum in 1991 noted in passing that the United States had abandoned the types of development projects that were the bedrock of aid since the 1960s: housing, infrastructure, and industry.[38] Following the 1972 earthquake, planners built their vision of a modernized Managua around housing victims to integrate them into urban industry, tying the new Managua with the rest of the country with new highways that would foster commerce. The new policies in the 1990s instead focused on macroeconomic problems of balance of payments, privatization of property held by the state after the Sandinista period, and the reduction of the size of the state itself. Though aid reached historically high levels, balance of payments and currency support were invisible.[39]

Previous planners had expected the economic infrastructure itself, the hardware of a modern economy, to foster the outlooks and attitudes conducive to modernization. Planners had also emphasized community development and decentralization to foster democratic participation in the economy and politics. Programs of the 1990s worked more directly on forging a "democratic culture."[40] The offspring of Reagan's call for a "democratic revolution," groups like the National Endowment for Democracy worked not at promoting grassroots political development but at influencing elites to participate in liberal democracy. These groups directed aid to anti-Sandinista groups to counterbalance the superior organization and political commitment of the FSLN, which, despite having lost the election, remained the most cohesive party.[41] Political aid was built around a two-party democratic model, even though Nicaragua's political landscape was characterized by intense fragmentation. Planners envisioned that political competition would behave like market competition, and judicious foreign aid was necessary to steer both.

In place of the grandiose aid projects of the age of modernization, US projects in the 1990s began to emphasize their assistance to a damaged and insecure population. Aid programs had once been criticized for ignoring the needs of small business owners, especially in the failed attempt to reconstruct Managua. No more. In the developmentalist language of the day, microenterprise, thanks to its very vulnerability, became the most robust capitalist redoubt.[42] Bush administration policies put great emphasis on equating poverty and permanent handicap in the context of a war-torn country. New foundations, one of which was started in the name of former CIA director and Contra war architect William J. Casey, directed special attention toward Contra war veterans with disabilities.[43] There were also programs aimed at "orphans" of the war, though administrators could not discover a sufficient number of these orphans to disburse the aid.[44] The language of specific infirmity built into the aid program prohibited assistance to otherwise needy children who did not qualify.

The presence in power of the first elected female head of state in the Americas might have boded well for women's participation in politics and the economy. The abandonment of the androcentric models of development propagated by both US development agencies and the revolutionary government seemed poised to give way to new possibilities for women's liberation.[45] Agencies charged with fostering women's participation noted however that "the fact that the nation's President is a woman does not appear to influence the role of women in the private sector," and women continued to suffer higher unemployment and lower pay than men.[46] Feminists in the country had during the revolutionary period and civil war deliberately subordinated many of their demands to the needs of the revolutionary cause, though women's groups within trade unions like the Asociación de Trabajadores del Campo had achieved significant gains for rural working women.[47] After the war ended, these groups would begin to assert themselves once again, even crossing old divides between right and left to develop an autonomous feminist agenda.[48]

USAID integrated the feminist critique of development with its emphasis on entrepreneurship. Just as aid agencies began acknowledging that the old development model had caused grave ecological damage, USAID also recognized that "growth-driven strategies do not necessarily benefit women entrepreneurs, producers or workers."[49] Aid agencies had been mandated since the 1970s to encourage women's participation in development as part of the "basic human needs" doctrine.[50] The critique of development that had originally encouraged the direction of aid toward the private sector to combat inequality and dictatorship would later provide one of the chief weapons in the US war against the Sandinista state.[51] Similarly, the feminist critique of development helped both to undermine the state-controlled economy and also to divide leftist groups opposed to neoliberal development.

Women were hardest hit by programs to shrink government services and privatize industry, as women were often first to be fired from government positions and newly private companies.[52] Health and education services that had targeted women were cut as well.[53] USAID used the occasion of the drastically changed development horizon to redefine the new state of debility in the economy as an opportunity for women. The growth of programs for microcredit offered an opportunity to combine directives to help "the poorest of the poor" with the mandate to foster entrepreneurship in petty trade, "where women predominate."[54] Aid was most often directed toward individual entrepreneurs, undercutting the cooperative movement that the revolutionary period had fostered.[55] Administrators noted ruefully that the microcredit programs offered little opportunity for "graduation" from microcredit to traditional loans, thus undercutting any possibility for long-term growth.[56] Consonant with the turn away from programs to encourage national industry, USAID also encouraged the growth of *maquila* manufacturing, which isolated industrial development in a free trade zone that activists argued "functions as if it were another country, with completely distinct laws."[57] *Maquilas* provided large concentrations of women workers, whom aid could reach more easily, but administrators acknowledged the reduced ability for women workers to organize.[58]

Aid administrators praised the growth of women's groups emerging outside the traditional party and union system, which administrators claimed favored "constructive methods" over "confrontation."[59] Though US aid agencies did not, as in El Salvador, funnel large amounts of money into groups with historic ties to guerrilla movements, they did encourage contact between right and left women's groups, encouraging them to develop a "minimum agenda" of consensus premised on the exclusion of divisive issues such as abortion.[60] As the center grew, the unity of the FSLN began to fracture, fueled in part by increasing demands by female members for inclusion in the governing structures of the party.[61] Even as women's groups were calling for new forms of recognition for the difference of their struggle from traditional class issues, the central government would revive Latin America's quintessential form of government-sponsored identity politics, *mestizaje*, to restrain dissent and form a new governing coalition.

Elite Negotiation and *Mestizaje*'s Rebirth

Nicaragua's political culture during the age of development had been suffused by a series of concepts by which planners and politicians at the local and international level had attempted to organize the country's transition to modernity. Writers on the left like Sergio Ramírez lamented that these ideas were the stalking horses of imperialism, meant to disguise under the cover of benevolent technocracy the imposition of US imperial power.[62] Conservatives like Pablo Antonio Cuadra asserted that the left was simply replacing one set of foreign concepts with another, imposing the ideas of Marxism-Leninism from Russia and Cuba on Nicaragua's soil. In the 1990s, in response to fears of the imposition of yet another alien regime—this time the macroeconomic strictures of a "neoliberal republic"—local elites added what they saw as a uniquely Latin American concept to the political lexicon to insulate their national culture from an alienating world order.

The term *concertación* in Nicaragua came into use to name the process of reconciliation of right and left begun at the end of the 1980s. It would also name the two sets of negotiations in the early 1990s that set the terms for social peace in the country. In distinction to the model of parliamentary democracy regnant in many western European countries that emphasized political parties and conflictual debate, the term evoked a corporatist model of governance rooted in Hispanic tradition.[63] The term had come into vogue throughout Latin America only in the mid-1980s with the creation of the Concertación de Partidos por la Democracia, the alliance of parties in Chile that came together to oppose the Pinochet dictatorship. The term was also used in Mexico to denote "direct dialogue and partnership between the executive and different interest groups."[64] In the 1990s the word would be applied to the peace process between right and left throughout Central America to name political negotiations from the municipal to national level.[65] The model for such processes of *concertación* was the "pactos de Moncloa," a series of agreements between representatives of business, government, and labor that helped restore democracy in Spain after the dissolution of the Franco dictatorship.[66] Though US leaders had learned from Portugal and Spain the power of using aid to promote pluralism and undermine the left, Latin Americans saw in the Iberian transition models for resistance.

The first Nicaraguan revolutionary junta in 1979 had been formed along a corporatist model, one constructed not around local representatives of business, labor, and politics but rather turned outward to the international forces with which different sectors of Nicaragua's political elite were allying themselves.[67] The junta soon dissolved under pressure from Sandinistas to pursue more revolutionary policies and the Reagan administration campaign to roll back the revolution, and its dissolution represented an end to the truce between the conservative and radical elites. According to Francisco Mayorga, the process of *concertación* in Nicaragua began in earnest in 1988 as an attempt to reconstruct the lost consensus of the revolutionary moment in the aftermath of the announcement by the Soviets that they would be withdrawing their aid from Nicaragua.[68] The first steps in that direction were taken by the group known as the Commission on the Recovery and Development of Nicaragua (CORDENIC), which worked with the commission set up by Senator Terry Sanford of South Carolina. Though the group cooperated with US politicians, it set itself apart from groups like Consejo Superior de Empresa Privada (COSEP), which openly allied itself with the foreign policy of the US government. Dismissed as "COSEP heroes and martyrs" (the formula used for naming many Sandinista mass organizations) by Contra supporters such as Enrique Bolaños, CORDENIC made little headway in reconciling the private sector with the Sandinista government, though members such as Antonio Lacayo did succeed in getting confiscated property returned.[69] Most important, these representatives had both strong ties to the private sector and with the Sandinista government, which would make possible the transition of 1990.[70]

Though the first attempt at *concertación* of elites at the end of the 1980s failed, the successful transition between the Ortega and Chamorro governments can be attributed to the dialogue already begun. The strongest indication that the new government would follow the spirit of local *concertación* rather than the vision of a US imperialism was the decision of President Chamorro to retain Humberto Ortega, brother of the outgoing president, as head of the military. The Chamorro government signed a protocol of transition with the Sandinistas that left Ortega as military chief and gave Doña Violeta direct authority over the military instead of creating a minister of defense. The creator of this understanding, which alienated Contra supporters even as it made possible a peaceful government transition, was Antonio Lacayo, Doña Violeta's son-in-law and minister to the president in the new government. According to some observers, the new government had not ushered in a new order but rather, in the words of Arturo Cruz, re-created the Tercerista alliance, the coalition of revolutionary and Conservative elites that made the revolution possible.[71]

The decision to retain Ortega as head of the military assured the loyalty of the large Sandinista army but did not satisfy the large numbers of remaining Sandinista supporters. Further, the decision infuriated US politicians and the Nicaraguan right.[72] Though the cabinet named by the new government contained a cross section of the dispersed coalition of the UNO, the members who belonged to the leadership of COSEP resigned. In the first months of the government, the right wing of the Chamorro coalition, represented by Vice-President Virgilio Godoy and the Contra adviser Alfredo César, turned against Doña Violeta's presidency. The government announced sweeping cuts to public budgets, downsizing the military, privatizing state-owned property, and instituting a program of monetary stabilization known as the Mayorga plan. FSLN supporters took to the streets in protest and paralyzed the city of Managua.

In response to the deterioration of support for the new regime, the government announced it would hold a series of meetings, named the "Concertación," in the fall.[73] Held at Managua's Universidad Nacional Autónoma de

Nicaragua (UNAN), the Concertación brought together representatives of Sandinista-dominated labor unions and agricultural organizations with the more conservative groups centered on COSEP. The first meeting established the terms of social peace, with the government agreeing to acknowledge the power of the FSLN's base of workers and campesinos as legitimate political actors whose gains during the revolution could not be overturned overnight. The FSLN for its part recognized the authority of the government and began to rein in its base's resistance to the imposition of economic restructuring.

The expression *concertación*, though rooted in Hispano-American culture, was nonetheless subject to continuous interrogation by the elites who were attempting to formulate a new order in Nicaragua. *La Prensa* ran numerous editorials in which the authors attempted to define the expression in terms of "harmonization" or consensus. Elites looked to various models on which to base this consensus. Many saw Costa Rica, with its stable democratic government and thriving capitalist economy, as worthy of emulation. But workers' representatives worried that Costa Rica provided a dangerous model for labor relations, given its quiescent working class.[74] Other authors suggested that *concertación* should be modeled on western Europe's social democracy and a vision of nationalist capitalism.[75] Sandinista intellectuals began to promote a social democratic vision of their party's future, implicitly accepting the new regime but splitting the party as a movement for democratization of its ranks gathered force.[76] Though the United States was a major driving force behind pushing the neoliberalization of Nicaragua, intellectuals refused to acknowledge the United States as a model for their own society.

While harmony and consensus were often used as synonyms for *concertación*, numerous authors evoked another of *concertación*'s connotations: sexual congress. *La Prensa* suggested the necessity of creating a *"cama de la concertación,"* suggesting the possibility of a marriage between the right, the FSLN, and the new government.[77] The rector of UNAN and prominent political philosopher Alejandro Serrano Caldera was charged with overseeing the first Concertación accords. Serrano Caldera went to great lengths to distinguish *concertación* from another important phenomenon in Nicaraguan life, *pactismo*. The various Somoza dictators had created a series of "pacts" with the conservative elite that granted Somoza ultimate power while giving the elite a share of the spoils. *Concertación* would instead establish what Serrano Caldera dubbed "unity in diversity," or a consensus that did not grant any party supreme power over the other.

In his writings and speeches on *concertación*, Serrano Caldera revived the notion of *mestizaje*. While the apostle of *mestizaje*, Pablo Antonio Cuadra, was emphasizing the contentious and unstable roots of the nation's racial heritage,

Serrano Caldera returned to a more benign vision of the mixture of Spanish and indigenous culture in Nicaragua, a romanticized indigeneity in which Indian roots lay safely in the past. He conjured an image of tranquil Indians among the forests and volcanoes of Nicaragua, part of its nostalgic scenery rather than a living reminder of the tortured roots of the country's contemporary political and racial order.[78]

The first Concertación was touted as a success by the Chamorro government. Despite facing the explicit opposition of the right gathered around COSEP and the left around the FSLN, the government showed itself able and willing to engage in the types of compromises and negotiations necessary to maintain a social peace, albeit a tenuous one, in the urban center of Managua where the FSLN and Managuan workers proved capable of paralyzing the city if their interests were ignored. In response to massive civil unrest in the first months after the inauguration of Chamorro and the beginnings of the program of monetary stabilization, the government moderated its macroeconomic adjustment and replaced the controversial head of the Central Bank, Francisco Mayorga, who was closely associated with neoliberal financial strictures. Though Antonio Lacayo vehemently denied that he had created a "co-government" with the FSLN, as his opponents claimed, many spoke of a "marriage" between elites that was making possible a semblance of order in the country.[79]

Both the Sandinistas and the Chamorro government advertised their newfound modus vivendi as a broad social consensus, not a power-sharing agreement. Nonetheless, the fruits of their cooperation were exhibited both in close Sandinista cooperation with the presidency in the National Assembly and in Nicaragua's international affairs. Much as the Sandinista government had used the concept of "diversified dependency" to reach out for aid to ideologically different parts of the world, the Chamorro government's newly diversified *concertación* enabled it to attract aid from more countries than the United States. One of the promises of the Chamorro campaign had been that her government would put an end to the US embargo of Nicaragua and bring back not only US economic support but also that of its allies in Western Europe and Japan. The government fulfilled that promise, though at the price of disavowing the World Court decision holding the United States liable for damages in the Contra war. Moreover, in September 1990 Daniel Ortega traveled to Stockholm and participated in a conference of social democratic nations attempting to form an alternative to the Washington-controlled apparatus of the World Bank and International Monetary Fund.[80] The agreement between the FSLN and Chamorro's government opened the possibility of Nicaragua receiving both US aid and aid from countries less interested in drastic macroeconomic change and government downsizing.

Propiedad in the New Nicaragua

As elites gathered at UNAN to make their *"cama de la concertación"* and restore a semblance of order, the countryside remained a confused tangle of unrest and violence. Ten years of civil war had displaced thousands of campesinos, many of whom had fought for the government or joined the Contra forces in the name of conflicting visions of Nicaragua's future. After the end of the war, thousands of Contra supporters returned to the countryside from camps in Honduras and Costa Rica. The demobilization of the Ejército Popular Sandinista (EPS) also meant that its forces, too, would return to the land. Though the government used the promise of land to pacify these demobilized troops, many of them proved ready and willing to take matters into their own hands and reclaim territory for themselves. Groups known as *recontras* and *recompas* used their military skills to seize contested land or demand the government redress their grievances. Eventually groups known as *revueltas* would put aside their past ideological differences, claiming that the new elite government had abandoned those on both sides who had served as cannon fodder in the Contra War and creating their own ideological *mestizaje*.

The dispute over property was not confined to the peasant classes. One of the central aims of the Sandinista revolution was to wrest political and economic power and property from the Somoza family and its allies. With the onset of elite disaffection from the revolution, the government also began to expropriate land and enterprises whose owners had either fled the country or were believed to be deliberately decapitalizing their property to drag down the economy. The Chamorro government aimed to privatize the state holdings gathered by the revolutionary government, to reduce the size of the government and appease the strictures of international forces that demanded privatization in return for assistance with the country's overwhelming international debt.[81]

In the months between Chamorro's election and her inauguration, the Sandinista-controlled government engaged in a rapid process of titling of lands and houses, granting deeds to individuals and cooperatives that had benefited from the land reform.[82] The government also gave titles to the houses in Managua that the Sandinista elite had confiscated from the exiled rich and distributed to the Sandinista leadership. This process became pejoratively known as the "Piñata," cast by the opposition as the distribution of the spoils of the state to a small revolutionary elite who disguised their avarice in the name of social justice.[83] The Sandinista elite who had benefited from the Piñata claimed that their primary purpose was to preserve the gains made by Nicaragua's poor during the revolution. They asserted that they were entitled to maintain their luxurious residences, once owned by members of Somoza's elite, because they had received no salary during their service to the revolution. Their houses were small recompense for their service to their country. Many of their families had even donated property to the state as part of the revolutionary cause.[84]

The revolution had distributed large amounts of land to Nicaragua's landless. The emphasis on the distribution of private property, however, had not been an initial priority in the revolutionary experiment. In the early years after 1979, the government did not redistribute the land expropriated from Somoza but gathered it in state-controlled farms or workers' cooperatives to maintain economies of scale. Agrarian Minister Jaime Wheelock and others, who saw their goal as modernizing Nicaragua's agriculture while also carrying out redistribution to the poor, argued that these state farms were necessary to maintain an efficient export economy and carry out revolutionary programs. With the onset of the Contra war, the government became conscious that one of the chief demands of rural Nicaraguans was access to land. Beginning in 1983, the government began a program of distribution and titling to stanch the tide of campesinos turning against the revolution. Though it was too late to win the affection of many rural Nicaraguans, this program represented an acknowledgment that the revolutionary enthusiasm so palpable among the urban poor was much less solidly rooted in the countryside.[85]

During the decade-long war, the FSLN maintained that the primary motivating factor in the uprising against the revolution was manipulation by the United States and its allies in the oligarchy and the former Somocista elite. In the early 1990s, members of the Sandinista elite began to acknowledge that there remained a gulf between the revolutionary program and its ostensible beneficiaries in rural Nicaragua.[86] Former revolutionary official Alejandro Bendaña traced the roots of the Contra war to a "*tragedia campesina*" in which the aims of the revolution conflicted with the desires of ordinary Nicaraguans for land.[87] Other members of the FSLN elite fit this critique of the agrarian policies of the revolution within a larger critique of their revolutionary aims in general. They blamed the modernizing pretensions of the vanguard, manifest in the directorate of nine Sandinista comandantes, for subverting the democratizing power of the revolution.[88] These FSLN members acknowledged that the mixed economy and plural politics touted as the distinguishing characteristic of Nicaragua's revolution in distinction to that of Cuba had been "tactics that adorned the surface," rather than ends in themselves.[89] These members of the elite nonetheless held that democratization, though not originally a primary goal, was one of the most worthy results of the revolution.[90] This process of self-criticism among the revolutionary elite would prefigure a split within the ranks of the FSLN, as one wing would attempt to carry out a democratization of the party apparatus itself, while more orthodox forces would try to maintain continuity through the power of the party's most prominent leader, Daniel Ortega.

The social democratic wing of the FSLN, in recognizing the party's failures in the countryside, also muted the party's former insistence on the importance of imperialism. Party leaders recognized that they had structured their ideology around perpetual war against the United States.[91] According to Sergio Ramírez, the first sign of the danger this posed to the revolutionary project was in the government's construction of an airstrip north of Lake Managua that would enable the use of MiG fighter jets in the country's defense. The distortion to the economy of such a massive project and the leadership's desire for other symbols of modernization set in motion the inflationary spiral that would eventually wreck the economy. Former revolutionary leaders thus acknowledged that their own vision of "takeoff," mimicking the corrupt modernization of the Somoza era, had poisoned the revolution's project from the beginning.[92]

Sandinista intellectuals like Orlando Nuñez, who played an important role in articulating the revolution's aims for an international audience in the 1980s, argued that the party's self-critique went too far in legitimizing the peasant uprising against the revolution. He acknowledged the validity of aspects of the Sandinista internal critique, recognizing that many campesinos had rejected the revolutionary vision.[93] He claimed that the central dispute was not over land, however, but over the government's attempt to set agricultural prices, effectively using the *campo* to subsidize the city. He also pointed out that, notwithstanding the thousands of campesinos that had flocked to the Contra cause, many thousands also fought as volunteers or conscripts in the EPS against Contra and US aggression.[94] Academics studying Nicaragua during the 1990s likewise began to discover the importance of property in Nicaraguan history. Scholars began to uncover a desire among the country's campesinos to be masters of their own domain rather than beneficiaries of modernizing projects.[95] Jeffrey Gould discovered that many of Nicaragua's campesinos had maintained indigenous roots through control of communal land. Though not private property, this form of ownership was nonetheless antithetical to the modernizing efforts of both capitalist individualism and Sandinista cooperativism.[96]

The second Concertación, in July 1991, manifested a new elite consensus about the importance of private property. The government agreed to acknowledge campesino rights to lands won during the revolution. The government also created a process whereby Managua's poor could receive title to their houses, and the Sandinista elite could compensate former owners of their homes. The government maintained its commitment to privatization of state-owned enterprises but granted workers a share of ownership. Privatization, the government argued, could set off a virtuous cycle of property ownership. The money from the selling of private properties would be used to finance bonds to compensate the properties' former owners. Nuñez and others touted government acknowledgment of workers' right to a share of their enterprises as a victory for the left against the forces of neoliberalism and the strictures of the International Monetary Fund.[97] Others worried that the workers' endorsement of privatization would garner them only the crumbs of the cake being divided by the elite.[98]

The government heralded the victory of consensus over the disintegrating forces in the countryside by publishing transcripts of the second Concertación's proceedings. The transcripts show a contentious debate between the representatives of the major sectors of the economy, with both revolutionary and conservative organizations claiming to represent business and labor. One representative pointed out a major limitation of the corporatist model of *concertación*: the representatives of business, labor, and landowners might come to an accord, but who would speak for the continually growing numbers of unemployed in landless as the government continued to lay off thousands of workers and privatized companies reduced their workforce?[99] Daniel Nuñez broached the topic of armed bands of demobilized soldiers displacing peasants from their land, but the recording was cut in mid-sentence.[100]

Some attendees wondered aloud what the ultimate foundation of the *concertación* was. If it was merely a consensus between elites, then why should nonelites believe it would be respected? Lacayo staked the ability of the Chamorro government to stay in power on *concertación*, but in a democratic polity, the current government was by nature transitory. "Well," the representative of the Congreso Permanente de Trabajadores wondered, "these things are disconcerting, because it's unknown with whom one is agreeing [*concertando*], because if today we agree [*concertar*] with a group from the ministry and they say they can be run out at any moment, then we remain disconcerted, wondering with whom we're agreeing [*concertando*]."[101]

Critics claimed that beneath the ostensible transparency of *concertación* lay an elite contract to divide spoils rather than preserve the gains of the revolution.[102] David Close points out that criticism of the government privatization was muted in the Sandinista press, suggesting that the party was benefiting from the distribution of goods and property.[103] Conservatives like Pablo Antonio Cuadra, whose vision of national identity was premised on a profound relationship between the peasantry and land, recognized the legitimacy of giving those peasants title to property. He worried, however, that the privatization program was less about granting workers and peasants their rights than about divvying up the goods of a disintegrating state. *Property* in land, he argued, was the root of *propriety*, the ability to use freedom in a manner constructive for society.[104] He also warned against *concertación*, which would be to "harmonize [*concertar*] good and evil."[105] The temporary consensus around the importance of property gave the government a respite from social unrest. But the ruling fiction of *concertación* was that elite agreement could forge a stable peace on the solid foundation of territory. Yet Nicaragua's history proved time and again that the stability of elite pacts and the ground itself could be subject to forces beyond the country's territorial boundaries.

Sustainable Development and Modernization's Legacy

As Managua's elite engaged in a homegrown process of *concertación*, another new concept colonized the rhetoric of development. Though its roots could be traced back to eighteenth-century German forestry science, "sustainable development" had come to prominence in the intellectual and policy circles of international development only in 1987.[106] The publication of the Brundtland Commission report, headed by a prominent Scandinavian politician, warned of the disastrous environmental effects of unchecked industrial and agricultural development. The report warned not only of the irreversible consequences of unchecked economic growth but also of its counterproductive nature. The potential short-term gains of pro-growth policies were being offset by environmental degradation that destroyed the fertility of the soil and made the ultimate symbols of modernity, urban cityscapes, unlivable.[107]

These symptoms were manifest in Nicaragua. Agronomists and ecologists pointed out that the rapid deforestation on what had long been considered Nicaragua's frontier was bringing very little cultivable land into production. The use of pesticides for cash crops like cotton was degrading the quality of the soil and drinking water, making the diversification of the country's economy more difficult. The city of Managua, where industrialization had concentrated for half a century, had destroyed its most valuable source of drinking water, Lake Managua or Xolotlán, by dumping industrial chemicals and human waste into the water. The process of decentralization of the city set off by planners in the 1970s was draining the other sources of potable drinking water, making it possible to envision Managua becoming a desert sitting between two of the region's largest freshwater lakes.[108]

There had been isolated movements toward an ecological understanding of Nicaragua's environmental problems in earlier decades. Somoza had passed bills regulating forestry and fishing, some of which were pushed by activists like Bernard Nietschmann, but those served mainly to centralize the Somoza family's economic control of those industries.[109] The revolution attracted the enthusiasm of progressives from around the world and promoted a progressive image with innovative environmental programs to counteract counterrevolutionary propaganda. The creation of a peace park between Costa Rica and Nicaragua, a demilitarized zone of ecological protection called Si-a-paz, was one such innovative project.[110] Solidarity activists also promoted numerous small ecological projects to link peace and development.[111] In recognition of this work, the "Fate of the Earth" congress proposed Nicaragua as the site of its annual meeting in 1989.[112] The conflict on the east coast showed that such environmental rhetoric could also be turned against the government. Indigenous rights activists argued that the sustainable ecological practices of the Miskito Indians were endangered by the modernist development practices of the Sandinista government, legitimizing the Miskito counterrevolutionary struggle.[113]

After the end of the war many Sandinistas, finding themselves outside government, began to recast themselves as environmentalists, following in the footsteps of European socialists who had made the transition from "red" to "green" in the 1970s and 1980s. New NGOs sprang up proposing to protect indigenous, women's, and campesino rights as means to social justice and environmental sustainability. Even Tomás Borge, Sandinista minister of the interior, attempted to recast himself as an environmental activist. The prorevolutionary magazine *Semana Comica*, which often mocked the pretensions of the revolutionary elite, printed comics showing former radicals replacing the violence in the name of socialism with violence in the name of ecological justice.[114] The political magazine *Semanario,* headed by Sergio Ramírez and Edmundo Jarquín, representatives of the social democratic tendency of the FSLN, also began a supplement entitled *Oikos*, funded by a Dutch NGO, which publicized environmental problems in the country.[115] Even the business school INCAE began to argue that sustainable development was good for entrepreneurship.[116]

Concurrently in the United States, the Clinton administration consecrated sustainable development as the new concept around which its developmentalist ideology would be centered. Most of Secretary of State Warren Christopher's major foreign policy speeches featured the term, without ever explicitly defining it.[117] USAID frantically attempted to integrate the expression with the grab bag of developmental tools and concepts the agency used to legitimate its practices. This effort was more necessary as administrators recognized that USAID, which had been created during the Cold War as a tool of the Alliance for Progress, would have to justify its continued existence in a post–Cold War world.[118] The planners at USAID attempted to incorporate this new concept, like other concepts before it, into their lexicon of development before the idea had been extensively defined. Early studies of how to incorporate sustainable development included environmental sustainability but broadened the concept to include health issues, sustainable economic growth, and even democratization.

The 1994 report *Theory and Practice in Sustainability and Sustainable Development* attempted to summarize USAID's findings on the meaning of this new concept for aid practice. Setting in relief the self-referential nature of sustainability discourse, the report defined sustainability as "a *measure* of how the growth, maintenance, or degradation of a resource or set of resources affects a population's ability to sustain itself." Sustainability was also "a *property* of processes, investments, technologies and systems," a "fluid and ever-changing" series of "*tradeoffs and substitutions* among resources and systems as valuation and access change over time."[119] Economic, environmental, and social sustainability were mutually dependent. Democratic governance and free market capitalism were prerequisites both for economic growth and for accountability of government to ensure equitable distribution and to evaluate the environmental consequences of development.

Sustainability also had more direct relevance to the day-to-day functioning of the aid bureaucracy. Central to the new practice of sustainability as applied by USAID was "benefit sustainability." "Within the development community," the report finally recognized, "sustainability refers to the ability of benefit flows to be maintained after project funding ceases." Benefit sustainability meant that projects to bring health services, agricultural assistance, democratic culture, and the myriad other types of assistance USAID was funding in Latin America needed to somehow continue after funding by donors ended. Though Nicaragua was a major recipient of US development assistance in the 1990s, such aid was premised on an eventual end to such outside assistance. This was the old concept of "self-help" repackaged for a post–Cold War world. As foreign aid budgets were rapidly shrinking, Nicaragua needed to put itself on a sound economic and political footing to continue its democratic transition in the 1990s. Many reports set the creation of macroeconomic stability, policies to attract foreign investment, side by side with the creation of environmental stability, the promise of a continually predictable and exploitable natural environment to fuel economic growth. Though the central importance of economic growth was always emphasized, gone was the central metaphor of economic takeoff leading to economic and political independence.

Most projects could be described as conforming to this mandate on the issues of environmental and democratic sustainability. Project managers touted their programs' role in helping raise Nicaragua's poor from grinding poverty and instilling in them a sense of self-worth and self-determination. On the issue of "benefit sustainability," administrators were more pessimistic. Officials warned that an early end to programs could leave beneficiaries with little recourse without the expertise of the aid apparatus to assist them.[120] Whereas once programs had imagined development assistance helping create a democratic industrial proletariat and independent small farmers, planners now recognized the difficulty of carrying out even such basic programs as child survival in Nicaragua's new order. Because a major component of the US project to restructure Nicaragua was the downsizing of the government, administrators could no longer expect a central government bureaucracy to take their place once funding came to an end.

The concept of "sustainable development" captured the frayed strands of the once tightly woven tapestry of modernization theory but failed to provide a convincing alternative vision for the future for poorer countries. Whereas aid programs in the 1960s had been explicit about the need to create sound government planning agencies around a centralized power, in the 1990s planners no longer counted on national or local government to intervene and replace the functions of international aid. In Nicaragua political development programs did attempt to foster municipal government, but this was part of a project to assist a political movement around anti-Sandinista crusaders Arnoldo Alemán and Virgilio Godoy that subverted the central government they believed was colluding with the FSLN.[121] The US government could no longer rely on the ostensibly beneficial functions of central military power either, as the Chamorro government had built its stability on the maintenance of a nationalized but still fundamentally Sandinista military. Instead, US agencies premised aid on the creation of a stable political climate for investment, in which opening Nicaragua's economy to the world would obviate the need for the centralized government power fundamental to the old vision of modernization. Such a stable order, tentatively forged through *concertación*, would still depend on the unpredictable political climate in Washington.

Gioconda Belli, one of the most important writers of Nicaragua's revolutionary generation, expressed in her novel *Waslala* what she saw as postrevolutionary Nicaragua's precarious condition in the age of sustainable development. She describes the inhabitants of her fictional Nicaragua set in an imaginary future as "maintaining themselves in a rounded [*redondo*] time, that turned in circles around itself . . . desiring modernity but not able to acquire it. They didn't have the means [*medios*]."[122] The country's last remaining resource was its environment itself. Rich countries paid money to preserve oxygen-producing forests intact, while also using the country as a dumping ground for toxic waste.[123] Meanwhile, the possibility of utopia had retreated to another dimension, and the sale and consumption of illegal drugs provided the only means for "takeoff."

Politics, Property, and the New Precarity

The central tenet of the new political and economic order promoted by the United States was that economic and political restructuring would make possible new international investment that could provide jobs. These jobs would then provide the needy population with access to the newly privatized government services of health and education. The foundation of such new investment would be a stabilized system of property rights and protections, which the *concertación* process had attempted to institute. The Chamorro government had, however, proved itself more willing to compromise with the forces of the FSLN than many members of the US government thought appropriate. According to Antonio Lacayo, he was warned by undersecretary of state Bernard Aronson that maintaining Humberto Ortega as head of an essentially Sandinista military would jeopardize US assistance. Aronson warned that Senator Jesse Helms (Republican of North Carolina), who held a powerful position on the Senate Foreign Relations Committee, could hold up assistance to Nicaragua if US demands were not met.[124] The Bush administration did in fact hold up assistance to Nicaragua in 1992, in response to Helms's concerns that Sandinistas were still in power in Managua. Though the Chamorro government maintained its commitment to keeping the social peace through cooperation with the FSLN, funds were eventually reinstated.

Concertación instituted a compromise between past and future: it acceded to US demands for a long-term restitution of confiscated property and the privatization of state holdings, while also recognizing the land distributions carried out during the revolution.[125] In response, Helms's staff issued a report called *Nicaragua Today* in August 1992.[126] The report was based on the testimony of members of Nicaragua's exile community who had moved to Miami during the 1980s, many of whom had become naturalized US citizens. These exiles, some of whom were former associates of the Somoza regime, returned to Nicaragua in the 1990s and demanded restitution. The report asserted that the US government was obliged by law to refuse economic assistance to Nicaragua until all property claims were met. More sensationally, the report held that despite the victory of the US-supported candidate, Nicaragua was still under control of the "communist" Sandinistas. It asserted that Violeta Chamorro was a figurehead: Lacayo and Ortega were in total control of the country. Not only were they continuing to arm the still unresolved conflict in El Salvador, but they were also carrying out a program of assassination of demobilized Contra forces.

Helms had allies. Many of the demobilized Contra forces felt they had been abandoned by the US government after the election of 1990. The believed that they should be recognized as a victorious army, not victims of a humanitarian crisis in need of resettlement to "development poles" and given charity by US aid organizations. Contra supporters asserted that Helms was the only American who remained loyal to their army. Helms, in turn, is alleged by Lacayo to have offered to bring about a US invasion of Nicaragua should the demands of property claimants and the Contra supporters not be met.[127]

The incoming Clinton administration immediately showed itself unwilling to heed the senator's warnings. In his confirmation hearings as secretary of state, Warren Christopher evaded Helms's direct allegations against the Chamorro government and spoke highly of the government's efforts to create a distribution of property that would satisfy all claimants.[128] Nonetheless, the 1994 Helms-Gonzalez amendment to the Foreign Assistance Act mandated that the US government deny assistance from US organizations, and veto assistance from international organs like the World Bank and International Monetary Fund, to any government that did not immediately resolve property demands to the satisfaction of the claimants. In response, the Clinton administration issued a "national interest waiver," claiming that US interests would be severely harmed by denying aid to Nicaragua. The State Department instituted a yearly review of Nicaragua's progress on resolving property claims that would affirm that the country was satisfying the demands of claimants.[129] The potential for total revocation of the financial support from the United States and financial organizations created an annual existential threat to the stability of Nicaragua's economy.

The Helms debacle highlights the paradox of power in the "neoliberal republic" that US power was creating in Nicaragua. Commentators have asserted that the United States bungled its attempt to impose a neoliberal entrepreneurial elite in Nicaragua after the 1990 election, undermining the central government's power because of latent anti-Sandinista feeling. "One should not overestimate the intelligence of US officials," William Robinson writes, implying that smarter politicians could have saved the neoliberal program.[130] The United States, however, confronted something unprecedented in its long history of involvement in Nicaragua, a genuinely democratic government that was not opposed in principle to US involvement in its governance but was nonetheless interested in constructing an autonomous politics around Latin American rather than US models.

US aid programs that promoted sustainable development helped create expectations of economic betterment on the part of local populations but were also premised on dismantling both central government power and the aid apparatus itself. In the 1970s, in concert with its allegiance to modernization theory, the United States relied on the ultimate authority of a military strongman to preserve order in the face of the expected political and economic changes in the country. In the 1990s, the regime of structural adjustment could not promise anyone the central power once held by either the Somozas or the Sandinistas. Helms and his allies were compelled to assert that Nicaragua had not undergone a democratic transition at all but was rather still dominated by communism: the Cold War was not in fact over. The compromise that was created, ingenious in its simplicity, was to institute a regime in which the United States held ultimate veto power over whatever government was in power in Managua by the threat to withhold all international aid. The country could maintain the unpredictable processes of democratic negotiation, while the United States maintained its status as final arbiter over Nicaragua's precarious territory.

Epilogue

Repetition, Alliance, and Protest in Contemporary Nicaragua

In his novel *Managua, Salsa City*, Franz Galich describes the peregrinations of a former elite soldier in the Sandinista liberation movement who navigates the seedy underworld of neoliberal Nicaragua after the fall of the revolutionary order in 1990. In Galich's world, former idealists have succumbed to baser instincts and now fight for survival in the dystopian space of a physically unreconstructed and morally debased urban landscape:

> *Miren Managua de día: quedó así desde el terremoto cuando Dios y el Diablo se echaron una tercia y como Dios perdió, se retiró a sus alturas y el Diablo se quedó con el derecho de seguir gobernando en Managua, porque ya hacía años, en el otro terremoto, el Diablo también había ganado, pero más antes ya había ganado, cuando la guerra contra los gringos, en el norte, en las Segovias . . . Pero lo peor de todo es que después del terremoto se creyó que Dios podía ganar y finalmente volvió a perder y así seguirá pasando hasta el final de los siglos, donde Dios tal vez logre vencer al Diablo.*[1]

For Galich, an internationalist who moved to Nicaragua during the revolution to help build utopia, the revolution began as a struggle for control of Nicaragua's political and economic destiny in the face of US power but became a metaphysical contest between God and the Devil. And the Devil seemed to be winning.

Galich's concern with the repetition of Nicaragua's historic struggles became manifest in April 2018, when a burgeoning opposition movement confronted an FSLN that had returned to power and governed Nicaragua for the past decade. Protesters took to the streets chanting the slogan "Ortega, Somoza, son la misma cosa." They sought to recreate an antidictatorial alliance of the right and left against what they dubbed the new Somocismo, echoing the very practice of alliance formation that had brought the FSLN to power decades before. The explosion of opposition to the Ortega regime in 2018 marked a rapid turnaround, as over the prior two decades Ortega and the FSLN had succeeded in building a broad coalition of local and international support that made Nicaragua part of Latin America's "pink tide" of resurgent leftist governments.[2]

The rise of the current Ortega regime and the subsequent unraveling of its support must be situated within the longer history of resistance and negotiation centered on projects for economic and political development shaped by Nicaragua's relations with the United States. With Ortega's 2006 election, Nicaragua joined elected governments from Venezuela to Brazil as part of Latin America's "counter-hegemonic alternative" to the neoliberal world order promoted by the United States since the end of the Nicaraguan revolution.[3] Ortega's return reflects the most recent attempt on the part of Nicaraguans to negotiate their country's precarious position against a changing international landscape. By the 2000s, few believed in the promises of developmental transformation that had structured in succession the Somoza government, the FSLN's revolutionary project, and the neoliberal program of the 1990s. US aid programs and ongoing threats to terminate them continued to exert power without offering promises of economic or political takeoff. Like the governments of many countries affected by the pink tide, the Ortega government responded to the situation by building a political coalition around a new "grand narrative about the path toward modernity" that combined neoliberal policies with promised structural changes in the style of older developmental programs.[4] The Ortega government also resurrected a dream of economic transformation through an infrastructural megaproject—a new transoceanic canal—that has shaped Nicaraguan life for more than a century.

One of the most frequently noted vulnerabilities of the pink tide governments before the wave of protests and election losses that overtook them in the 2010s was these governments' overreliance on resource extraction, leading to pollution, corruption, and inequality that helped spark popular discontent. Nicaragua illustrates another dimension of the new development model these states attempted to create. In the absence of abundant resources such as the hydrocarbon wealth that fueled the economic boom elsewhere, Nicaragua under the FSLN attempted to leverage the country's territory itself, not for extraction but as a means of attraction. The government took part in two major initiatives that undergirded Latin America's resurgent left: the Alternativa Bolivariana para América Latina y el Caribe (ALBA) led by Venezuela, and the courting of China as both an export market and source of investment. While these alliances offered an alternative to US influence and intervention, a multiplication of alliances brought new possibilities for instability by allowing parties such as the FSLN to purchase popular and elite acquiescence to their growing power with an elusive promise of indefinite economic growth.

The signature project of the Ortega government, the Gran Canal Interoceánico de Nicaragua, proposed to use Chinese investment to counter the century-long hegemony of the United States over Latin American territory by constructing what its boosters called "the greatest engineering project in the history of humanity."[5] Ortega mobilized tools of local and international alliance formation shaped over a century of international cooperation and confrontation to bring about a decade of relative stability and prosperity. When the promise of economic development to resolve local political conflicts proved hollow, it brought Nicaragua's bloodiest protests in decades and provoked accusations that Ortega was recapitulating the country's history of authoritarianism and subjection. These developments led many protestors to call for repetition of the path of resistance and revolution, while also reviving local and international calls for US intervention in Nicaraguan affairs.

Nature, Power, and Cycles of Politics

Travelers to Nicaragua since the colonial period have commented on the twin blessing and curse of its natural endowments. The richness of the soil promised unlimited economic growth, while the position of the territory on a volcanic isthmus made it prone to natural disasters. The country's many volcanoes were symbols of its immense natural beauty and fertility, but also held the potential to reshape the political landscape by reshaping the physical. The instability of the nation's successive capitals, beginning with the destruction of the provincial capital of León in 1610 and culminating in the 1972 earthquake, loom large in the country's social imagination. Poverty and prosperity depend on the seasonal cycles of drought and rain that perpetually threaten to paralyze the country's agricultural export economy. Hurricanes and tidal waves have paralyzed the government, as in 1992 when a tsunami helped bring about a constitutional crisis. Natural forces also serve as a synecdoche for US power, as in the legend that a stamp depicting Volcán Momotombo sent to all US senators in 1902 caused the interoceanic canal to be built in Panama instead of in Nicaragua.

Catastrophe has defined the country's topography and its politics, and also informs the work of political commentators attempting to come to terms with the country's turbulent history. The rebellions and political crises that have wracked the country are often equated with natural disorder: "they repeat without end, the wars, the earthquakes, the volcanic eruptions," writes Carlos Vilas.[6] In a work on the country's natural disasters, Jaime Wheelock writes that "8 of 28 worst disasters in Latin America and the Caribbean from 1972 to 1998 were in Nicaragua, two of which were wars."[7] Observers spoke of Nicaragua's upheavals during the age of development as a "social earthquake."[8] They recognized that the international economic system was as unpredictable and uncontrollable as the weather, with consequences as dire.[9] Commentators often likened the frequency of intervention of the United States in Nicaragua's affairs as a dangerous cycle not unlike that of the natural world. Robert Pastor, responsible for US policy under Carter, originally titled his 1987 book on the United States and Nicaragua *Condemned to Repetition*. He retitled it *Not Condemned to Repetition* in the hopeful years after the 1990 election when many thought that the pattern of antagonism between the two countries, and between the United States and Latin America, had been broken.[10]

In much scholarship about the unexpected wave of democratization breaking over Latin America during the 1980s and 1990s, also conceived in cyclical terms, academics asserted that a democratic culture could be instilled by intraelite cooperation and a US government no longer inclined to support authoritarian regimes.[11] Looking inward, Nicaraguans expressed pessimism about the possibilities of what many saw as a legacy of inequality reaching back to the colonial period.[12] Members of the FSLN continued to question their program's ability to reach the country's peasantry, and new studies began to uncover a powerful legacy of indigenism that separated a small elite from the rest of the nation. The country's literature had once been marked by a rich interest in the legacy of indigenous culture and the profound durability of Nicaragua's folk tradition. The literature of the 1990s began to center instead around the anomie of urban life and consumer culture in the wake of political disillusion after the Sandinista revolution.[13]

The 1996 election provided observers some measure of promise that Nicaragua's democracy was beginning to consolidate. The peaceful transfer of power between the outgoing Chamorro administration and the stridently antiSandinista Arnoldo Alemán administration gave some hope that despite widespread allegations of electoral corruption, democracy was becoming ingrained in Nicaragua's culture. Pablo Antonio Cuadra expressed the dilemma that many saw in the return to power of Alemán, whose Liberal Party was in many ways

the heir of Somocismo. Cuadra felt compelled to support the campaign of
Alemán against the candidacy of Antonio Lacayo, son-in-law and chief adviser
to Violeta Chamorro.[14] For Cuadra, the principle that family members should
not succeed one another in office was essential to avoiding repetition of the
Somoza dynasty, causing him to distance himself from Lacayo despite his long
connections with the Chamorro family. Although he spoke favorably of the efforts of Alemán as mayor of Managua to revitalize the city, which included
erasing revolutionary monuments and artwork, he warned of the dangerous
legacy of *caudillismo* in the Liberal Party.[15] Alemán used his position as mayor to
portray himself as the agent of reconstruction undoing the legacy of both the
earthquake of 1972 and the civil wars of the revolutionary period. He received
the blessing of anti-Sandinista icon Cardinal Obando y Bravo, and the construction of a new cathedral south of the old downtown linked the resurgent
power of the Catholic Church with the civic improvement of Managua.[16]

Yet another catastrophe would soon uncover the limitations of Nicaraguan
political and economic stability. Hurricane Mitch struck in 1998, claiming
thirty thousand lives and causing billions in property damage throughout Central America. The worst tragedy, however, was in Nicaragua, where a mudslide
triggered by the rains buried two to three thousand inhabitants of the villages El
Porvenir and Roberto Rodriguez, perched precariously on the sides of Volcán
La Casita. Such living situations were common in Nicaragua, where the lack of
resolution of the land question pushed peasants to farm the sides of mountains
unreachable by modern farm equipment. This movement even spawned a literature in the canon of sustainable development, as planners attempted to help
campesinos make the most efficient use of their land on the *laderas*, the fertile
but highly unstable mountainsides of Central America's many volcanoes.[17]

The resonance between the latest tragedy and the earthquake of 1972 was
manifest as the press accused the Alemán administration of mishandling relief
funds and augmenting the president's personal power and wealth rather than
seeing to the needs of the population, leading to accusations that Alemán was
succumbing to the *caudillismo* of which Cuadra had warned. A swell of anti-
corruption sentiment spurred by the scale of the disaster caused Alemán's own
party to turn against him.[18] The United States gave large amounts of reconstruction assistance but offered little in the way of comprehensive change. Instead, the United States added yet another element of precarity to the country's
already fragile economic situation, a "transparency waiver" to accompany the
"property waiver" that threatened the total elimination of US and international assistance should satisfactory progress not be made in uncovering corruption.[19]

During the George W. Bush administration, Nicaragua once again became site of new experiments in US development policy. Unveiled after September 11 as part of a multipronged security strategy linking development with the War on Terror, the Millennium Challenge Corporation (MCC) offered aid to a small number of poor countries that met minimum standards on a number of development "indicators." This was pitched as a new "nonpolitical" approach to development, growing out of disillusionment with the manifest disaster of neoliberal shock policies in the 1990s not only in Nicaragua but in the post-communist world and Latin America. Rather than the old method of using aid to steer policy from within a country, as was the case for both modernization and neoliberal programs, the new method would "pull" nations toward desirable policies.[20] In the case of Nicaragua, however, aid continued to be aimed at internal political goals: keeping the Sandinistas out of power and continuing the process of returning property to the country's political exiles.

Rebuilding Managua *Terremoteada*

The events that brought Daniel Ortega to power in 2007 arose from the FSLN's nadir in the 1990s and responded to the situation of political precarity encouraged by the United States. Though a large part of the intellectual and cultural elite had left the FSLN by the 2000s, key figures with international training and technocratic expertise remained and continued to shape the party. Individuals connected to Nicaragua's Conservative nationalist tradition—whose practices of confrontation and accommodation with US power reached back before the Cold War—played a key role in negotiating agreements that reshaped the ideological foundations of Nicaraguan politics.

Dionisio Marenco helped arrange a pact between Alemán and Ortega that bridged the opposed leaders' ideological differences. A graduate of the Harvard-linked business school INCAE created during the Alliance for Progress, Marenco had helped create the youth movement that linked Conservative anti-Somoza politics with the FSLN. He took part in the events leading to the 1967 massacre in Managua, organizing cadres of militant students to counter Somocista paramilitaries. During the revolution, he served in the international commerce and planning departments, places where members of the Conservative elite exercised greatest influence.

The pact shielded Alemán and Ortega from prosecution in the face of growing calls for their prosecution for both public and private corruption.[21] The agreement helped put members of both parties in key positions in the electoral council and the auditor general's office, allowing party oversight of these key institutions. The two erstwhile antagonists also worked together to lower the proportion of the vote required for presidential election to 35 percent, making possible Ortega's surprise election victory in 2006 due to the continued support of his electoral base against a fragmented opposition. Marenco defended the practice of using covert negotiation to manage politics—"We aren't in Switzerland or Sweden, where they strictly comply with laws"—suggesting the necessity of extralegal measures in the absence of institutionalized rule of law.[22]

In addition to local pact-making, Marenco served as key intermediary for the international negotiation that would boost the Ortega government's international standing. The US government treated the return of Ortega to power with suspicion, and after controversial municipal elections in 2008 the United States began to threaten the removal of aid under the MCC. European governments also began to withdraw aid under accusations of voter fraud.[23] To replace this withdrawn aid, Marenco helped negotiate an agreement with Venezuela that would replace this foreign aid with oil sold at concessionary prices as part of Hugo Chávez's Alianza Bolivariana for an alternative international order in the hemisphere.[24] This aid helped boost the independence of the FSLN, as much of it was channeled through party-controlled businesses, granting the party the independence to act as benefactor in providing aid to poor communities through the FSLN's Consejos de Poder Ciudadano.[25]

Ortega won the 2006 election with only 38 percent of the vote, but in 2011 he would be reelected with more than 60 percent of the vote, demonstrating the president's ability to use his power to widen his political appeal. An influx of aid from Venezuela brought a new sense of prosperity that seems to have inured many Nicaraguans to the warnings of a resurgence of *caudillismo* and single-family rule coming most loudly from disaffected members of the FSLN, who began splitting from the party in the 1990s and formed their own organization, the Movimiento Renovador Sandinista (MRS).

Another important FSLN intellectual, Orlando Nuñez, worked to justify the alliance between right and left that undergirded Ortega's power. In his book *La Oligarquia*, Nuñez argued that Nicaragua's history was defined by the oligarchic control of the inheritors of Spanish conquest. Reprising an important theme of Sandinista intellectuals, Nuñez argued that Nicaragua had never managed to create a truly independent bourgeoisie but instead created only a "bourgeois nucleus of grand capital" that failed to achieve the relative autonomy of the comprador classes of South America described by dependency theorists. The oligarchy—composed most prominently of members of the Chamorro

clan—put family interests above national development and deliberately abet-
ted the nation's underdevelopment, necessitating a populist alliance of left and
right against a common oligarchic enemy. Nuñez also denounced the cultural
influence of the oligarchy that he and other FSLN intellectuals argued had
made itself a conduit for foreign influence through connections with NGOs.[26]
This argument served to delegitimize the FSLN's primary rival on the left,
the MRS, that party members denounced as working in league with the US
State Department to undermine Nicaragua's national culture.

The most visible element of the FSLN's resurgence was its use of newly
replenished party coffers to recreate a new visual syntax in Managua, linking
the country's history with a promised prosperity that fused elements of socialism and capitalism in a populist pastiche. The party since 2006 engaged in
reviving the iconography of the revolutionary period, much of which was suppressed during the 1990s, while also mixing it with the trappings of consumer
capitalism. The Ortega government engaged in a project of revitalizing the
old downtown of Managua that for many decades had languished as the city's
life moved to the periphery, as planned by US designers in the 1970s. Avenida
Bolívar, the downtown's main thoroughfare, was lined with dozens of giant
yellow metal trees, called "arboles de vida," that light up at night.[27] Though
many Managuans lamented what they saw as a waste of energy (Nicaragua had
one of the highest energy prices in Central America despite large subsidies
from Venezuela), the trees added a semblance of life and vitality to the national tragedy of the ravaged downtown area. The Avenida leads from Lake
Managua to the Loma de Tiscapa, former stronghold of the Somoza family,
which was turned into a park in which a dark silhouette of Augusto Sandino
overlooks the city. At the bottom of "La Loma" was erected an enormous portrait in lights of former Venezuelan president Hugo Chávez, who helped fund
Managua's new boom (figure 7.1).

Another part of the government's revitalization campaign was the development of Lake Managua's Malecón. Though the lake was devastated by industrial pollution from factories on its north shore, Managua's residents who could
afford the five-córdoba entrance fee to Puerto Salvador Allende and relatively
steep menu prices could now enjoy restaurants with cuisine from around the
world in a park dedicated to Chile's deposed socialist president. In the summer of 2014 the government also unveiled a replica version of Managua's old
downtown before the earthquake, with scale versions of the modernist buildings that once crowded the streets. Its aim was to pass the nostalgia of the city's
older generations for the lost symbols of a thriving consumerism to the young,
whom the government promised a new golden age of development. The only

Figure 7.1. Hugo Chávez overlooking Avenida Bolívar. Photo reprinted with permission of CCC Jairo Cajina.

reminder that the price of Managua's former economic glory was paid for with political freedom was the replica of the building that housed Somoza's personal newspaper, *Novedades*, painted in the same bright yellow of the *arboles de la vida* that sprouted around the city (figure 7.2).

Global *Mestizaje*, Local Schisms

A convergence of growing ecological consciousness and critiques of neoliberal governance became part of a widespread reconsideration of development in the 2000s. The concept of "resilience" became a locus of attraction for thinkers questioning both the liberal developmentalism of modernization and its neoliberal successor. Resilience thinking began as ecological critique in the 1970s, describing the adaptation of ecosystems to disasters both man-made and natural. This critique has come to play a key role in thinking about not only ecological stability but also social stability and security in what theorists describe as an ever more complex world.[28] In Nicaragua, debates over the fate of the nation and the role of the economic development centered on the possibility of both ecological and social resilience, which can be rendered in Span-

Figure 7.2. Mini-Managua in Paseo Xolotlán. Photo by the author, Managua, July 31, 2014.

ish as both the loan translation *resiliencia* but also the more familiar Nicaraguan concept of *resistencia*.

Conflict between economic development and environmentally based resistance arose from the Ortega government's boldest attempt to leverage geography into a domestic and international tour de force, the Gran Canal Interoceánico de Nicaragua, announced after Ortega's reelection to the presidency in 2011. The project was negotiated by Enrique Coronel Kautz, another descendant of Nicaragua's Conservative clans. Coronel Kautz was son of José Coronel Urtecho, member of the Granada-based vanguard movement that fused avant-garde poetics and corporatist hierarchy to attempt a regeneration of Nicaraguan cultural life in the 1930s. Influenced by the cultural nationalism of the vanguardists but preferring engineering to poetry, the Coronel Kautz brothers used their international training in agronomy to modernize the country's agriculture in the 1970s, working at the country's foremost exemplar of agro-industry, the Ingenio San Antonio.[29] During the revolution, they helped plan the revolution's efforts to transform Somoza-era land concentration into state-led agrarian modernization.[30] After the outbreak of the Contra War, critics argued that sidelining land redistribution in favor of an emphasis on large-scale agriculture and revolutionary cooperatives inspired by a modernist ethos had alienated the country's peasantry and helped fuel insurrection.[31]

Coronel Kautz worked with the Ortega government to negotiate an agreement with Chinese billionaire Wang Jing to build the most expensive engineering project in human history.[32] Nicaragua had been a site of proposed canal projects since its colonial era, and many members of the country's elite felt that a canal represented the country's "unique comparative advantage" necessary to compete in the global economy.[33] The canal project, like the alliance with Venezuela, served both to diversify Nicaragua's international alliances and to shore up the FSLN's domestic constituency. This ambitious project helped win over support for Ortega from groups such as COSEP that had been staunch enemies of the FSLN since the 1980s. According to Arturo Cruz Jr., the canal project appealed to members of the private sector who desired foreign investment but resented the US government's continued interference in local politics.[34]

The unlikely affinity between Ortega and COSEP led some observers to argue that a new model was developing in Nicaragua that fused old political forms with new economic structures. Despite its anti-American rhetoric, the FSLN embraced the free trade ethos promoted by the United States by passing a new free trade agreement, the Dominican Republic–Central America Free Trade Agreement (CAFTA-DR).[35] The FSLN also mitigated its militant image by changing its colors from strident red and black to cheery pastels while reconstructing strained relations with the Catholic Church. Ortega's wife Rosario Murillo, who had been the personal assistant of Conservative icons Pablo Antonio Cuadra and Pedro Joaquín Chamorro before the revolution, spearheaded both the party's makeover to assuage domestic antagonists and a campaign to market Nicaragua internationally as a safe tourist destination to rival neighboring Costa Rica. These moves led critics to assert that, rather than riding on the "pink tide" of leftist resurgence in Latin America, the FSLN was instead propagating its own "COSEP model" of governance that had little in common with its leftist origins. Though draped in appealing public relations imagery, critics asserted that Nicaragua had revived the corporatism of the past by fusing capitalism with authoritarian governance.[36]

The prospect of the transoceanic canal simultaneously stimulated an economic boom and divided Nicaragua's population. The canal deepened antagonisms between members of the country's elite, whose different factions all relied on the contradictory legacy of Nicaragua's nationalist intellectual tradition rooted in the corporatist values of the Conservative network that profoundly shaped the country's culture. Two of this nationalist tradition's key ideas—the ideal of Nicaragua's mestizo identity, and the idea of the national territory as the nation's most valuable resource—became focal points for divisions as the Ortega government's canal project unfolded.

The mestizo identity that undergirded Nicaraguan nationality, as Jeffrey Gould and others have argued, was premised on the erasure and expropriation of the country's indigenous populations. Critics such as Gould have pointed out that *mestizaje* was often deployed by nationalist elites as a way of imagining a harmonious fusion of European and indigenous populations, concealing the brutal fact of ongoing acts of conquest and violence. Nationalists such as Pablo Antonio Cuadra, who developed the idea of *mestizaje* into a Nicaraguan national ideal, did not, however, always suppress the violence of conquest. Cuadra argued in the 1930s that the incompletion of the Spanish conquest, caused by the liberalization of the Spanish empire, had left the Nicaraguan nation fragmented, particularly on the Caribbean coast where Miskito Indians maintained alternate forms of identity.[37] During the first Sandinista period in the 1980s, enthusiastic revolutionaries steeped in mestizo nationalism pushed for the incorporation of the east coast, causing a backlash among local populations.[38] The new canal project raised these problems anew, as the regime of autonomy granted to the east after the Contra War fit uneasily with the need for massive territorial upheaval the canal would require.

Critics of the canal mobilized a vision of national territory under threat of invasion, asserting that the Ortega government was inviting dangerous foreign influence into the country. The Universidad Centroamericana became an important locus for peaceful protests when the canal project was unveiled in 2014. In an exhibition called *Ciao Guapote* (a reference to a species of fish threatened by the canal) artists evoked fears that the dredging of Lake Nicaragua would destroy the lake's fragile ecosystem. Combining environmental critiques with Cold War iconography, artists juxtaposed pictures of Wang Jing, Mao, and Stalin, and students expressed their rage at the government's antidemocratic practices and the feared collusion of the country's elite.

On the day the canal agreement was signed, representatives of the cultural elite, including many members of the anti-FSLN MRS, gathered to hear a performance of Pablo Antonio Cuadra's *Cantos de Cifar*. Carlos Mejía Godoy y los de Palacagüina, Nicaragua's most iconic musical group, whose work is linked with the legacy of the revolution, performed a musical interpretation of Cuadra's ode to the "Gran Lago," Lake Nicaragua. In a series of tales of the humble Nicaraguans who ply the waters of the lake, Cuadra describes the essence of the country's national identity in a fusion of its campesinos and its landscape. Cuadra's work also associates the lake with the city of Granada, capital of the country's Conservative tradition. The building where these elites gathered embodied their vision of Nicaraguan culture and their place in it: the Centro PAC united the imperatives of commerce and art, selling national literature and boosting national culture through book presentations and cultural performances. The elite's gathering at that moment to listen to the ode to the Gran Lago was significant because only a week later the government of Daniel Ortega was scheduled to break ground on the first construction for the new interoceanic canal. In addition to representatives of the old elite, many disaffected former members of the FSLN, such as former vice president Sergio Ramírez, had rejected the turn toward *caudillismo* of Ortega and had begun instead to gather around the cultural nationalist vision propounded by Cuadra. Many believed that the canal, which would cut across Lake Nicaragua, would fracture the nation. The project would grant Ortega the power to continue in office indefinitely, pass on the presidency to his wife and children, and perhaps even subject the country once again to foreign power.

Antagonism to the canal project multiplied accusations that the Ortega government was recapitulating the history of Somocismo. Critics compared the likelihood of Ortega's subservience to the Chinese government—which was rumored to be behind the ostensibly private canal venture—to Somoza-era thralldom to the United States. While elites mobilized their cultural authority to resist the Ortega government, groups of campesinos were simultaneously forming organizations in rural Nicaragua that began converging on Managua, protesting the government's callous treatment of small farmers in appropriating land for the canal.[39]

The canal's boosters, by contrast, evoked a benign version of *mestizaje*, suggesting that the canal might heal divisions within the nation. Canal promoters had long argued that such a project could resolve the country's economic backwardness and cultural fragmentation. Even Cuadra in his youth had called the project of building a canal in Nicaragua his country's "geographic destiny," imagining this undertaking as a fulfilment of the unfinished Spanish colonial project.

For more than a century, the United States flirted with the possibility of building an alternative to the Panamanian route. In the 1960s, US officials buoyed expectations of a canal in order to boost support for the Alliance for Progress, helping cement Conservative support for Liberal president René Schick. Ideas for a canal continued to be raised during the 1980s and 1990s, as both right and left governments courted potential backers from around the world.[40]

Francisco Mayorga's novel *El filatelista* released as canal plans were being made public, reflects the intersection of canal boosterism with the *mestizaje* mythos.[41] Mayorga is most well known for having instituted the neoliberal monetary policies of the Chamorro years as president of the Banco Central, afterward serving as an official in the Inter-American Development Bank and as an adviser to the Ortega government. Mayorga portrays in fictional form the financial and political calculations that surround the canal's conception. His narrative device skews the tropes of literary *mestizaje*, which often involve the sexual connection between a local native and a foreigner: the central conceit of the novel is the story of two *internacionalistas* who meet in Nicaragua in the 1980s, conceive a daughter, and then are separated. The daughter, like the mestizo archetypes she is based on, plays a key role in nation-building in overseeing the legal and financial negotiations between the Nicaraguan government and the Chinese financial interests backing the canal. The legacy of the revolution is in its breeding a new generation of *internacionalistas*, now serving as handmaidens of high finance.

Mayorga's book, praised by former FSLN opponents such as Arturo Cruz Jr., imagines the canal as a means for Nicaragua to provoke the United States and survive unscathed, thanks to a fantastically reimagined international order. Interspersed with this story of international family romance is a description of the backroom discussions that created the canal. Mayorga not only describes Chinese and Nicaraguan negotiations but also imagines the potential response in the US capital, where there "circulates like a subtle breeze a power capable of unleashing the hurricane force of wars or recessions by the simple means of a vote." In his imagined encounter between US power brokers, the military threat of Chinese expansion in the western hemisphere is weighed against what Mayorga and the Ortega government describe as the needs of the inevitable growth in world trade that the Panama Canal will be unable to support. Mayorga asserts that the needs of global finance will overcome fears of global insecurity, and the financial capital of east and west will ultimately meet and mix harmoniously like the waters of the Atlantic and Pacific Oceans in Nicaragua.

Unlike the members of the cultural elite who met at the Centro PAC to critique the canal, other members of the country's financial elite gave their support to the project. Members of COSEP evoked the changing nature of global capital and the decentering of finance from the United States as reasons for inscribing a new global relationship with Asia on Nicaragua's territory. Critics asserted that instead of international harmony and national autonomy, the canal was more likely to turn Nicaraguan territory into a Chinese colony. One critic likened it to the Spanish conquest, and asserted that a new form of *mestizaje* would result in a "montón de chinitos [a ton of Chinese babies]."[42] One of the most persistent critiques of the canal warned of its disastrous environmental consequences.[43] The government asserted that the new investment that the canal would attract would give it the capacity to better the country's already dire environmental situation.[44] The government claimed that the strictures of neoliberalism stripped the state of its capacity to deal with environmental issues that are themselves a product of the growth of capitalism within the country. Only by allying itself to states not interested in undermining Nicaragua's sovereignty could the country overcome the nefarious influence of the United States, whose long hegemony in Nicaragua had the effects of a natural disaster.[45]

The US government made little comment on the canal project, except to criticize the lack of transparency of the negotiations behind the project. Instead the United States focused its attention on Nicaragua's three northern neighbors, Guatemala, Honduras, and El Salvador, which were wracked by gang violence and insecurity that Nicaragua was largely spared, in part thanks to its revolutionary legacy. Nonetheless, the Ortega government continued to provoke the United States, naming an advocate of Puerto Rican independence as Nicaragua's representative to an Organization of American States meeting, causing the meeting to shut down.[46] Within Nicaragua itself, the government faced a continual chorus of criticism not only from the cultural elite but also from campesinos slated to be displaced from their land. Meanwhile, the changing global environment threatened to undercut any potential economic utility of the canal, as global warming opened up a possible northwest passage through the Arctic, thanks to melting ice.[47] Critics argued that this possibility was irrelevant, as the canal was a hoax from its inception.[48]

April 2018

On April 18, 2018, the Nicaragua canal company HKND closed its offices in Hong Kong and did not make public a new forwarding address.[49] This was only the latest blow to the international connections Sandinista diplomacy had constructed during its latest decade in power. A year earlier, Venezuela had cut its oil subsidies to Nicaragua as the government of Nicolás Maduro faced economic and social calamity. Republican politicians in the United States also revived the threat of sanctions that had hung over the country since the 1990s with the Nicaragua Investment Conditionality Act (NICA), proposing sanctions against members of the regime and a boycott of international financial institution loans to the country in response to FSLN corruption.

The end of the canal company had been a long time in the making, but its ignominious demise was overshadowed by events that it had helped set off. The same day HKND's offices closed, demonstrators gathered in front of Managua's Universidad Centroamericana to protest the Ortega government's announced plan to cut social security benefits. The demonstrations merged with other recent protests spurred by news of a massive wildfire in the Indio Maíz biological reserve and accusations of government failure to combat the environmental damage. Over the previous two years anti-Ortega groups led by civil society organizations, students, and campesinos galvanized by the canal issue had transformed their anticanal message into a broad critique of abuses by the Ortega regime. Protesters gathered to fell the *arboles de vida* in acts of collective protest. The April protests quickly moved beyond Managua, as anti-Ortega groups constructed "tranques" all over the country in an attempt to force Ortega to step down. Clashes between protestors, police, and government-sponsored paramilitary groups spiraled into the worst violence in Nicaragua in decades.

The protests, killings, and jailing of dissidents begun in April 2018 set off a wave of accusations and counteraccusations that centered on the question of foreign influence in Nicaragua. Ortega supporters accused the protests of being managed by groups funded by Washington's National Endowment for Democracy, which had fostered anti-Sandinista politics since its creation in the 1980s. Anti-Ortega groups in turn argued that government repression was paid for by a decade of Venezuelan funding and that ALBA-linked governments had provided paramilitaries that committed numerous extrajudicial atrocities.

After the government successfully dismantled the tranques and protests became more peaceful, the anti-Ortega movement faced a difficult task of self-definition. Anti-Ortega groups that grew out of the 2018 protests successfully formed a mass movement, Azul y Blanco, named after the colors of the national flag. Within this movement, no single political tendency proved dominant, as with other recent decentralized protest movements relying on social media mobilization. COSEP's enthusiasm for the Ortega government waned as the canal project lost momentum, and the April protests led it to join other civil society groups in an Alianza Cívica to push for a negotiated transition. Organizations once critical of the precarity imposed by US intervention now sought sanctions to punish associates of the regime and force a reckoning. Advocates of a grassroots style of protest critiqued the overreliance on foreign intervention and expressed fears that undemocratic pact-makers were once again attempting to manage Nicaragua's democracy.[50]

The continuing influence of the United States in Central America demonstrates how economic and political structures created over the past century continue to shape local conflict. The recurrence of local and international alliance creation and dissolution characterizing Nicaragua's recent history can be best understood as an attempt to bolster the country's precarious position within a shifting geopolitical tableau. The dynamics of alliance formation take place within an international context that gives these pacts their local force and causes local political struggles to resound abroad. The trajectory of Nicaragua's politics from the 1960s to the present has been marked by its leaders' use of such alliances to turn their country's geographic position into an exploitable resource in lieu of natural resources available elsewhere. Decades of intervention by the United States in Nicaragua helped create the country's precarity, as well as modes of resistance that continue to shape national and international life. Sandinismo's transformations correspond to attempts to create alternative international alliances to both manage and mitigate international influence. The rise of the latest Ortega regime and its subsequent unraveling must be understood as only the most recent attempt on the part of Nicaraguan elites to negotiate their country's position at the center of the Central American isthmus—between North and South America, between the Atlantic and Pacific Oceans, and between tectonic plates—in the context of endemic instability and inequality in the international order.

Notes

Introduction

1. "¿Las catástrofes, pues, son nuestra historia . . . ?—Peor que eso. Nosotros mismos somos una catástrofe producto de una suma de catástrofes, porque cuando estas azotan a otros pueblos arrasan campos y ciudades, pero la identidad de las gentes se conserva, y eso no ha ocurrido aquí." Chamorro, *Richter 7*, 64.

2. Williams, *The Tragedy of American Diplomacy*.

3. The idea of the "age of development" comes from María Josefina Saldaña-Portillo, *The Revolutionary Imagination in the Americas and the Age of Development*.

4. Offner, *Sorting Out the Mixed Economy*; Krippner, *Capitalizing on Crisis*; Mirowski, *Never Let a Serious Crisis Go to Waste*; Slobodian, *Globalists*.

5. Benjamin, "Central Park," 34.

6. This new international order is of course in sharp contrast to the New International Economic Order: "Toward a History of the New International Economic Order," special issue, *Humanity* 6, no. 1 (Spring 2015).

7. Coronel Urtecho, *Reflexiones sobre la historia de Nicaragua*, 16.

8. Greenberg, *Manifest Manhood*.

9. Gobat, *Empire by Invitation*.

10. Grandin, *Empire's Workshop*.

11. LeoGrande, *Our Own Backyard*.

12. Grandin, *Empire's Workshop*.

13. T. Graydon Upton, "'Operation Pan America'—the Hidden Catalyst," National Security Files—Regional Security, John F. Kennedy Library, Boston, Massachusetts, Box 215.

14. Taffet, *Foreign Aid as Foreign Policy*.

15. "Latin America Guidelines of United States Policy and Operations," May 1962, National Security Files—Regional Security, Kennedy Library, Box 216.

16. Ramírez, *Balcanes y volcanes y otros ensayos y trabajos*, 95.

17. Moscoso, *The Alliance for Progress*.

18. Immerwahr, *Thinking Small*.

19. Policy Planning Council, "The Principle of Self-Determination," March 12, 1962, Record Group (RG) 59, General Records of the Department of State, Bureau of Inter-American Affairs, Subject and Country Files (IAA-SCF) 1955–1963, Box 5, National Archives and Records Administration, College Park, Maryland (NARA).

20. Luis Somoza Debayle speech, JFKPOF-122-017, Papers of John F. Kennedy, Presidential Papers, President's Office Files, Countries; Nicaragua: General, 1961–1963, Kennedy Library.

21. "Memorandum of Conversation for the Files," February 9, 1967, RG 59, Bureau of Inter-American Affairs/Office of Central American Affairs, Records Relating to Nicaragua, 1963–1975, Box 4, NARA.

22. US Agency for International Development, *U.S. Overseas Loans and Grants: Obligations and Loan Authorizations, July 1, 1945–September 30, 2015*.

23. The revolt against this "bourgeois spirit" is analyzed in Gobat, *Confronting the American Dream*.

24. "Con el Panamericanismo únicamente Hemos Logrado los Americanos ser Tributarios de la Gran Nación del Norte." Cuadra, *Hacia la cruz del sur*, 64.

25. Cuadra, *Breviario Imperial*, 1.

26. Delgado Aburto, *Márgenes recorridos*, 13.

27. Solís, *Pablo Antonio Cuadra: Itinerario*, 40.

28. Vasconcelos, *La raza cósmica*.

29. Gould, *To Die in This Way*.

30. Saldaña-Portillo, *The Revolutionary Imagination in the Americas and the Age of Development*.

31. Toynbee, *A Study of History*, Volume 8.

32. Walter, *El régimen de Anastasio Somoza, 1936–1956*.

33. Conservatives often associated *zelotes*, based on the Zealots of ancient Judea, with the militant left, even though the Conservatives themselves used similar tactics. Pablo Antonio Cuadra, "Vuelve Navidad," *La Prensa*, December 20, 1970; Humberto Belli, "Cristianismo y Sandinismo," in Cruz and Velázquez, *Nicaragua, regresión en la revolución*, 198.

34. Stephen Henighan emphasizes the "three-way union" between "ostracized Conservative oligarchs," radicalized "professionals from Liberal families," and guerrillas from "poor or lower-middle-class families." Henighan, *Sandino's Nation*.

1. The Alliance for Progress on the Doubtful Strait

1. Cardenal, *El estrecho dudoso*, 5, 56.

2. José Coronel Urtecho, "Prologo," in Cardenal, *El estrecho dudoso*; Rostow, *The Stages of Economic Growth*.

3. Castro, *Second Declaration of Havana*.

4. Levinson and Onís, *The Alliance that Lost its Way*; Alba, *Alliance without Allies*.

5. On US policy as counterrevolution, see Grandin and Joseph, eds., *A Century of Revolution*; Gambone, *Capturing the Revolution*.

6. Ameringer, *The Democratic Left in Exile*.

7. Field, *From Development to Dictatorship*; Latham, *Modernization as Ideology*; Taffet, *Foreign Aid as Foreign Policy*.

8. *John F. Kennedy: Containing the Public Messages, Speeches, and Statements of the President*, 172.

9. Ameringer, *The Caribbean Legion*.

10. Pedro Joaquín Chamorro, *La Prensa* (*LP*), March 14, 1961.

11. Dosman, *The Life and Times of Raúl Prebisch.*

12. "Task Force report to President-Elect Kennedy on immediate Latin American problems and recommendations for immediate action," December 13, 1960, Berle Papers, Subject Files 1946–71, Box 94, Franklin Delano Roosevelt Presidential Library.

13. Schwarz, *Liberal: Adolf A. Berle and the Vision of an American Era*; Ameringer, *Don Pepe: A Political Biography of José Figueres of Costa Rica.*

14. Greg Grandin, "Your Americanism and Mine: Americanism and Anti-Americanism in the Americas," *American Historical Review* 111, no. 4 (1 October 2006): 1042–1066.

15. A. A. Berle to George C. McGhee, June 13, 1961, RG 59, Task Force on Latin America, Subject and Country Files, 1961, Box 2, National Archives and Records Administration (NARA), College Park, Md.

16. Berle cited his own role in formulating major inter-American resolutions at Montevideo (1933), Buenos Aires (1936), and Chapultepec (1945) as authority. A. A. Berle, Memorandum for the Secretary, March 22, 1961, RG 59, Task Force on Latin America, Subject and Country Files, 1961, Box 2, NARA.

17. Maldonado, *Luis Muñoz Marín.*

18. Schoultz, *In Their Own Best Interest.*

19. Declaration of San Jose, March 28, 1961, RG 59, Task Force on Latin America, Subject and Country Files, 1961, Box 2, NARA.

20. José Figueres, May 2, 1961, RG 59, Task Force on Latin America, Subject and Country Files, 1961, Box 1.

21. Arthur Schlesinger Jr. Memorandum, April 10, 1961, RG 59, Task Force on Latin America, Subject and Country Files, 1961, Box 3, NARA.

22. Schlesinger, *Thousand Days,* 768–769, quoted in Schmitz, *Thank God They're on Our Side.*

23. Schoultz, *That Infernal Little Cuban Republic,* 155.

24. Abraham Lowenthal, "Foreign Aid as a Political Instrument: The Case of the Dominican Republic," *Public Policy* 14 (1965): 141–160; Patrick J. Iber, "'Who Will Impose Democracy?': Sacha Volman and the Contradictions of CIA Support for the Anticommunist Left in Latin America," *Diplomatic History* 37, no. 5 (2013): 995–1028.

25. See US Department of State, *Foreign Relations of the United States (FRUS), Foreign Relations, 1964–1968: Volume XXXI–South and Central America; Mexico.*

26. Pedro Joaquín Chamorro, "César viene de Oriente," *LP,* May 28, 1961.

27. Pfeiffer, *Official History of the Bay of Pigs Operation,* vol. II.

28. Walter, *El régimen de Anastasio Somoza.*

29. Szulc, *Twilight of the Tyrants.*

30. Charles W. Anderson, "The Political Future of Nicaragua," August 1959, Robert Alexander Papers, Box 69, Rutgers University Archives, New Brunswick, NJ; Pedro Joaquín Chamorro, "Una Carta a los Compañeros de La SIP," *LP,* October 12, 1961.

31. Kay, *Latin American Theories of Development and Underdevelopment.*

32. Hansen, *Central America: Regional Integration and Economic Development.*

33. Grunwald, Wionczek, and Conroy, eds., *Latin American Integration and U.S. Policy.*

34. Eisenhower, *The Wine is Bitter.*

35. "US Losing Role in Central American Integration Movement," August 18, 1960, RG 59, Central Decimal File, 1960–63, Box 2339, NARA; *Task Force Report on Economic Integration in Central America* (Washington: USAID, February 1962).

36. "AID's 'New Look' in Central America," February 2, 1962, ARA/OAP, Subject and Country Files, 1955–1963, Box 5, NARA.

37. Millikan and Rostow, *A Proposal: Key to an Effective Foreign Policy.*

38. Berle and Jacobs, eds., *Navigating the Rapids*, 756.

39. A. A. Berle to Richard Goodwin, June 13, 1961, RG 59, Task Force on Latin America, Subject and Country Files, 1961, Box 1, NARA.

40. "The Amounts and Kinds of Development Assistance for Latin America: A Four-Year and a Ten-Year Look," Papers of President Kennedy, National Security Files, Regional Security, Box 216, John F. Kennedy Library (JFK).

41. Draft Memorandum from the Consultant to the Task Force on Latin America (Gordon) to the President's Assistant Special Counsel (Goodwin), March 6, 1961, *FRUS, 1961–1963: Volume XII—American Republics.*

42. "Weeka #34," August 28, 1965, RG 59, Central Foreign Policy Files 1964–1966, Box 2511, NARA.

43. Cruz, *INCAE: los años formativos.*

44. Dan H. Fenn Jr. Personal Papers, Box 52, JFK.

45. Antonio Monte C., "Patrimonialismo y clientelismo del régimen somocista en la implementación del Mercado Común Centroamericano en Nicaragua (1960–1972)," *Revista de Historia* 29 (2013), 37–58.

46. "Anti-Castro Activities and Organizations," JFK Assassination Collection Reference System, CIA Segregated Collection, Box 36, NARA.

47. Ralph C. Estrada, "The Alliance for Progress in Nicaragua," November 18, 1963, WHCF-FO Box 31, Lyndon Baines Johnson Library (LBJ).

48. "Inmensa tarea en el Rio Coco," *LP*, March 11, 1961.

49. Carlos Cuadra Pasos, "Intervención," *Revista Conservadora*, May 1962.

50. Pedro J. Chamorro, "Mister Poncio Pilato," *LP*, March 22, 1967.

51. Lowenthal, "Foreign Aid as a Political Instrument."

52. "Material for Presidential Briefing on Alliance for Progress," February 15, 1962, ARA/OAP, Subject and Country Files, 1955–1963, Box 5, NARA.

53. "Nicaragua Strategy Statement," February 23, 1963, RG 59, ARA/Asst. Secretary & US Coordinator Alliance for Progress, Subject and Country Files, 1962–1975, Box 2, NARA.

54. Henighan, *Sandino's Nation*; Millet, *Guardians of the Dynasty*, 37.

55. Esgueva Gómez, *Elecciones, reelecciones y conflictos en Nicaragua, 1821–1963.*

56. Gómez, *Autoridad/cuerpo/nación.*

57. Mendieta Alfaro, *Olama y Mollejones.*

58. This group included Carlos Fonseca, founder of the FSLN. Baltodano M., *Memorias de la lucha sandinista.*

59. Lily Soto, *Nicaragua: el desarrollo histórico de los partidos políticos en la década del 60*, 90.

60. Chamorro Cardenal, *Estirpe sangrienta*; Guido, *Noches de tortura.*

61. "Nicaragua: Personalities—Pedro Joaquín Chamorro, 1957–1977," Box 45, Papers of Frances R. Grant, Rutgers University Special Collections.

62. Walker, *The Christian Democratic Movement in Nicaragua*, 29.

63. Fleet, *The Rise and Fall of Chilean Christian Democracy.*

64. Luis A. Somoza D., "El partido Liberal Nacionalista y sus afinidades y discrepancias con los otros partidos," *Revista Conservadora*, July 1966.

65. "'La Calle Atravesada', símbolo de los gobiernos plutócratas," *LP*, November 20, 1961.

66. Diego Manuel Chamorro, "Balance del Partido Conservador y complejo de culpa de algunos jóvenes conservadores," *Revista Conservadora*, August 1962.

67. Pedro Joaquín Chamorro, "Las comunidades que se están redimiendo por si solas," *LP*, November 2, 1963.

68. "Primer reparto agrario beneficia campesinos," *LP*, November 7, 1961.

69. Pablo Antonio Cuadra, "'La Prensa' cumple su programa social," *LP*, July 28, 1961.

70. Managua to Secretary of State, April 5, 1962, Papers of President Kennedy, National Security Files, Countries, Box 143A, JFK.

71. Otilio Ulate, "Respuesta al presidente Somoza," *Revista Conservadora*, January 1961.

72. Rabe, *Eisenhower and Latin America*, 106.

73. Felipe González, "The Experience of the Inter-American Human Rights System," *Victoria University of Wellington Law Review* 40, no. 1 (June 2009): 103–125.

74. Emilio Álvarez Montalván, "No intervención vs. democracia representativa," *Revista Conservadora*, January 1962.

75. Cuadra Pasos, "Intervención."

76. Leonte Herdocia, "Exposición documental," *Revista Conservadora*, October 1962.

77. "Estoy seguro que sabréis cumplirla, en la misma medida enérgica, noble y valiente con que supisteis actuar en la otrora esclavizada Republica Dominicana."

78. "Discussion of election prospects and current situation with leader of Nicaraguan opposition party," June 29, 1962, RG 59, ARA/OAP, Records Relating to Nicaragua 1958–1962, Box 2, NARA.

79. Col. Guillermo Rivas Cuadra to Major General A. Somoza D., June 16, 1962, RG 59, ARA/OAP, Records Relating to Nicaragua 1958–1962, Box 2, NARA.

80. Managua to Secretary of State, August 28, 1962, National Security Files, Countries, Box 143a, JFK.

81. Martin for Ambassador, September 5, 1962, Papers of President Kennedy, National Security Files, Countries, Box 143A, JFK.

82. Adolf A. Berle to Fernando Aguero, July 9, 1962, RG 59, Bureau of Inter-American Affairs, Subject Files: 1961–1963, Box 22, NARA.

83. Bracken to Brown, May 3, 1962, May 31, 1962, RG 59, Bureau of Inter-American Affairs, Subject and Country Files, 1955–1963, Box 5, NARA.

84. Memorandum: Current Political Situation in Nicaragua, Bracken to Martin, May 31, 1962, RG 59, Bureau of Inter-American Affairs, Subject and Country Files, 1955–1963, Box 5, NARA.

85. Letter from Adolf Berle to Luis Manuel Debayle, July 9, 1962, RG 59, Bureau of Inter-American Affairs, Subject Files: 1961–1963, Box 22, NARA.

86. "Guidelines for Policy and Operations," October 1962, RG 59, Policy Planning Staff, Country Files, 1957–1962, Box 40, NARA.

87. "Summary Review of Current Threat to Government of Nicaragua from Exile Bands and Domestic Political Situation," September 19, 1962, RG 59, ARA/OAP, Subject and Country Files, 1955–1963, Box 1, NARA.

88. Santa-Cruz, *International Election Monitoring, Sovereignty, and the Western Hemisphere.*

89. Walker, *The Christian Democratic Movement*, 30.

90. "La alianza para el retroceso," *LP*, October 10, 1963.

91. Aaron Brown to Lansing Collins, December 11, 1963, RG 59, ARA/OAP, Subject and Country Files 1955–1963, Box 6, NARA.

92. Task Force on Latin America Meeting, February 16, 1961, RG 59, Task Force on Latin America, Subject and Country Files, 1961, Box 1, NARA.

93. Kathleen Horkan-Lopez, "USAID Support for Development Finance Institutions in Central America" (Washington, DC: USAID, September 29, 1998).

94. "Un programa para enfrentarse a problemas del área tan cuidadosamente planeado como en ningún parte del mundo," *Revista Conservadora*, May 1964.

95. "Material for Presidential Briefing on Alliance for Progress," February 15, 1962, ARA/OAP, Subject and Country Files, 1955–1963, Box 5, NARA; "CASP Revisions relating to AID," June 23, 1967, RG 59, Central Foreign Policy File 1967–1969, Box 2369, NARA.

96. Immerwahr, *Thinking Small*.

97. Handwritten note, RG 306, Office of the Assistant Director for Latin America, Country Files for Nicaragua 1953–1971 (OADLA-CFN), Box 2, NARA.

98. *El Ex-Becario Nicaragüense* 43 (January 1965), Biblioteca Álvaro Argüello Hurtado S.J., Instituto de Historia de Nicaragua y Centroamerica.

99. "Comité pro-Alianza," *LP*, April 6, 1963.

100. *El Ex-Becario Nicaragüense*, 43.

101. Baltodano, *Memorias de la Lucha Sandinista*, vol. 2.

102. "Weeka #28," July 13, 1963, RG 59, Central Foreign Policy Files, 1963, Box 3995, NARA; Reinaldo Antonio Téfel, "Contestaciones de la encuesta," *Revista Conservadora*, February 1963.

103. Aaron S. Brown to Charles R. Burrows, December 23, 1966, RG 59, ARA/OAP, Records Relating to Regional Matters, 1962–1974, Box 2, NARA.

104. Andrew B. Wardlaw, *The Operations of the Central American Common Market* (Washington, USAID, 1966).

105. Nicaraguan Strategy Statement, February 3, 1965, RG 59, ARA/Asst. Secretary & US Coordinator Alliance for Progress, Subject and Country Files, 1962–1975, Box 10, NARA.

106. Walker, *The Christian Democratic Movement*, 19.

107. "Mr. Zavala's Visit," July 7, 1965, RG 59, ARA/Office of the Director for Central America, Records Relating to Regional Matters, 1962–1974, Box 1, NARA.

108. Pedro Joaquín Chamorro, "El 'patroncito' y el empresario," *LP*, June 9, 1963.

109. "Página socioeconómica," *LP*, March 6, 1963.

110. "Nicaragua: Plan of Action," February 11, 1965, RG 59, Bureau of Inter-American Affairs, Asst. Secretary and US Coordinator Alliance for Progress, Subject and Country Files, Box 10, NARA.

111. "El canal por Nicaragua," *Revista Conservadora*, March 1964.

112. "Weeka #23," June 12, 1965, RG 59, Central Foreign Policy Files, 1964–1966, Box 2511, NARA.

113. Aaron S. Brown, "Voter Registration in Nicaragua Indicates Probable Fraud," January 7, 1967, RG 59, Central Foreign Policy File 1967–1969 Box 2366, NARA.

114. "Regional Economic Integration," Administrative Histories, Box 2, LBJ.

115. Hapgood, ed., *The Role of Popular Participation in Development*.

116. Sandoval, ed., *From the Monastery to the World*.

117. Cardenal, *Las ínsulas extrañas: memorias II*.

118. Gould, *To Lead as Equals*.

119. Pablo Antonio Cuadra, "La parábola del séptimo hijo," *LP*, January 15, 1967.

120. "Se funda una cooperativa en el archipiélago de Solentiname," *LP*, May 21, 1967.

121. Cardenal, *Las ínsulas extrañas*.

122. "Botes para archipiélago de Solentiname," *El Ex-Becario* 80 (February 1968), 56.

123. Michael Dunne, "Kennedy's Alliance for Progress: Countering Revolution in Latin America," *International Affairs* 92:2 (March 2016), 435–452.

124. "Excelentísimo Señor presidente de la republica de Nicaragua y Comandante General de las Fuerzas Armadas, General de División Don Anastasio Somoza Debayle," December 9, 1967, RG 59, Bureau of Inter-American Affairs, Asst. Secretary and US Coordinator Alliance for Progress, Subject and Country Files, Box 4, NARA.

125. Aaron S. Brown, Memorandum, October 21, 1966, RG 59, ARA/OAP, Records Relating to Nicaragua 1963–1975, Box 4, NARA.

126. Aaron S. Brown to Charles R. Burrows, December 23, 1966, RG 59, ARA/OAP, Records Relating to Regional Matters, 1962–1974, Box 2, NARA.

127. Brown to Burrows, document 90, *FRUS, Volume XXXI—South and Central America; Mexico, 1964–1968*.

128. Asociación de Militares Retirados y Oficiales de Combate (AMROCS).

129. "22 January 1967 Movement by Conservative Opposition Party," February 1, 1967, RG 306, Office of the Assistant Director for Latin America, Country Files for Nicaragua 1953–1971 (OADLA-CFN), Box 2, NARA.

130. "Opposition Party Criticism of AMROCS and Overtures to Guardia National," November 17, 1966, OADLA-CFN, Box 2, NARA.

131. "22 January 1967 Movement by Conservative Opposition Party."

132. "Further Talk with Bishop Chavez on Nicaraguan Crisis," January 1967, OADLA-CFN, Box 2, NARA.

133. "Memorandum of Conversation for the Files," February 9, 1967, RG 59, Bureau of Inter-American Affairs/Office of Central American Affairs, Records Relating to Nicaragua, 1963–1975, Box 4, NARA.

134. Cardenal, *Las ínsulas extrañas*.

2. Decentering Managua

1. Sergio Ramírez, "De las propiedades del sueño (I)," in *De tropeles y tropelías* (1972).

2. Sergio Ramírez, "De las propiedades del sueño (II)," in *De tropeles y tropelías* (1983).

3. Vilas, *The Sandinista Revolution*, 101; Diederich, *Somoza and the Legacy of US Involvement in Central America*.

4. David Wall, "City Profile: Managua," *Cities* 13 (1996). On contemporary Managua's class character, see Dennis Rodgers, "A Symptom Called Managua," *New Left Review* 49 (January–February 2008).

5. Cullather, *The Hungry World*, 242.

6. Wendell Pritchett, "Which Urban Crisis: Regionalism, Race, and Urban Policy, 1960–1974," *Journal of Urban History* 34 (2008), 266–286.

7. Vivian Bickford-Smith, "Introduction: The Case for Studying Cities and Nationalisms," *Journal of Urban History* 38 (2012), 855.

8. Wardlaw, "The Operations of the Central American Common Market."

9. Nicaraguan Strategy Statement, February 3, 1965, RG 59, ARA/Asst. Secretary & US Coordinator Alliance for Progress, Subject and Country Files, 1962–1975, Box 10, NARA.

10. Durham, *Scarcity and Survival in Central America*.

11. Rama, *La ciudad letrada*; Lerner, *The Passing of Traditional Society*, 60.

12. Perlman, *The Myth of Marginality*.

13. Rockefeller, *The Rockefeller Report on the Americas*.

14. Bautista Lara, *La urbanización de Managua*.

15. Walter, *The Regime of Anastasio Somoza, 1936–1956*.

16. Wall, "City Profile: Managua," 47.

17. Ortega R., *Reconstrucción histórica y gráfica de Managua anterior al terremoto de 1972*.

18. "1967 Nicaragua Country Analysis and Strategy Paper," RG 59, Bureau of Inter-American Affairs/Office of Central American Affairs, Records Relating to Nicaragua, 1963–1975, Box 4, NARA.

19. "Organizan cuerpo femenino de policía," *LP*, March 30, 1974.

20. "Address by Richard M. Nixon to the Bohemian Club," document 2, *FRUS, 1969–1976: Volume I—Foundations of Foreign Policy, 1969–1972*.

21. Hinton, *From the War on Poverty to the War on Crime*, 37; Suri, *Henry Kissinger and the American Century*, 167–170.

22. Conversation among President Nixon, the President's Assistant for National Security Affairs (Kissinger), the President's Assistant (Haldeman), and Secretary of the Treasury Connally, Washington, June 11, 1971, *FRUS, 1969–1976: Volume E-10—American Republics.*

23. Memorandum from the President's Assistant for National Security Affairs (Kissinger) to President Nixon, Washington, May 7, 1969, *FRUS, 1969–1976: Volume E-10—American Republics.*

24. Diederich, *Somoza and the Legacy of US Involvement in Central America.*

25. Henry Kissinger, Memorandum for the President, Subject: "Letter from Turner Shelton," April 10, 1970, National Security Council Files; Name Files, Box 834, Richard M. Nixon Library (RMN).

26. Bob Houdek, Memorandum for General Haig, July 29, 1970, National Security Council Files; Name Files; Governor Scranton to Sonnenfeldt, Helmut, Box 834, RMN; Lake, *Somoza Falling.*

27. Téfel, *El infierno de los pobres.*

28. Pablo Antonio Cuadra, "Pájaros del dulce encanto," *LP*, April 26, 1970.

29. Pedro Joaquín Chamorro, "La vivienda de mi Hermano," in *La Patria de Pedro* (Managua: La Prensa, 1981).

30. Cardenal, *Sacerdote en la revolución: memorias, tomo I*, 235.

31. The estimates of the dead ranged from 2,000 to 20,000, with most settling at the middle number of 10,000. R. Kates, J. E. Haas, D. J. Amaral, R. A. Olson, R. Ramos, and R. Olson, "Human Impact of the Managua Earthquake," *Science* 182 (December 7, 1973): 984.

32. US Agency for International Development, *Case report: Nicaragua-earthquake, December 1972.*

33. "Super-bid due in Nicaragua," *Wrecking and Salvage Journal* 7 (July 1973), 9. Erick Aguirre, *Un sol sobre Managua* (Managua: HISPAMER, 1998), 63.

34. Paul J. Dosal, "Natural Disaster, Political Earthquake: The 1972 Destruction of Managua and the Somoza Dynasty," in Buchenau and Johnson, eds., *Aftershocks.*

35. Memorandum from George W. Phillips, January 5. 1973, RG 59, Inter-American Affairs, Records Relating to Nicaragua, 1963–1975 (DSIAA-RRN), Container 6, NARA.

36. Conversation among Nixon, Kissinger, and Haldeman, document 43, *FRUS, 1969–1976: Volume E-10—American Republics.*

37. White House Telephone, Conversation #035-013; 12-27-1972, White House Tapes, RMN.

38. Executive Office Building, Conversation #380-001a; 12-28-1972, White House Tapes, RMN.

39. Haas, Kates, and Bowden, eds., *Reconstruction following Disaster*, 69.

40. Haas et al., *Reconstruction following Disaster*, 108–109.

41. Inter-agency Group staff notes on FY 1975–1976 Nicaragua CASP, RG 59, Inter-American Affairs, entry a1 5734: Records Relating to Nicaragua, 1963–1975, Container 7, NARA.

42. Chamorro, *Diario politico.*

43. Chamorro, *Richter 7.*

44. Pedro Joaquín Chamorro, "Carta sobre Managua," *LP*, January 19, 1974.

45. Haas et al., *Reconstruction following Disaster*, 988–989.

46. July 73 P-Reel, Subject: 1974–1975 CASP, RG 59, Central Foreign Policy Files, Created 7/1/1973–12/31/1976, Documenting the period 7/1/1973–12/31/1976, NARA.

47. Maddick, *Democracy, Decentralisation and Development.*

48. Rondinelli, *Secondary Cities in Developing Countries.*

49. US Agency for International Development, *Nicaragua—Rural Development Sector Loan* (Washington, DC: USAID, 1975); "Conversation with President Somoza concerning rural development," September 30, 1975, RG 59, Central Foreign Policy Files, 7/1/1973–12/31/1976 (CFPF), NARA.

50. US Agency for International Development, *Community Development—Nicaragua* (Washington, DC: USAID, 1974).

51. Immerwahr, *Thinking Small*.

52. *Executive Seminar on Social and Civic Development: Title IX of the United States Foreign Assistance Act, Antigua, Guatemala, June 1–6, 1969* (Washington, DC: Brookings Institution 1969); Testimony of James R. Fowler, July 23, 1969, Foreign Assistance Act of 1969, Hearings Before the House of Representatives Committee on Foreign Affairs, 1201.

53. *Foreign Assistance Act of 1973* (Washington, DC: GPO, 1973), 77–88. US Agency for International Development, *Implementation of "New Directions" in Development Assistance: Report to the Committee on International Relations on Implementation of Legislative Reforms in the Foreign Assistance Act of 1973* (Washington, DC: GPO, 1975).

54. "Courtesy call on General Somoza by General Wm. Rosson, CINCSO, 3-17-1973," CFPF, NARA.

55. Managua 4069, Subj: CNI Negotiations, from Amembassy Managua to Secstate, October 73, RG 59, Inter-American Affairs, Entry A1 5734: Records Relating to Nicaragua, 1963–1975, Container 6, NARA.

56. Letter from Leland Warner to Stuart Lippe, March 15, 1973, RG 59, Inter-American Affairs, entry a1 5734: Records Relating to Nicaragua, 1963–1975, Container 7, NARA.

57. Memorandum from President Nixon, Washington, March 5, 1970, *FRUS 1969–1976, Volume IV—Vietnam*.

58. "Memorandum for the Development Assistance Executive Subcommittee, Subject: Intensive review request, loan title: earthquake recovery–reconstruction/deconcentration," NCF, Box 10, pp 8, 13, NARA.

59. Karen L. Remmer and Gilbert W. Merkx, "Bureaucratic-Authoritarianism Revisited," *Latin American Research Review* 17 (1982): 3–40.

60. Rostow, *Politics and the Stages of Growth*, 245.

61. Mann, *Evaluation of Managua Reconstruction Planning*.

62. Mann, *Evaluation of Managua Reconstruction Planning*.

63. Peattie, *Planning: Rethinking Ciudad Guayana*; Téfel, *El infierno de los pobres*.

64. Mann and von Moltke, *Report on a Process of Planning and Urban Design for the Reconstruction and Development of Managua*.

65. Everingham, *Revolution and the Multiclass Coalition in Nicaragua*, 113.

66. Amembassy Managua to Department of State, "Comments on the Succession," August 3, 1968, Central Foreign Policy File 1967–1969, Box 2369, NARA.

67. Sánchez S. and Terán G., *Sobre la descentralización*.

68. US Agency for International Development, *Nicaragua urban sector loan-Managua*, 10–12.

69. 1973STATE062298, "Managua reconstruction: IBRD Panel," April 1973, CFPF, NARA.

70. J. Osborn, "Geographic/demographic problems of post-earthquake development in Nicaragua," 14 CFPF, NARA.

71. "International Advisory Panel on Reconstruction and Redevelopment of the Managua Region," March 1973, cited in Alcira Kreimer, "Post-Disaster Reconstruction Planning: The Cases of Nicaragua and Guatemala," *Mass Emergencies* 3 (1978): 23–40.

72. Viceministerio de Planificación Urbana de Nicaragua, *Informe Nacional de Nicaragua*.

73. US Agency for International Development, *Proposal and Recommendations for the Review of the Development Loan Committee, Nicaragua-Program Loan, 1-31-73* (Washington, DC: USAID, 1973).

74. "La reconstrucción oficial de Managua," *LP*, August 11, 1974.

75. "Supplementary CASP Guidance—Nicaragua," DSIAA-RRN, NARA.

76. "Memorandum for the Development Assistance Executive Committee, from: USAID/Nicaragua, Subject: Intensive Review Request, Loan Title: Earthquake Recovery—Reconstruction/Deconcentration," pp. 8, 13, RG 286, Box 10: URB Urban Development Program FY1974 (Nicaragua), Country Files, compiled 1973–1975, NARA.

77. On the application of this philosophy in the United States, see Cohen, *A Consumer's Republic*.

78. "Un recorrido por la nueva," *LP*, September 5, 1974.

79. "Las Américas: tercera ciudad de Nicaragua," *LP*, August 1, 1974.

80. Harrison Wehener, "Housing," NCF, Box 10, NARA.

81. Charles Dean, Letter to *Washington Post*, May 23, 1973, NCF, Box 10, NARA.

82. "US Relief Housing on Way to Becoming Managua Slum," *Washington Post*, May 18, 1973, A17.

83. "Community Development in Las Américas," October 17, 1973. NCF, Box 10, NARA.

84. James Theberge, "Nicaragua—Economic Performance in 1975 and Prospects for 1976," March 31, 1976, RG 59, Microfilm, P76049-1377, NARA.

85. "Informe oficial sobre desastre en Las Américas," *LP*, March 7, 1974.

86. "'Las Américas' reconstrucción con cantinas," *LP*, February 21, 1974.

87. "Rebelión en Las Américas," *LP*, October 8, 1974.

88. Spalding, *Capitalists and Revolution in Nicaragua*; Everingham, *Revolution and the Multiclass Coalition*.

89. US Agency for International Development, *AID Loan No. 524-L-028—Program Loan* (Washington, DC: USAID, 1977), 2.

90. Memorandum of Conversation, 8-20-73, RG 286, Box 10: URB Urban Development Program FY1974 (Nicaragua), Country Files, compiled 1973–1975, NARA.

91. Memorandum of conversation, August 20, 1973, NCF, Box 10, NARA.

92. Laínez, *Terremoto '72*, 7.

93. Diederich, *Somoza and the Legacy of US Involvement*.

94. "Nacionalicemos la reconstrucción," *LP*, March 10, 1974.

95. Pedro Joaquín Chamorro, "Un comentario al 'grito de Matagalpa'," *LP*, March 13, 1974.

96. "Somoza-viviendas, que significa?," *LP*, March 30, 1974.

97. Letter from Leland Warner to Stuart Lippe, 3-15-73, RG 59, Bureau of Inter-American Affairs, Office of the Deputy Assistant Secretary, Subject and Country Files, compiled 1968–1975, Box 7, NARA.

98. 1967 Nicaragua Country Analysis and Strategy Paper, RG 59, Bureau of Inter-American Affairs/Office of Central American Affairs, Records Relating to Nicaragua, 1963–1975, Box 4, NARA.

99. Memorandum of Conversation, 9-4-73, RG 286, Country Files, compiled 1973–1975, URB Urban Development Program FY1974 (Nicaragua), Box 10, NARA.

100. "Desarrollo urbano de Managua," *Revista Conservador* 16 (March 1967): 2–10.

101. Managua to Department of State, "Economic and Commercial Highlights, May 1974," RG 286, Country Files, compiled 1973–1975, URB Urban Development Program FY1974 (Nicaragua), Box 10, NARA.

102. Chamorro, *Diario político*, 102.

103. Chamorro, *Richter* 7.

104. Walker, *The War in Nicaragua*.

105. Cuadra, *El nicaragüense*, 90.

106. Pablo Antonio Cuadra, "Nuestro capital y la burbuja del nicaragüense," *El nicaragüense* (Managua: Editorial Hispamer, 2007), 197.

107. Cuadra, *El nicaragüense*, 198.

108. Managua to State, "Elections 1974: The Governing Liberals," 11-9-73, P740005-1798, Microfilm, RG 59, NARA.

109. Laínez, *Terremoto '72*, 7.

110. Laínez, *Terremoto '72*, 153.

111. Laínez, *Terremoto '72*, 150.

112. Francisco Laínez, *LP*, December 28, 1974.

113. Rosario Murillo, "Colonos 74 sub-viven en 'Las Américas,'" *LP*, August 28, 1974.

114. David E. Mutchler, "Adaptations of the Roman Catholic Church to Latin American Development: The Meaning of Internal Church Conflict," in Smith, ed., *The Roman Catholic Church in Modern Latin America*, 207.

115. "'El Paraíso' de Fundeci: un modelo piloto de urbanización comunitaria," *LP*, August 18, 1974.

116. "De mil viviendas constará ciudadela El Paraíso-León," *LP*, March 4, 1974.

117. "Un formidable proyecto social," *LP*, February 22, 1974.

118. Baltodano M., *Memorias de la lucha sandinista*.

119. Most accounts locate the beginning of this alliance later, after insurrection had begun. Everingham, *Revolution and the Multiclass Coalition in Nicaragua*, 110–137.

120. Cardenal, *Sacerdote en la revolución*, 235.

121. "Managing international disasters—Guatemala: hearings and markup before the Subcommittee on International Resources, Food, and Energy of the Committee on International Relations," House of Representatives, 94th Cong., 2nd sess., on H.R. 12046, February 18 and March 4, 1976, p. 18.

3. Dis-integrating Rural Development

1. Pablo Antonio Cuadra, "Un campesino ha venido a escribir este editorial," *LP*, October 29, 1977.

2. LaFeber, *Inevitable Revolutions: The United States in Central America*; Pastor, *Not Condemned to Repetition*; Castañeda, *Utopia Unarmed*.

3. Gobat, *Confronting the American Dream*, 259.

4. Robert Culbertson, "Letter from Matagalpa," February 20, 1975, RG 59, Bureau of Inter-American Affairs/Office of Central American Affairs, Records Relating to Nicaragua, 1963–1975, Box 4, NARA, pp 3–5.

5. Culbertson, "Letter from Matagalpa," 11.

6. Taffet, *Foreign Aid as Foreign Policy*, 176.

7. Latham, *Modernization as Ideology*, 151–207.

8. Cullather, *The Hungry World*.

9. Weisman, *Daniel Patrick Moynihan: A Portrait in Letters*, 134; see also Samuel P. Huntington, "The Bases of Accommodation," *Foreign Affairs* (July 1968).

10. US Agency for International Development, Development Assistance Program, *Central America, Book 5, Chapter X—Nicaragua* (Washington, DC: USAID, 1973).

11. US Agency for International Development, *Central America, Book 5, Chapter X—Nicaragua*.

12. Pedro Joaquín Chamorro, "Desconcentrar y descentralizar," *LP*, March 2, 1974. "Discurso Pronunciado por Don Marco A Zeledón," March 1, 1974, RG 59, Microfilm, P-Reel P740033-0978, NARA.

13. US Agency for International Development, *Nicaragua–Rural Education Development Program* (Washington, DC: USAID, 1977), 6.

14. In 1977, 1.8% of farms accounted for 48% of land. Testimony of Dr. W. Richard Smith, US Congress, House Committee on International Relations, Subcommittee on International Development, *Rethinking US Policy toward the Developing World: Nicaragua,* 95th Cong., 1st sess., October 18, 1977, 15.

15. "Inter-American Bank lends $8.3 million for land settlement project," September 27, 1973, RG 286, Country Files, compiled 1973–1975, URB Urban Development Program FY1974 (Nicaragua), Box 10, NARA.

16. Gould, *To Lead as Equals.*

17. Baltodano M., *Memorias de la lucha Sandinista*; Memo from Ambassador Harry Shlaudeman to Secretary of State, "Humberto Ortega Historian," August 1990, Declassified Documents Database; Blandón, *Carlos Fonseca, sacrificado.*

18. USAID itself acknowledged that wherever roads had been used to open new lands, peasants have been driven from their land. "Project: Rio Blanco-Siuna Road, US $32 Million," October 19, 1977, RG 286, USAID Mission to Nicaragua/Development Planning Division, P799: Subject Files 1971–1981, NARA, p. 3.

19. US Agency for International Development, *Implementation of "New Directions" in Development Assistance.*

20. Testimony of Fernando Cruz, former USAID official, in Subcommittee on International Development, *Rethinking United States Foreign Policy toward the Developing World: Nicaragua.*

21. Victor Ruttan attributes this process to the influence of the Nixon Doctrine, which downplays the antagonism of the US Congress. Ruttan, *United States Development Assistance Policy.* On the influence of NGOs: Macekura, *Of Limits and Growth.*

22. Latham, *Modernization as Ideology,* 206; Clapp, *Significant Cases in Integrated Rural Development Experience,* 14.

23. Ralph C. Estrada, "The Alliance for Progress in Nicaragua," November 18, 1963, WHCF-FO Box 31, LBJ.

24. Testimony of Dr. W. Richard Smith, *Rethinking US Policy toward the Developing World,* 14.

25. Letter from James L. Gorman to Ambassador Theberge, September 25, 1975, RG 286, Nicaragua Subject Files 76–78, Box 1, NARA.

26. Turner Shelton, "Nicaraguan Rural Development Sector Loan I," June 1975, RG 286, Country Files, compiled 1973–1975, AGR, Agricultural Development Program FY1976 (Nicaragua), Box 10, NARA, p. 16.

27. Memo from John Barton, "The Institutional Image of USAID/Nicaragua: Some Thoughts and Suggestions," October 3, 1975, RG 286, USAID Mission to Nicaragua/Development Planning Division, P799: Subject Files 1971–1981, NARA, p. 2.

28. Clapp, *Significant Cases in Integrated Rural Development Experience,* 40. US Congress, Senate, Committee on Foreign Relations, Subcommittee on Western Hemisphere Affairs, *Latin America,* 95th Cong., October 4, 1978.

29. Clapp, *Significant Cases,* 22.

30. US Congress, House Committee on International Relations, Subcommittee on International Organizations, *Foreign Assistance Legislation for Fiscal Year 1979 (Part 4),* 95th Cong., March 7, 1978, 88.

31. The separation of the economic and military function of the Guardia was new; its creators had initially imagined that Guardia members might provide the basis for a middle class. Gobat, *Confronting the American Dream,* 205.

32. Report of conversation with Edmundo Jarquín, May 12, 1977, RG 286, USAID Mission to Nicaragua/Development Planning Division, P799: Subject Files 1971–1981, NARA. Chamorro, *Diario Político,* 118.

33. Robert E. Culbertson, "INVIERNO, Politics and Security," October 1, 1975, RG 286, Nicaragua Subject Files 76–78, Box 1, NARA.

34. James Theberge, "Conversation with President Somoza Concerning Rural Development (INVIERNO) Loan and Internal Security," September 30, 1975, RG 286, Nicaragua Subject Files 76–78, Box 1, NARA.

35. James Gorman, "INVIERNO," September 25, 1975, RG 286, Nicaragua Subject Files 76–78, Box 1, NARA.

36. On the separation of military function from civilian function in granting of aid and the difficulty of making the distinction: US Congress, House Committee on International Relations, Subcommittee on International Organizations, *Human Rights in Nicaragua, Guatemala, and El Salvador: Implications for US Policy*, June 8 and 9, 1976, 202–203. For the testimony of a Department of Defense spokesman, see p. 741.

37. CIA, National Foreign Assessment Center, "Nicaragua: An Appraisal of the Guardia Nacional," May 1978, NLC-24-39-5-31-4, Remote Archives Capture Project (RAC), Jimmy Carter Presidential Library, Atlanta, GA.

38. Gobat, *Confronting the American Dream*, 217–218.

39. Carlos M. Vilas, "Family Affairs: Class, Lineage and Politics in Contemporary Nicaragua," *Journal of Latin American Studies* 24, no. 2 (May 1992), 309–341; Stone, *The Heritage of the Conquistadors*.

40. Everingham, *Revolution and the Multiclass Coalition in Nicaragua*.

41. Gobat, *Confronting the American Dream*, chapter 7.

42. This phenomenon is well documented in numerous revolutionary memoirs, such as those of Gioconda Belli, Sergio Ramírez, and Fernando Cardenal.

43. Cuadra, *Breviario Imperial*.

44. Vegas-Latapie, *Memorias políticas*, 253.

45. Cuadra, *Otro rapto de Europa*, 110.

46. Cuadra, *Otro rapto de Europa*, 17.

47. Pablo Antonio Cuadra, "El 12 de octubre y nuestra identidad," *LP*, October 15, 1977.

48. Author's interview with Víctor Alemán Ocampo, Managua, 2014; Stephen White, "An Interview with Pablo Antonio Cuadra," *Northwest Review* 23 (1985), 74–91.

49. Sergio Ramírez blames Pedro Joaquín Chamorro's political failure on his personal antagonism toward members of his class; Ramírez, *Adiós muchachos*.

50. Coronel Urtecho, *Conversación con Carlos*.

51. Coronel Urtecho, *Tres conferencias a la empresa privada*, 12.

52. Coronel Urtecho, *Tres conferencias a la empresa privada*, 128.

53. Coronel Urtecho, *Tres conferencias a la empresa privada*, 23.

54. Coronel Urtecho, *Tres conferencias a la empresa privada*, 75.

55. Coronel Urtecho, *Tres conferencias a la empresa privada*, 44.

56. "La conquista de España de 'Perjúmenes,'" *LP*, September 18, 1977.

57. "Más sobre Mejía Godoy," *LP*, December 4, 1977.

58. Ferrero Blanco, *La Nicaragua de los Somoza*, 205.

59. "Cardenal enfermo en Paris," *LP*, December 18, 1977.

60. Ramírez, *Balcanes y volcanes y otros ensayos y trabajos*, 169.

61. These workshops would later inspire much debate over the relation between the party, the peasants, and artistry. Wellinga, *Entre la poesía y la pared*.

62. Fernando Cardenal, *Sacerdote en la revolución*, 123.

63. Cabezas, *Fire from the Mountain*.

64. Ferrero Blanco, *La Nicaragua de los Somoza*, 347–348.

65. For an example of *LP* outlining similarities of the FSLN, the Catholic Church, and UDEL: "Quién son el FSLN," *LP,* October 19, 1977.

66. Jaime Chamorro C. "El mito de comunismo" *LP,* April 28, 1978.

67. Randall, *Sandino's Daughters,* 80–93.

68. Miguel Angel Borgen, "Una anécdota que calza en el caso de Amada . . . ," *LP,* June 23, 1974; "Democracia y pluralismo: gran apoyo a Amada, PJCh y a impugnación," *LP,* October 21, 1974.

69. Gobat, *Confronting the American Dream,* 243.

70. "Más repudio a tráfico de plasma," *LP,* October 6, 1977.

71. Pablo Antonio Cuadra, "El valor de la sangre," *LP,* November 26, 1977.

72. Pablo Antonio Cuadra, "Un faro en la noche," *LP,* August 24, 1974.

73. US Congress, House Committee on International Relations, Subcommittee on International Organizations, *Human Rights in Nicaragua, Guatemala, and El Salvador: Implications for US Policy,* 94th Cong., 2nd sess., June 8 and 9, 1976, appendix 7.

74. For the assertion that Obando advocated armed rebellion: Pezzullo, *At the Fall of Somoza,* 105.

75. Diederich, *Somoza and the Legacy of US Involvement in Central America,* 128–129.

76. US Congress, Subcommittee of the Committee on Appropriations, *Foreign Assistance and Related Agencies Appropriations for 1978, Part 3, Special Hearings of Public Witnesses,* 95th Cong., 1st sess., 1977.

77. House Committee on International Relations, *Human rights in Nicaragua, Guatemala, and El Salvador.*

78. Chamorro, *Diario Político,* 184–192.

79. Chamorro, *Diario Político,* 108.

80. "Y dicho todo esto, espero con la consciencia tranquila y el alma llena de paz, el golpe ya usted me tiene destinado." Pedro Joaquín Chamorro, "Reacción epistolar frente a la amenaza," *LP,* October 4, 1977.

81. The metaphor of a "crusade" came from the policy's critics, most notably Muravchik, *The Uncertain Crusade.* For a more recent understanding, see Keys, *Reclaiming American Virtue.*

82. "Human Rights," Memo from Anthony Lake to Cyrus Vance, February 4, 1977, RG 59, P9, Policy Planning Staff, Office of the Director, Records of Anthony Lake, 1977–1981, Box 2, NARA.

83. Moyn, *The Last Utopia,* 151–158.

84. Pastor, *Not Condemned,* 63.

85. Commission on United States–Latin American Relations, *The Americas in a Changing World: A Report of the Commission on United States–Latin American Relations* (New York: Quadrangle, 1975).

86. Secretary of State Cyrus Vance, January 31, 1977, document 18, *FRUS, 1977–1980: Volume I—Foundations of Foreign Policy.*

87. NSC Meeting, October 19, 1979, NLC-24-61-8-7-3, RAC, Carter Library.

88. An argument for the "symbolic value" of cutting aid to Somoza is found in Memo from Mark Schneider to Steve Oxman, September 23, 1977, RG 59, Office of the Deputy Secretary, Records of Warren Christopher, 1977–1980, Box 38, NARA.

89. On the conservative turn in human rights policy: Hauke Hartmann, "US Human Rights Policy under Carter and Reagan, 1977–1981," *Human Rights Quarterly* 23 (May 2001), 402–430; Pastor, *Not Condemned,* 55–59.

90. Petras and Morley, *US Hegemony under Siege,* 128–131.

91. Owen J. Lustig, USAID/RDD, "Thoughts on our mission paper," January 18, 1978, RG 286, Nicaragua Subject Files 76–78, Box 1, NARA.

92. Mauricio Solaún, "Proposed Education Loan to Nicaragua," April 23, 1978, RG 286, Nicaragua Subject Files 76–78, Box 1, NARA.

93. Subcommittee on International Organizations, *Foreign Assistance Legislation for Fiscal Year 1979 (Part 4),* 96.

94. Letter from W. Michael Blumenthal to Senator James Abourezk July 28, 1978, RG 59, Records of Warren Christopher, 1977–1980, Human Rights-Nicaragua II, NARA, Box 40.

95. On moving the United States toward a "post-aid" relationship: Memo from Robert Pastor to Zbigniew Brzezinski, March 4, 1977, Zbigniew Brzezinski Collection (ZB), Subject File, Box 24, Carter Library.

96. "Minutes of Policy Review Committee on Nicaragua," November 13, 1978, NLC-15-35-5-5-7, RAC, Carter Library.

97. Memo from Robert Pastor to Zbigniew Brzezinski, August 29, 1978, NLC-17-34-4-1-1, RAC, Carter Library.

98. On the possibility of channeling aid through religious organization to delegitimize governments: US Congress, House Committee on International Relations, Subcommittee on International Development, *Rethinking United States Foreign Policy toward the Developing World*, 95th Cong., 1st sess., October 18, 1977, 26.

99. Ruttan, *United States Development Assistance Policy*, 228–230.

100. Booth, *The End and the Beginning: The Nicaraguan Revolution*, 102.

101. Memo on "Nicaragua Operational Program Grants," RG 59, Office of the Deputy Secretary, Records of Warren Christopher, 1977–1980, Box 38, NARA.

102. James Theberge, "New Initiatives in Human Rights," January 5, 1976, RG 286, Nicaragua Subject Files 76–78, Box 1, NARA.

103. On using private voluntary organizations to bypass the central government: Letter from Julius Schlotthauer to David Jickling, January 25, 1978, RG 286, USAID Mission to Nicaragua/Development Planning Division, P 799: Subject Files 1971–1981, NARA.

104. "Los derechos humanos en Nicaragua: encuesta," *Revista Conservadora del Pensamiento Centroamericano* 155 (April-June 1977): 10–33.

105. Approximately twelve of the twenty-three respondents spoke out in favor of private NGOs in channeling aid, though some argued that a larger structural change needed to accompany such an initiative.

106. It is striking that only one of the twenty-three respondents mentioned the Catholic Church as a proper channel for aid to the poor. In marked contrast, in the 1920s, the Caballeros Católicos were central to elite activism. Gobat, *Confronting the American Dream*, 184.

107. "Los derechos humanos en Nicaragua: encuesta," 28.

108. "Los derechos humanos en Nicaragua: encuesta," 15.

109. Michel Gobat traces this concern to the Guardia's displacement of the oligarchy's authority in the countryside.

110. Pablo Antonio Cuadra, "Las venas de nuestra nacionalidad siguen sangrando", *LP*, November 5, 1977.

111. Chamorro Cardenal, *Los Somoza: una estirpe sangrienta*, 188.

112. Wilfredo Montalván, "Nuestra lucha, la G.N., y los Estados Unidos," *LP,* February 2, 1978.

113. Francisco Fiallos Navarro, "La Guardia Nacional; ¿un ejército de ocupación?," *LP*, September 6, 1978.

114. Testimony of Father Miguel d'Escoto, Subcommittee on International Organizations, *Foreign Assistance Legislation for Fiscal Year 1979 (Part 4),* 106.

115. Cardenal, *Sacerdote*, 216.

116. Ramírez, *Adiós Muchachos*, 155–156.

117. Memo from Robert Pastor, "Nicaragua: Your Questions about Political Futures," September 7, 1978, ZB, Subject File, Box 36, Carter Library; "Minutes of Policy Review Committee on Nicaragua," November 13, 1978, NLC-15-35-5-5-7, RAC, Carter Library.

118. Ramírez, *Adios Muchachos*, 117.

119. Ambassador Maurice Solaún, "Nicaraguan Disaster and AID Programs," September 22, 1978, RG 286, USAID Mission to Nicaragua/Agriculture & Rural Dev. Division, Subject File: 1971–1984, Box 4, NARA.

120. Vilas, *The Sandinista Revolution*; Farhi, *States and Urban-based Revolutions*.

121. NSC meeting on "US Policy to Nicaragua," September 4, 1978, ZB, Subject File, Box 36, Carter Library.

122. Pastor, *Not Condemned*, 133.

123. From Secretary of State to Ambassador Bowdler, July 1979, NLC-16-117-2-32-8, RAC, Carter Library.

124. Barrios de Chamorro, *Dreams of the Heart*.

4. Pluralism, Development, and the Nicaraguan Revolution

1. Chamorro Cardenal, *El enigma de las alemanas*.

2. Joseph and Grandin, *A Century of Revolution*.

3. Prashad, *The Poorer Nations*.

4. Grandin, *Empire's Workshop*; Robinson, *Promoting Polyarchy*; Guilhot, *The Democracy Makers*; Pee, *Democracy Promotion, National Security and Strategy*.

5. Lefeber, *Inevitable Revolutions*.

6. On the international dimensions of Latin American corporatism, see Wiarda, *Corporatism and National Development in Latin America*; O'Donnell, Schmitter, and Whitehead, eds., *Transitions from Authoritarian Rule*.

7. On the internal relations within the junta and the FSLN's dominant role: Christian, *Nicaragua, Revolution in the Family*.

8. José Coronel Urtecho to Sergio Ramírez, August 7, 1979, Sergio Ramírez Papers (SR), Box 36, Princeton University, Princeton, NJ.

9. "Programa del Gobierno de Reconstrucción Nacional," Vertical File, Instituto de Historia de Nicaragua y Centroamerica (IHNCA), Managua.

10. Alejandro Bendaña, "The Foreign Policy of the Revolution," in Walker, ed., *Nicaragua in Revolution*.

11. On the relationship between pluralism and solidarity among nonaligned nations, see Rao, *Third World Protest*.

12. US Agency for International Development, *A Decade of Development*, 24.

13. Harmer, *Allende's Chile and the Inter-American Cold War*; "Allende and Lanusse Agree On 'Ideological Pluralism,'" *New York Times*, July 25, 1971.

14. William Jesse Biddle and John D. Stephens, "Dependent Development and Foreign Policy: The Case of Jamaica," *International Studies Quarterly* 33, no. 4 (December 1989): 411–434.

15. Jarquín Calderón, *Pedro Joaquín: ¡juega!*, 253, 278; "El pluralismo político: única respuesta a la crisis," *LP*, August 2, 1978.

16. Letters of José Coronel Urtecho, SR, Box 36.

17. Ramírez, *Adiós Muchachos*.

18. Ramírez, *¿Te dió miedo la sangre?*

19. Carlos Fonseca to Sergio Ramírez, "Comité de Solidaridad con el pueblo de Nicaragua," November 15, 1975, SR, Box 37.

20. Willy Brandt to Sergio Ramírez, October 11, 1978, SR, Box 58.

21. Rother and Larres, eds., *Willy Brandt and International Relations*.

22. Eusebio Mujal-Leon, "European Socialism and the Crisis in Central America," in Wiarda, ed., *Rift and Revolution.*

23. Eusebio Mujal-Leon, "The West German Social Democratic Party and the Politics of Internationalism in Central America," *Journal of Interamerican Studies and World Affairs* 29, no. 4 (Winter 1987–1988): 89–123.

24. Assmann, ed., *El juego de los reformismos,* 148.

25. Ana Mónica Fonseca, "From the Iberian Peninsula to Latin America: The Socialist International's Initiatives in the First Years of Brandt's Presidency," in Rother and Larres, eds., *Willy Brandt and International Relations.*

26. Schori, *Escila y Caribdis.*

27. Bernd Rother, "Cooperation between the European and Latin American Moderate Left in the 1970s and 1980s," in Rother and Larres, eds., *Willy Brandt and International Relations.*

28. See chapter 1.

29. One of these organizations, the Centro de Estudios Democráticos de América Latina, was the successor of the Institute for Political Education founded by Figueres and funded by the CIA in the early 1960s: Francisco Morales H., "45 años de CEDAL," *Cambio Político,* November 26, 2013.

30. Roelofs, *Foundations and Public Policy.*

31. Amembassy San José to Secstate Washdc, "Friedrich Ebert Foundation (FES) Representative on Central American Matters," September 4, 1979, Access to Archival Databases (AAD), NARA.

32. Pastor, *Not Condemned to Repetition.*

33. Address by Bernt Carlsson, Managua, July 19, 1980, SI, Box 1145.

34. Seminario Internacional de Solidaridad con Nicaragua, "Documento Final: Consideraciones, Conclusiones y Recomendaciones," SI, Box 1144.

35. "Proyecto para la conformación del Frente Amplio Antidictatorial en Nicaragua," February 1978, SR, Box 58.

36. Castañeda, *Nicaragua: contradicciones en la revolución.*

37. Vanden and Prevost, *Democracy and Socialism in Sandinista Nicaragua,* 103.

38. John R. Nellis, "Algerian Socialism and Its Critics", *Canadian Journal of Political Science* 13 (September 1980): 481–507.

39. Frank, *Reflections on the World Economic Crisis.*

40. Arturo J. Cruz Jr., "Nicaragua: Somocismo and the Sandinista Revolution," Oliver North Files, Box 2, Reagan Library, Simi Valley, California.

41. Norman Uphoff, "Political Considerations in Human Development," in *Implementing Programs of Human Development.*

42. They organized around the Frente Amplio Opositor: "FAO Documento No. 1: Proyecto de J. Zavala—Icaza Tijerino," n.d., SR, Box 52.

43. Vargas, ed., *La Crisis de la Democracia en Costa Rica.*

44. "Perspectivas de la democracia en América Latina: el caso de Nicaragua," May 1979, SI, Box 1144.

45. "Mexican Policy towards Nicaragua," August 21, 1979, FCO 160/65, British National Archives, London, England. On Mexico's support for the revolution: Ramírez, *Adiós Muchachos.* On tensions between the United States and Mexico: *Las razones y las obras: gobierno de Miguel de la Madrid: crónica del sexenio 1982–1988.*

46. "Soviet Ambassador to Cuba Vorotnikov, Memorandum of Conversation with Raul Castro," September 1, 1979, History and Public Policy Program Digital Archive, TsKhSD, f. 5, op. 77, d. 833, ll. 63–67; trans. Elizabeth Wishnick, at http://digitalarchive.wilsoncenter.org/document/111249.

47. "International aspects of today's Nicaraguan panorama," August 16, 1979, Socialist International Papers (SI), Box 1144, International Institute of Social History, Amsterdam.

48. Pastor, *Not Condemned to Repetition*.

49. Velázquez, *Nicaragua: Sociedad Vivil y Dictadura*, 80.

50. Viron P. Vaky, "Everything Is Part of Everything Else," in "America and the World 1980," *Foreign Affairs* 59, no. 3 (1980), 617–647.

51. On this covert funding, see Kagan, *A Twilight Struggle*.

52. Amembassy Bonn to Secstate Washdc, "Christian Democracy and the Democratic Opening in Central America," September 7, 1979, AAD.

53. Chamorro Cardenal, *La Prensa, Republic of Paper*, 15.

54. This funding was channeled through the University of Central America: Papers of the Nicaragua Information Center, Box 5, Bancroft Library, University of California, Berkeley.

55. Claribel Alegría to Sergio Ramírez, September 21, 1978, SR, Box 36.

56. Miguel d'Escoto "Introduction," in Millett, *Guardians of the Dynasty*.

57. Saldaña-Portillo, *The Revolutionary Imagination in the Americas and the Age of Development*.

58. Henighan, *Sandino's Nation*; Cardenal, *La Revolución Perdida: Memorias Tomo III*.

59. Luciano Baracco, "The Nicaraguan Literacy Crusade Revisited: The Teaching of Literacy as a Nation-Building Project," *Bulletin of Latin American Research* 23, no. 3 (July 2004): 339–354.

60. Kirkendall, *Paulo Freire and the Cold War Politics of Literacy*; Guerra, *Visions of Power in Cuba*.

61. Cabezas, *La montaña es algo más que una inmensa estepa verde*; Vilas, "Family Affairs," 13.

62. Cardenal, *In Cuba*.

63. Cardenal, *Islas extrañas*, 118.

64. Cardenal, *Sacerdote en la Revolución*.

65. Arce Solórzano; Ruiz Muñoz; Membreño Rivera, *Nicaragua, un destino turístico*.

66. "Nicaragua: A country to be discovered," Nicaragua Collection (NC), Box 1, University of Miami, Miami, Florida.

67. Peace, *A Call to Conscience*.

68. On the paradoxical use of revolutionary solidarity for private ends: Paige, *Coffee and Power*, 301.

69. Conroy, *Nicaragua: Profiles of the Revolutionary Public Sector*.

70. Conversation between Tomás Borge and General-Major Fiedler, Berlin, November 5, 1980, John Koehler Files, Box 20, Hoover Institution.

71. SV to BC, Speech Notes re: Meeting of the Socialist International Committee for the Defense of the Revolution in Nicaragua, Managua, June 25, 1981, SI, Box 1147.

72. Harrington, *The Long-Distance Runner*.

73. "Últimos acontecimientos en Nicaragua," November 19, 1980, SI, Box 1145.

74. Willy Brandt to Felipe Gonzalez, June 2, 1981, e-Dossier #22, Cold War International History Project.

75. On US influence: David Kunzle, "Nicaragua's *La Prensa*—Capitalist Thorn in Socialist Flesh," *Media, Culture & Society* 6 (April 1984): 151–176. On intraelite conflict: Christian, *Revolution in the Family*. See also Carlos M. Vilas, "Nicaragua: A Revolution That Fell from Grace of the People," *Socialist Register* 27 (1991): 302–321.

76. Henighan, *Sandino's Nation*, 270.

77. Xabier Gorostiaga, "Some Aspects of Nicaragua's Economy," *Envío* 5, October 1988; Spalding, *Capitalists and Revolution in Nicaragua*.

78. José Coronel Urtecho to Pablo Antonio Cuadra, Pablo Antonio Cuadra Papers, Box 1, Benson Latin American Collection, University of Texas at Austin.

79. Christian, *Revolution in the Family*.

80. Pablo Antonio Cuadra, "Arquitectura y lenguaje," *LP*, June 7, 1980.

81. Whisnant, *Rascally Signs in Sacred Places*, 241.

82. Wellinga, *Entre la Poesia y la Pared*.

83. On the FSLN practice of replacing politically uncommitted professionals with internation-alists: Comments of Luis Medal of MIDINRA, Foro-Debate, Instituto Nicaragüense de Investigaciones Económicas y Sociales and Fundación Friedrich Ebert, Managua, Nicaragua, Undated, Nicaragua Subject Files, Box 3, Hoover Institution.

84. Gladys R. de Espinoza, "Los que fueron, los que deben volver y los que no deben partir," *LP*, June 24, 1980.

85. On the FSLN's internal deliberations on the role of professionals in the revolution: "Untitled memo on the role of professionals in the revolution," Moisés Hassan Papers, FSLN File, Hoover Institution, Stanford, California.

86. "FSLN quiere llevar profesionales de la mano," *LP*, March 27, 1981.

87. "Por el rescate democrático de la revolución nicaragüense," No 8, Sept 1982, Movimiento Democrática Nicaragüense, Alfonso Robelo Files, Box 5, Hoover Institution.

88. "Austria dice: democracia y pluralismo," *LP*, November 20, 1980.

89. "Robelo invitado a Alemania," *LP*, November 16, 1980.

90. "Yugoslavia, ayer, hoy, mañana," *LP*, June 9 1980.

91. Cruz Jr., *Memoirs of a Counterrevolutionary*, 192.

92. "Los Mayas de Europa," *LP*, August 1, 1981.

93. Pablo Antonio Cuadra, "Múnich, o la alegría de vivir," *LP*, August 15, 1981.

94. Cuadra's cultural anticommunism would influence figures such as Mario Vargas Llosa, for whom Nicaragua provided an impetus for embracing neoliberalism: Pablo Antonio Cuadra, "A Vargas Llosa se le escapó la historia," NC, Box 1.

95. Carlos Tünnermann Bernheim, "Los Problemas de Seguridad de la Cruzada Nacional de Alfabetización y Medidas de Seguridad que Convendría Tomar," May 7, 1980, SR, Box 61.

96. Molina Jiménez and Díaz Arias, eds., *Ahí me Van a Matar*.

97. Honey, *Hostile Acts*.

98. Iber, *Neither Peace nor Freedom*.

99. Brandt, *North-South: A Programme for Survival*.

100. "Cancun Bilateral Meeting between the Prime Minister and the Mexican President," October 14, 1981, PREM 19/698, British National Archives.

101. López Portillo, *Mis tiempos*, 1117.

102. Transcript of Meeting between US Secretary of State Alexander M. Haig and Carlos Rafael Rodriguez, December 8, 1981, Document 111221, CWIHP.

103. Prashad, *The Poorer Nations*.

104. "North-South Conference at Cancun," *Envío* 6, November 15, 1981; SI, Box 1146.

105. Council for Inter-American Security, *A New Inter-American Policy for the Eighties*.

106. Kirkpatrick, *Dictatorships and Double Standards*.

107. "Interim Report on the Bureau on Inter-American Affairs and Related Bureaus and Policy Areas," Department of State Memorandum, December 1, 1980, El Salvador, 1977–1984, ES00893, Digital National Security Archive.

108. On the failure of the general strike thanks to government reforms and the importance of the "modern businessman": Luigi Einaudi et al., "Draft of Department of State Special Report," "El Salvador: Democracy of Dictatorship?," April 1981, Roger Fontaine files, RAC 6, Reagan Library.

109. Instituto Centroamericano de Administración de Empresas, "Estudio del Sector Privado de Centro América y Panamá" (Washington, DC: USAID, November 1981).

110. On the US inability to deal directly with El Salvador's oligarchy: Message from American Embassy San Salvador, April 1982, "The Powers behind the Politicians," NSC Executive Secretary

El Salvador Box 47, Reagan Library; Raymond Bonner, *Weakness and Deceit: U.S. Policy and El Salvador* (New York: Times Books, 1984).

111. National Security Council Meeting, February 10, 1982, NSC 00040, Box 3, Reagan Library; Bakan, Cox, and Leys, eds., *Imperial Power and Regional Trade*.

112. Jean G. Zorn and Harold Mayerson, "The Caribbean Basin Initiative: A Windfall for the Private Sector," *Lawyer of the Americas* 14 (Winter 1983): 523–556. Other efforts to achieve greater visibility for the initiative included President's Task Force on International Private Enterprise, *Report to the President*; US House of Representatives, Foreign Affairs Committee, Private Enterprise Initiative, 11; Bandow, ed., *U.S. Aid to the Developing World*.

113. Mark F. McGuire and Vernon W. Ruttan, "Lost Directions: US Foreign Assistance Policy since New Directions," *Journal of Developing Areas* 24 (January 1990): 127–180.

114. For many years, P. T. Bauer was the most prominent critic of such aid. Bauer, *Equality, the Third World, and Economic Delusion*.

115. "CBI Status Report—Conclusions of an Inter-Agency Review of CBI Implementation in Five Beneficiary Countries," April 25, 1986, FO003-02, WHORM Subject Files, Reagan Library.

116. Peter Preston, "The Cancun Summit," November 4, 1981, FCO 59/1797, British National Archives.

117. "Mini-plan Marshall, un Tema Escabroso," *LP*, May 29, 1981.

118. On US economic warfare: E. V. K. Fitzgerald, "An Evaluation of the Economic Costs to Nicaragua of U.S. Aggression: 1980–1984," in Spalding, *The Political Economy of Revolutionary Nicaragua*.

119. On the distancing of the CBI from the Marshall Plan and its status as "carrot and stick": "NSC Discussion Paper: U.S. Policy in the Caribbean Basin," NSC 00010, 28 May 1981, NSC Executive Secretary, Reagan Library; "Press Briefing by Secretary of State Alexander Haig," October 21, 1981, FCO 59/1807, British National Archives.

120. McGuire and Ruttan, "Lost Directions," 142.

121. US Agency for International Development, *AID Congressional Presentation Fiscal Year 1983, Annex III, Latin America and the Caribbean* (Washington, DC: USAID, 1982), 89; Richard Newfarmer, "A Look at Reagan's Revolution in Development Policy," *Challenge* 26 (October 1983): 34–43.

122. Interview with Marshall D. Brown, *United States Foreign Assistance Oral History Program Foreign Affairs Oral History Collection* (Arlington, VA: Association for Diplomatic Studies and Training, 1996).

123. On the use of funds to support the private sector and as "bargaining chip" with the government: US Agency for International Development/El Salvador, *The Caribbean Basin Initiative in El Salvador: A Plan for Private Sector Development* (San Salvador: USAID, July 1982), 109. On the condition of Economic Support Funds aid to Salvador support for land reform and private sector: Memo from Secretary of State to USAID missions in Latin America, "LAC Experience with ESF," December 1983, RG 286, Agency for International Development, USAID Mission to Nicaragua/Executive Office, Entry P796, General Records 1979–1984, Container 4, ARC#6277025, NARA.

124. US Congress, Committee on Foreign Affairs, Subcommittee on Inter-American Affairs, *The Caribbean Basin Policy*, 97th Cong., 1st sess., July 14, 21, and 28, 1981.

125. Carothers, *In the Name of Democracy*.

126. "Figueres' Associate Suggests USG Aid Eden Pastora," June 25, 1979, 1979SANJO02691, AAD.

127. Harrington, *The Long-Distance Runner*, 161.

128. Edén Pastora to Humberto Ortega, June 26, 1981, SR, Box 61.

129. Clarridge, *A Spy for All Seasons*.

130. Constantine Menges, "Central America and Its Enemies," *Commentary*, August 1981.

131. "Central America Options and Strategy," April 11, 1981, National Security Council Executive Secretary, Box 91282, Reagan Library.

132. Clarridge, *A Spy for All Seasons*, 217.

133. "Sandinista Violations of Human Rights," John G. Roberts Files, Box 48, Ronald Reagan Library.

134. "Pronóstico sobre la contrarrevolución que encabeza Edén Pastora," SR, Box 61.

135. Mario Soares to Willy Brandt, May 12, 1982, SI, Box 1147.

136. Carlos Andres Perez to Willy Brandt, July 13, 1981, SR, Box 61.

137. Cruz, *Crónicas de un Disidente*.

138. Cruz, *Memoirs*, 184.

139. Cameron, *My Life in the Time of the Contras*, 21.

140. Ronald Radosh, Penn Kemble, and Bruce Cameron were the primary publicists for this tendency.

141. Bruce Cameron and Penn Kemble, "From a Proxy Force to a National Liberation Front," February 1, 1986, Digital National Security Archive: Iran-Contra Affair.

142. A reference to Contra leader Adolfo Calero. Cameron, *My Life*, 109.

143. Bureau for Latin America and the Caribbean, USAID, "The Central American Initiative, A Preliminary Status Report Draft," February 1986, RG 286, Records Relating to the National Bipartisan Committee on Central America (Kissinger Commission), 1984–1987, Box 4, NARA.

144. "Address to the Nation on United States Assistance for the Nicaraguan Democratic Resistance," June 24, 1986, quoted in Grandin, *Empire's Workshop*.

145. LeoGrande, *Our Own Backyard,* 469–475.

146. Cruz, *Memoirs*, xiv, 218.

147. Ramírez, *Adiós Muchachos*, 112.

148. Grandin, *Empire's Workshop*, 82.

5. Retracing Imperial Paths on the Mosquito Coast

1. Squier described his journey in a pseudonymous fictional account: Bard, *Waikna*.

2. The description of the journey is in Nietschmann, *Caribbean Edge*.

3. Explanations for the explosion of conflict on the eastern shore blame the FSLN's modernizing programs, US covert interference, Miskito "contradictory consciousness," and Miskito nationalism: Theodore Macdonald, "The Moral Economy of the Miskito Indians: Local Roots of a Geopolitical Conflict," in *Ethnicities and Nations: Processes of Interethnic Relations in Latin America, Southeast Asia, and the Pacific*; Ortiz, *Blood on the Border*; Hale, *Resistance and Contradiction*; Baracco, *Nicaragua: The Imagining of a Nation*.

4. On the international indigenous movement: Brysk, *From Tribal Village to Global Village*; Niezen, *The Origins of Indigenism*; Yashar, *Contesting Citizenship in Latin America*.

5. Becker, *Indians and Leftists in the Making of Ecuador's Modern Indigenous Movements*.

6. On the politics of ecology: Escobar, *Territories of Difference*.

7. Ferguson, *The Anti-Politics Machine*.

8. Wolfgang Gabbert, "The Kingdom of Mosquitia and the Mosquito Reservation," in Baracco, ed., *National Integration and Contested Autonomy*. Other smaller indigenous groups spoke Sumu (now called Mayangna) and Rama.

9. Bryan and Wood, *Weaponizing Maps*.

10. On the Somoza regime's cultivation of small farmers and limited worker autonomy: Gould, *To Lead as Equals*. For a discussion of the coexistence of "high" modernism and alternative modernization projects in Guatemala: Way, *The Mayan in the Mall*.

11. On Somoza-era policies on the east coast: Vilas, *State, Class, and Ethnicity in Nicaragua*.

12. Inter-American Economic and Social Council, *The Charter of Punta del Este.*

13. Arthur Schlesinger, Jr, "Memorandum for the President," March 10, 1961, Papers of President Kennedy; National Security Files; Regional Security, John F. Kennedy Library, Box 215.

14. "Indians in Latin America," January 14, 1963, Bureau of Inter-American Affairs, Office of Central American and Panamanian Affairs, Subject and Country Files 1955–1963, RG 59, NARA, Box 5.

15. "Conversation on July 27, with IDB Operation Officer for Nicaragua," July 27, 1973, Box 10: URB Urban Development Program FY1974 (Nicaragua), Country Files, compiled 1973–1975, RG 286: Records of the Agency for International Development, 1948–2003, NARA.

16. Memorandum, 1/13/75, RG 286, Country Files, compiled 1973–1975, Agricultural Development Program FY1974 (Nicaragua), Box 9, NARA. On the creation of Nicaraguan *mestizaje*: Gould, *To Die in This Way.*

17. Interdepartmental Regional Group for Inter-American Affairs, "Policy & Action Paper—Nicaragua, 1966," RG 59, Bureau of Inter-American Affairs/Office of Central American Affairs, Entry #A1 5734: Records Relating to Nicaragua: 1963–1975, NARA, p 6.

18. Helms, *Asang.*

19. Author's interview with Maria Zuñiga, who worked with the Peace Corps and with Father Gregory Smutko, who advocated for indigenous rights under Somoza, Managua, September 29, 2014.

20. Author's interview with Armstrong Wiggins, founding member of Misurasata, Washington, D.C., June 2013; Luciano Baracco, "From Developmentalism to Autonomy: The Sandinista Revolution and the Atlantic Coast of Nicaragua," in Baracco, ed., *National Integration and Contested Autonomy.*

21. Hale, *Resistance and Contradiction,* 208.

22. Bartolomé de las Casas was a sixteenth-century Dominican friar who denounced the horrific treatment of indigenous peoples by the Spanish conquistadores.

23. Cuadra, *Hacia la Cruz del Sur,* quoted in Vegas-Latapie, *Memorias Políticas,* 253.

24. "El Signo Imperial en lo Geográfico." Cuadra, *Breviario Imperial,* 135.

25. Patrick N. Theros, Memorandum: Trip to Puerto Cabezas, RG 59, Bureau of Inter-American Affairs/Office of Central American Affairs, Records Relating to Nicaragua, 1963–1975, Box 4, NARA. For the alternative explanation, see Jenkins Molieri, *El Desafío Indígena en Nicaragua,* 210–211.

26. On connections between FSLN programs and the previous regime, see Vilas, *Estado, Clase y Etnicidad.*

27. "Principles and Definitions of the JGRN and FSLN Regarding the Coast," *Envío* 4 (September 1981).

28. Jenkins Molieri, *El Desafío Indígena en Nicaragua.*

29. Its name meant "Miskitu, Sumu, Rama, and Sandinistas Together."

30. The most detailed examination of government policies is in Hale, *Resistance and Contradiction.*

31. Bartolome, *Declaration of Barbados.*

32. Macekura, *Of Limits and Growth,* 196–217.

33. Cultural Survival Inc., "Strengthening Pluralism: A Combined Human Rights/Grassroots Development Program for Indians of Latin America and the Caribbean Basin," RG 286, USAID/Bureau for SAme/Carib. Office of Democratic Initiatives, Closed Project Files; 1978–1991, Container 1, NARA.

34. Cultural Survival, "Proposal for Human Rights Projects among the Indians of Latin America," 13.

35. Proposal for Human Rights Projects among the Indians of Latin America, submitted by Cultural Survival, Inc., July 1979, NARA, RG 286, USAID Mission to Nicaragua/Human Resources Development Division, Subject Files, 1975–1981, Container 5.

36. Memorandum by Thomas J. O'Donnell, Deputy Chief of Mission, Attendance at part of MISURASATA's First Anniversary Celebration at Waspam, November 11, 1980, RG 286, USAID

Mission to Nicaragua/Human Resources Development Division, Subject Files, 1975–1981, Container 5, NARA.

37. Letter from Polly F. Harrison, USAID Regional Social Science Advisor, to Theodore MacDonald, Project Director Cultural Survival Inc., February 24, 1981, RG 286, USAID/Bureau for SAme/Carib. Office of Democratic Initiatives, Closed Project Files; 1978–1991, Container 10, NARA.

38. Letter from Roma Knee, LAC/DP/SD, to Gerald Wein, Acting Director USAID/Nicaragua August 7, 1981, RG 286, USAID/Bureau for SAme/Carib. Office of Democratic Initiatives, Closed Project Files; 1978–1991, Container 10, NARA.

39. Letter from Theodore Macdonald to Ernesto Cardenal, December 17, 1979, NARA, RG 286, USAID/Bureau for SAme/Carib. Office of Democratic Initiatives, Closed Project Files; 1978–1991, Container 10.

40. Baracco, "From Developmentalism to Autonomy."

41. Hale, *Resistance and Contradiction*, 202.

42. Philippe Bourgois, "Class, Ethnicity, and State among the Miskitu Amerindians of Northeastern Nicaragua," *Latin American Perspectives* 8 (Spring 1981), 22–39.

43. "By the same dialectic whereby ethnic reaffirmation results in a more integrated Nicaraguan socialist identity, regional autonomy for northern Zelaya could cement a firmer national unity in Nicaragua and hopefully some day in a Union of Socialist States of Central America." Bourgois and Grunberg, *La Mosquitia en la Revolución*.

44. Author's interview with Philippe Bourgois, Philadelphia, Pennsylvania, 2012.

45. Centro de Investigaciones y Documentación de la Costa Atlántica, ed., *Ethnic Groups and the Nation State: The Case of the Atlantic Coast in Nicaragua* (Stockholm: University of Stockholm, 1987).

46. Manuel, *The Fourth World*.

47. Bryan and Wood, *Weaponizing Maps*.

48. On the issue of mapping: Charles Hale, "'Wan Tasbaya Dukiara': Contested Notions of Land Rights in Miskitu History," in Jonathan Boyarin, ed., *Remapping Memory: The Politics of TimeSpace* (Minneapolis: University of Minnesota, 1994). On indigenous culture: MacDonald, "The Moral Economy of the Miskito Indians." On disputes within indigenist organizations: Means, *Where White Men Fear to Tread*.

49. Hale, "Wan Tasbaya Dukiara," 88.

50. Instituto Nicaragüense de la Costa Atlántica, INNICA, "Proyecto de reubicación de las comunidades Miskitas sobre la margen sur del Río Coco," March 1981, Instituto de Historia de Nicaragua y Centroamérica (IHNCA) Collection, Managua.

51. Garrard-Burnett, Lawrence, and Moreno, *Beyond the Eagle's Shadow: New Histories of Latin America's Cold War*.

52. Mac Chapin, "Evaluation of Aid-Supported Grants to Cultural Survival," 1979–1987, AID closed project files 78–91, Box 9, NARA.

53. Cultural Survival, Inc., "A Cultural Survival Manifesto: Towards a Theory of Participant Development and Cultural Pluralism within National State Structures," 1979–1987, AID closed project files 78–91, Box 9, NARA.

54. Letter from Theodore MacDonald, Projects Director of Cultural Survival Inc., to Otto Reich, Assistant Administrator, Bureau for Latin America and the Caribbean, December 21, 1982, RG 286, USAID/Bureau for SAme/Carib. Office of Democratic Initiatives, Closed Project Files; 1978–1991, Container 10, NARA.

55. Nietschmann, *Between Land and Water*.

56. Nietschmann, *Between Land and Water*.

57. Carl O. Sauer, quoted in Michael J. Watts, "Now and Then: The Origins of Political Ecology and the Rebirth of Adaptation as a Form of Thought," in Perreault, Bridge and McCarthy, eds., *The Routledge Handbook of Political Ecology*, 29.

58. Bernard Nietschmann, "Statement before the Organization of American States' Inter-American Commission on Human Rights, on the Situation of the Indians in Nicaragua," October 3, 1983, in US Department of State, *From Revolution to Repression: Human Rights in Nicaragua under the Sandinistas*.

59. Extensive documentation on an attempt by Nietschmann and Steve Tullberg to discredit the claims to indigenous heritage of Roxanne Dunbar Ortiz can be found in Carton 8, Bernard Nietschmann Papers, Bancroft Library, University of California, Berkeley.

60. Nietschmann, *The Miskito Nation, Nicaragua, and the United States*. For critiques of Nietschmann's work, see Philippe Bourgois and Charles Hale, "The Atlantic Coast of Nicaragua," in Snarr, ed., *Sandinista Nicaragua, Part 1*; Pineda, *Shipwrecked Identities*.

61. Letter from Bernard Nietschmann to Orrin Hatch, April 11, 1984, Carton 8, Bernard Nietschmann Papers, Bancroft Library.

62. On Nietschmann's influence within these fields: William M. Denevan, "Bernard Q. Nietschmann, 1941–2000: Mr. Barney, Geographer and Humanist," *Geographical Review* 92 (January 2002): 104–109.

63. Armstrong Wiggins, "Colonialism and Revolution—Nicaraguan Sandinism and the Liberation of the Miskito, Sumu, and Rama Peoples: An Interview with Armstrong Wiggins," *Akwesasne Notes* 8, no. 4 (1981): 4–15.

64. Bernard Nietschmann, "Economic Development by Invasions of Indigenous Nations," *Cultural Survival Quarterly* 10, no. 2 (1986): 2–12.

65. Nietschmann, *Between Land and Water*.

66. "Militarization: The Environmental Impact," The Environmental Project on Central America—Epoca/Green Paper Number Three, in Nicaragua Information Center Files, Box 9, Bancroft Library.

67. Nietschmann, *The Unknown War*, chapter 1.

68. Bernard Nietschmann, "The Miskito Nation and the Geopolitics of Self-Determination," in Bernard Schechterman and Martin Slann, eds., *The Ethnic Dimension in International Relations* (Westport: Praeger, 1993).

69. Manuscript of Bernard Nietschmann, "Fourth World Revolution: With Yapti Tasba Guerrillas Fighting the Sandinista Revolution," Bernard Nietschmann Papers, Bancroft Library, chapter 9.

70. Manuscript of Bernard Nietschmann, "Fourth World Revolution," 375.

71. The term *Boland Amendment* refers to three amendments created by Representative Edward Boland, the first of which was attached to the Defense Appropriations Act of 1983.

72. Ameringer, *The Caribbean Legion*.

73. Nietschmann, manuscript of "Fourth World Revolution," 381–385.

74. Dinges, *Our Man in Panama*.

75. Nietschmann, manuscript of "Fourth World Revolution," 369.

76. Carlos Alemán Ocampo y Hilberto Lopez y Rivas, "Sandinismo y 'cuarto mundo,'" Colección Carlos Alemán Ocampo, IHNCA.

77. Frühling, González, and Buvollen, *Etnicidad y Nación*.

78. Rodolfo Stavenhagen, quoted in Héctor Díaz-Polanco and Kelley Swarthout, "*Neoindigenismo* and the Ethnic Question in Central America," *Latin American Perspectives* 14 (Winter, 1987): 87–100.

79. Hans Petter Buvollen, "Autonomy: Tactic and Self-Determination, the Sandinista Policy towards the Indigenous Peoples of Nicaragua," *Caribbean Quarterly* 36 (June 1990): 98–112.

80. Nietschmann, *The Unknown War*, 74. Charles Hale, attributing Sandinista acquiescence to Miskito autonomy as the result of the revolution's self-critique rather than its failures on the battle-field, renders Rivera's statement as "Ethnic groups run restaurants. . . . We are a people," omitting the crucial mention of an Indian army. Hale, *Resistance and Contradiction*, 214.

81. One of these was US-based Indian activist Russell Means.

82. For another perspective on negotiations: Reyes and Wilson, *Rafaga*.

83. Nietschmann, manuscript of "Fourth World Revolution," 529.

84. The issue of the limits of "recognition" as a basis for indigenous politics has become prominent in recent scholarship. Coulthard, *Red Skin, White Masks*.

85. Julio Tresierra, "Mexico: Indigenous Peoples and the Nation States," in Donna Lee Van Cott, ed., *Indigenous Peoples and Democracy in Latin America* (New York: St. Martin's, 1994), 206.

86. Maria Luisa Acosta, "Encroaching upon Indigenous Land: Nicaragua and the 'Dry Canal,'" in Jentoft, Minde, and Nilsen, eds., *Indigenous Peoples*; Ceferino Wilson, "La demarcación y titulación de tierras casi concluye, la etapa de saneamiento nos exige mucha madurez," *Envío* 362 (May 2012).

87. Goett, *Black Autonomy*.

88. US Agency for International Development, "Nicaragua Project Paper, Natural Resources Management," 38.

89. World Wildlife Fund grant proposal, "Miskito Kupia: Miskito Coast Protected Area," March 1991, Nicaragua Subject Files, Box 13, Hoover Institution Archive, Stanford, California.

90. Bernard Nietschmann, "Protecting Indigenous Coral Reefs and Sea Territories, Miskito Coast, R AAN, Nicaragua," in Stevens, ed., *Conservation through Cultural Survival*.

91. Bernard Nietschmann, "The Miskito Nation and the Geopolitics of Self-Determination," in Schechterman and Slann, eds., *The Ethnic Dimension in International Relations*, 38.

92. USAID Officer of the Inspector General Interview with Jurij Homziak, USAID Project Officer, Carton 24, Bernard Nietschmann Papers, Bancroft Library.

93. *Nicaragua Project Paper: Natural Resources Management* (Washington, DC: USAID, 1991), Annex F.

94. For another description of the contested nature of indigenous land claims at odds with Nicaragua's central government, and the role of self-defense, see Mark Jamieson, "Territorial Demarcation and Indigenous Rights in Eastern Nicaragua: The Case of Kakabila," in Baracco, *National Integration and Contested Autonomy*; Anja Nygren, "Nature as Contested Terrain: Conflicts over Wilderness Protection and Local Livelihoods in Rio San Juan, Nicaragua," in Anderson and Berglund, eds., *Ethnographies of Conservation*.

95. On Miskito social conditions in the area after the conservation project: Farrell, *Nicaragua Before Now*.

96. "Congressional Delegation Ballenger Conversations with President Chamorro and Minister of the Presidency Lacayo," Managua 2751, April 1991, Declassified Documents Reference System.

6. Institutionalized Precarity in Postwar Nicaragua

1. Pablo Antonio Cuadra, "'Espacios': en busca de una ecología del espíritu," *LP*, June 15, 1989.

2. Ramírez, *Confesión de Amor*, 57.

3. On the contradictions between modernization and identity in Latin America more broadly, see Svampa, *Debates Latinoamericanos*.

4. Robinson, *Transnational Conflicts*, 75.

5. On neoliberal utopianism in Nicaragua: Chávez, *Nicaragua and the Politics of Utopia*.

6. Sheppard, *The Persistent Revolution*; Munck, *Latin America: The Transition to Democracy*.

7. New Partnerships Working Group, *New Partnerships in the Americas: The Spirit of Rio*, 9.

8. Irene Selser, "Las contradicciones de un modelo: entrevista con Julio Valle-Castillo," *Nuevo Amanecer Cultural*, May 25, 1990.

9. The "surprising" nature of the outcome has received the most attention, though supporters of the UNO coalition frequently claim to have predicted the results. Bernard Aronson claims that the lack of knowledge by the US government of the election outcome is a "myth" created by Robert Pastor. What is beyond doubt is that the outcome was truly surprising to many supporters of the Sandinista government. Interview with former undersecretary of state Bernard Aronson, 2014.

10. Guillermoprieto, *The Heart that Bleeds*.

11. Kagan, *A Twilight Struggle*.

12. On US support for Chamorro: Robinson, *A Faustian Bargain*.

13. One congressman asserted that Violeta would make a good queen, though not a good president. US Congress, House Committee on Foreign Affairs, Subcommittee on Western Hemisphere Affairs, *Democracy and Reconciliation in Nicaragua: A Critical Assessment*, 103rd Cong., February 4, 1993, p. 5.

14. Memorandum of Conversation, "Discussion of Pending AID Loans with Nicaraguan Minister of Public Works," November 2, 1962, RG 59, Bureau of Inter-American Affairs, Office of Central American and Panamanian Affairs, Subject and Country Files, 1955–1963, Box 5, NARA.

15. A discussion of the movement from modernization to democratization is found in Guilhot, *The Democracy Makers*, 115.

16. Thomas Carothers, "The End of the Transition Paradigm," *Journal of Democracy* 13 (2002).

17. Karen Kampwirth, "The Mother of the Nicaraguans: Doña Violeta and the UNO's Gender Agenda," in "Women in Latin America, Part 2," *Latin American Perspectives* 23 (Winter, 1996): 67–86.

18. Richard Boudreaux, "Nicaragua's 'Family' Style Bridges Political Chasms," *Los Angeles Times*, May 5, 1990.

19. Pedro Xavier Solis, interview with the author, Managua, October 30, 2014.

20. On Sandinista attempts to gain the allegiance of the elite, and Reagan's cultivation of an alternative entrepreneurial internationalism, see chapter 3.

21. Ignacio Fonseca, "'El Fierro de los Chamorros' en la Era Sandinista," *LP*, October 17, 1989.

22. Bernard Aronson, telephone interview with the author, September 6, 2014.

23. Vilas, "Family Affairs," 309–341; Nuñez, *La Oligarquía en Nicaragua*.

24. Vilas, *Between Earthquakes and Volcanos*.

25. Bruce Nichols, "Rubberband Humanitarianism," *Ethics in International Affairs* 1 (March 1987): 191–210.

26. Baker, *The Politics of Diplomacy*, 56.

27. Santiago Murray, "Building towards Reconciliation," *Américas* 44:3 (1992): 52.

28. Brown, *Causes of Continuing Conflict in Nicaragua*.

29. Brown, *The Real Contra War*.

30. Author interview with Pedro Xavier Solis; "Pulso de la Semana," *Semanario*, October 30, 1991.

31. Wheelock, *Raíces Indígenas de la Lucha Anticolonialista en Nicaragua*. For more on *mestizaje*, see Jeffrey Gould, *To Die in This Way*; Williams, *The Other Side of the Popular*, 26.

32. "La Imprescindible Pero Inestable Célula de la Familia," *LP*, February 3, 1990.

33. Pablo Antonio Cuadra, "Sobre política y peces," *LP*, June 25, 1991.

34. "Policy and Action Paper—Nicaragua," RG 59, Bureau of Inter-American Affairs/Office of Central American Affairs, Records Relating to Nicaragua; 1963–1975, Container 3, NARA.

35. See chapter 4.

36. Nicaragua, Ministerio de Acción Social, *Propuesta Política Nacional de Población*.

37. US Agency for International Development, "Nicaragua Action Plan FY 95–FY 96," 42; Rubén Pasos, "Contener la Migración Campesina," *LP*, July 15, 1991.

38. US Agency for International Development, "Country Development and Strategy Statement, USAID/Nicaragua 1991–1996."

39. Nathan and Associates, *Final Report: Evaluation of USAID/Nicaragua Economic Support and Recovery Programs I, II, and III*.

40. US Agency for International Development, *Nicaragua Project Paper: Strengthening Democratic Institutions*, 15.

41. "Audit of the Nicaragua Assistance Program Funded by Public Law 101-302 and Fiscal Year 1991 Appropriations as of September 30, 1991" (Washington, DC: USAID, 1992), 90.

42. OIT / INATEC, *La Microempresa en Nicaragua y su Potencial de Desarrollo*.

43. Papers of William J. Casey, Box 395, Hoover Institution Archive.

44. "Displaced Children and Orphans in Nicaragua" (Washington, DC: USAID: 1993), 2.

45. On the feminist critique of development: Scott, *Gender and Development*.

46. US Agency for International Development, *Nicaragua Private Sector Support Project: Assessment of Private Sector Initiatives*, 53–54.

47. Kampwirth, *Latin America's New Left and the Politics of Gender*, 8.

48. Kampwirth, *Feminism and the Legacy of Revolution*; Ana Criquillon, "The Nicaraguan women's movement: feminist reflections from within," in Sinclair, ed., *New Politics of Survival*; Luciak, *After the Revolution*.

49. "Activity design document (redacted version): SO2, IR 2.2" (Washington, DC: USAID, 2005), 18.

50. This mandate was enacted in law with the 1973 Percy Amendment to the Foreign Assistance Act.

51. See chapter 2.

52. Babb, *After Revolution*.

53. Metoyer, *Women and the State in Post-Sandinista Nicaragua*.

54. Nathan Associates, Inc., *Assistance to Resource Institutions for Enterprise Support*, 46.

55. US Congress, Subcommittee on the Western Hemisphere of the Committee on International Relations, *An Evaluation of Democracy in Nicaragua*, 104th Cong., 1st sess., November 8, 1995, p. 12.

56. Nathan Associates, Inc., *Assistance to Resource Institutions for Enterprise Support*, 55.

57. Quote from Ligia Orozco, in "Welcome to the Free Trade Zone," *Envío* 150 (January 1994).

58. Joeckes and Moayedi, *Women and Export Manufacturing*, 43.

59. US Agency for International Development, *Women in Development Technical Assistance Project, Economic Opportunities and Labor Conditions for Women: Perspectives from Latin America: Guatemala, El Salvador, Honduras*, 18–20.

60. Ilja A. Luciak, "Gender Equality and Electoral Politics on the Left: A Comparison of El Salvador and Nicaragua," *Journal of Interamerican Studies and World Affairs* 40: 1 (Spring 1998): 48.

61. Babb, *After Revolution*, 32.

62. Ramírez, *Balcanes y Volcanes*.

63. Wiarda, *Corporatism and Comparative Politics*.

64. "Carlos Salinas and Mexico's New Era of Solidarity and *Concertación*," in Sheppard, *Persistent Revolution*.

65. Ríos, *Concertación de Actores Locales para el Desarrollo Integral del Municipio de Totogalpa*.

66. Valdez, *La Fascinación por la Moncloa*. Moulian, *Chile actual*; Williams, *The Other Side of the Popular*; Álvarez Montalván, *Cultura Política Nicaragüense*.

67. See chapter 3.

68. Francisco J. Mayorga, former Nicaraguan Central Bank president, interview with the author, Managua, December 4, 2014.

69. Antonio Lacayo Oyanguren, former minister to the president, interview with the author, Managua, August 24, 2014.

70. "Concertación económica y socialismo," *Envió*, March 1989; Spalding, *Capitalists and Revolution*.

71. Arturo Cruz Jr. and Consuelo Cruz Sequeira, "The Crisis of the Clans," *New Republic*, May 21, 1990.

72. Aronson interview, 2014.

73. Alejandro Baca Muñoz, "Pacto social y dialogo nacional," *LP*, September 4, 1990.

74. Gustavo Porras and José Espinosa, "Pacto social vs concertación," *El Nuevo Diario*, May 18, 1990; Pedro Antonio Rodriguez, "¿Es viable el capitalismo socialdemócrata, no salvaje, en Nicaragua?," May 23, 1990.

75. Serrano Caldera, Alejandro. *La Nicaragua posible: por un proyecto nacional: 4 Foro de Política Nacional, realizado en la Universidad el 13 y 14 de marzo de 1992* (Managua: Universidad Nacional Autónoma de Nicaragua [UNAN], 1992).

76. Edmundo Jarquín, "Reducción o reforma del estado," *Semanario*, August 1991.

77. "Concertación: un proceso complejo," *LP*, September 11, 1990.

78. Serrano Caldera, *La Unidad en la Diversidad*.

79. In an interview with the author in 2014, Lacayo still denied the existence of a "cogovernment" and then proceeded to compare the split between the government and the FSLN with the breaking up of a marriage. Lacayo interview, 2014.

80. Martínez Cuenca, *Sandinista Economics in Practice*.

81. Mark Everingham, "Agricultural Property Rights and Political Change in Nicaragua," *Latin American Politics and Society* 43, no. 3 (Autumn 2001): 61–93.

82. David Close claims the failure to legalize property relations was caused by Sandinista disdain for bourgeois legality and their inability to imagine ever having to cede power. Close, *Nicaragua: The Chamorro Years*, 162.

83. Pablo Antonio Cuadra, "Debajo de la hojarasca," *LP*, July 25, 1991.

84. "Entrevista: Wheelock Habla sobre Propiedad," *Semanario*, July 4, 1991.

85. Saldaña-Portillo, *The Revolutionary Imagination in the Americas*.

86. Luis Carrión, *Barricada*, June 20, 1990, quoted in Kagan, *Twilight Struggle*, 228.

87. Bendaña, *Una Tragedia Campesina*.

88. Martínez Cuenca, *Sandinista Economics in Practice;* Sergio Ramírez, *Adiós Muchachos;* Hassan, *La Maldición del Güegüense*.

89. López Castellanos and Ramírez, *La ruptura del Frente Sandinista*, 12.

90. Ramírez, *Adiós Muchachos*, 112–113; Ortega Saavedra, *La Odisea por Nicaragua*.

91. Aguirre, *La Espuma Sucia del Río*, 41.

92. Ramírez, *Adiós Muchachos*.

93. Orlando Núñez Soto, "Los Profetas del Pasado y los Campesinos de la Tragedia," *Barricada*, September 4, 1991; Eduardo Baumeister, "'La Tragedia Campesina' y un Debate Necesario," *Barricada*, September 15, 1991.

94. Núñez Soto, *La Guerra y el Campesinado en Nicaragua*, 33.

95. Charlip, *Cultivating Coffee*; Paige, *Coffee and Power*; Gobat, *Confronting the American Dream*.

96. Gould, *To Die in This Way*.

97. Orlando Núñez Soto, "Réquiem para el Caos en Nicaragua," *Nuevo Amanecer Cultural*, November 13, 1993.

98. Saldomando, *El Retorno de la AID.*

99. José Espinoza of CPT, in *Concertación Económica y Social, Fase II.*

100. Intervención de Daniel Nuñez, *Concertación Económica y Social, Fase II*, 11.

101. "Entonces, esas cosas desconciertan, porque uno no sabe con quién está concertando, porque si hoy concertamos con un grupo de ministros y dicen que lo pueden correr en cualquier momento, entonces nosotros nos quedamos desconcertados, que con quien estamos concertando. Incluso él no está aquí." Cassette 4, Intervención de CPT, *Concertación Económica y Social, Fase II*, 15.

102. For a critique of the mythical transparency in the Chilean context: Moulian, *Chile Actual.*

103. Close, *Nicaragua.*

104. Pablo Antonio Cuadra, "El Espíritu de Propiedad," *LP*, June 14, 1991.

105. Pablo Antonio Cuadra, "Al Paso que Vamos," *LP*, January 31, 1991.

106. Scott, *Seeing Like a State.*

107. World Commission on Environment and Development, *Our Common Future* (Oxford: Oxford University Press, 1987).

108. Jaime Incer Barquero, "Managua y sus Problemas Ecológicos," *LP*, June 25, 1990.

109. Jaime Incer Barquero, former Nicaraguan minister of environment, interview with the author, Managua, August 21, 2014; Nietschmann, *Caribbean Edge.*

110. Annis, *Poverty, Natural Resources, and Public Policy in Central America*, 49.

111. Tecnica Papers, Bancroft Library.

112. David Brower papers, Bancroft Library.

113. See chapter 4.

114. Fontanarrosa, "Boogie 'el Aceitoso,'" *Semana Comica*, January 1, 1991.

115. "La Catástrofe nos Amenaza," *Oikos Semanario*, October 10, 1991.

116. Latin American Center for Competitiveness and Sustainable Development, *Competitiveness in Central America: Preparing Companies for Globalization.*

117. Christopher, *In the Stream of History.*

118. "Mission Director's Narrative," USAID/Nicaragua Annual Budget Submission (Washington, DC: USAID, 1993), 4.

119. Emphasis in original. *Theory and Practice in Sustainability and Sustainable Development,* (Washington, DC: USAID, 1994).

120. US Agency for International Development, *PVO Child Survival Grants Program*, 13–14.

121. The NED supported programs to strengthen specifically "democratic political parties" and radio in "support of democracy," code words for anti-Sandinista groups. US Agency for International Development, *USAID/Nicaragua Semi-annual Project Status Report April 1, 1994–September 30, 1994*, 28–29; "USAID's Strategy in Nicaragua," *Envío* 142 (May 1993).

122. Belli, *Waslala*, 68.

123. Belli, *Waslala*, 86. Bernard Nietschmann also accused Steadman Fagoth of inviting "toxic waste dumpers" to the newly created Región Autónoma Atlántica Norte, where Fagoth had become minister for natural resources. "Fourth World Revolution: With Yapti Tasba Guerrillas Fighting the Sandinista Invasion," 547, Bernard Nietschmann Papers, Bancroft Library, University of California, Berkeley, California.

124. Lacayo Oyanguren, *La difícil transición Nicaragüense*, 150.

125. Even the US Government Accountability Office recognized the difficulty in processing the many complicated land claims. Government Accountability Office, *Aid to Nicaragua: US Assistance Supports Economic and Social Development* (Washington DC: GPO, 1992), 64.

126. *Nicaragua Today: A Republican Staff Report to the Committee on Foreign Relations* (Washington, DC: GPO, 1992).

127. Lacayo Oyanguren, *La difícil transición Nicaragüense,* 320.

128. US Congress, Senate Committee on Foreign Relations, *Nomination of Warren M. Christopher to Be Secretary of State,* 103rd Cong., January 13th and 14th, 1993.

129. John Maisto, former US ambassador to Nicaragua, telephone interview with the author, October 31, 2014.

130. Robinson, *Promoting Polyarchy.*

Epilogue

1. "Look at Managua by daylight: it's been like this since the earthquake [in 1972] when God and the Devil arm wrestled and as God lost, he went back upstairs and the Devil kept the right to keep governing Managua, because years ago, in the other earthquake [in 1931], the Devil had also won, but even before that he had already won, during the war with the gringos, in the north, in the Segovias [the Sandino rebellion]. . . . But worst of all is that after the earthquake [in 1972] they thought that God could win and finally lost again and that will keep happening until the end of time, where God could maybe beat the Devil." Galich, *Managua, Salsa City.*

2. Lievesley and Ludlam, eds., *Reclaiming Latin America.*

3. Chodor, *Neoliberal Hegemony and the Pink Tide in Latin America.*

4. Leiva, *Latin American Neostructuralism,* xix.

5. "Noticias de Nicaragua," *Envío* 423 (June 2017).

6. "Se Repiten Infinitamente las Guerras, los Terremotos, las Erupciones Volcánicas." Vilas, *El Legado de una Década,* 18.

7. Incer Barquero and Wheelock Román, *Desastres Naturales de Nicaragua,* 9.

8. *Nuevo Amanecer,* January 16, 1993.

9. Padre Uriel Molina Oliú, "Los pobres trazan nuestro camino," *Nuevo Amanecer Cultural,* December 4, 1992.

10. Pastor, *Condemned to Repetition* and *Not Condemned to Repetition.*

11. Guilhot, *The Democracy Makers,* 115.

12. Alvarez Montálvan, *Cultura Política Nicaragüense.*

13. "En la última instancia su conquista está relacionada con la revelación mitificada de un 'colonialismo interior benéfico,' el que da posibilidades de existencia a la nación." Delgado Aburto, *Márgenes Recorridos.*

14. Lacayo Oyanguren, *La Difícil Transición Nicaragüense,* 705.

15. Pablo Antonio Cuadra, "Al Paso que Vamos," *LP,* January 31, 1991.

16. The cathedral was funded by Domino's Pizza mogul Tom Managhan. Peter J. Boyer, "The Deliverer: A Pizza Mogul Finds a Moral Crusade," *New Yorker,* February 19, 2007.

17. F. Torres, "El concepto de sostenibilidad en el desarrollo agropecuario," in *Seminario Agricultura Sostenible en las Laderas Centroamericanas* (San José, CR: Instituto Interamericano de Cooperación para la Agricultura, 1991).

18. Katherine Isbester, "Nicaragua 1996–2001: Sex, Corruption, and Other Natural Disasters," *International Journal,* 56 (Autumn 2001): 632–648.

19. Horn, *Lessons Learned.*

20. Steven Radelet, "From Pushing Reforms to Pulling Reforms: The Role of Challenge Programs in Foreign Aid Policy," in Kaul et al., eds., *The New Public Finance.*

21. Ortega was accused of sexually abusing his stepdaughter, Zoilamérica Narvaez.

22. Dionisio Marenco, "Conozco bien la historia del Frente Sandinista, pero tal como están las cosas no logro imaginar su futuro," *Envío* 318 (September 2008).

23. Nils-Sjard Schulz, "Nicaragua: A Rude Awakening for the Paris Declaration," *FRIDE Comment*, November 2007.

24. Marenco, "Conozco bien la historia del Frente Sandinista."

25. James C. McKinley Jr., "Nicaraguan Councils Stir Fear of Dictatorship," *New York Times*, May 4, 2008.

26. "Jaime Wheelock responde a Orlando Núñez," *Radio Primerísima*, July 27, 2007.

27. Managuans nicknamed these "arbolatas," tin trees or perhaps canned trees.

28. Chandler, *Resilience.*

29. Gould, *To Lead as Equals.*

30. Coronel Kautz, *El Espíritu de Mis Padres.*

31. Saldaña-Portillo, *The Revolutionary Imagination in the Americas.*

32. "Noticias de Nicaragua," *Envío* 423 (June 2017).

33. Marenco, "Conozco Bien la Historia del Frente Sandinista."

34. Cruz served as Nicaraguan ambassador to the United States after Ortega's 2007 return. Interview with author, 2013.

35. Spalding, *Contesting Trade in Central America.*

36. Carlos F. Chamorro, "¿'Modelo Cosep', o el régimen de Ortega?," *Confidencial*, January 2, 2018.

37. Cuadra, *Entre la Cruz y la Espada.*

38. Hale, *Resistance and Contradiction.*

39. "Protests erupt in Nicaragua over interoceanic canal," *Guardian*, December 24, 2014.

40. Van der Post, *El Largo y Sinuoso Camino.*

41. Mayorga, *El Filatelista.* The title is reference to the legend that Panama was chosen as canal site over Nicaragua after a US senator circulated copies of a Nicaraguan stamp depicting one of the country's imposing volcanos.

42. Meeting of Cristianos Nicaragüenses por los Pobres, 2014. Lara Gunderson, personal email communication, August 23, 2014.

43. Academia de Ciencias de Nicaragua, *El Canal Oceánico por Nicaragua.*

44. Speech of Telémaco Talavera, Instituto de Historia de Nicaragua y Centroamérica, Universidad Centroamericana, September 10, 2014.

45. Interview by author with Arturo José Cruz Sequeira, Managua, September 2, 2014.

46. "The River That Must Be Crossed and the Stones That Must Be Felt For," *Envío* 403 (February 2015).

47. Victor Campos, "The Canal Will Jeopardize Our Ability to Cope with Climate Change," *Envío* 401, December 2014.

48. Sergio Ramírez, "Un cuento chino," *El Tiempo*, June 15, 2013.

49. "Nicaragua Canal Project Dealt New Blow," *Confidencial*, April 28, 2018.

50. Sarah Sklaw, "The Youth Leading Nicaragua's Uprising, One Year Later," *NACLA Report*, April 18, 2019.

Bibliography

Archives, Personal Papers, and Manuscript Collections

American Friends Service Committee Archives. Philadelphia, Pennsylvania.

Association for Diplomatic Studies and Training. Arlington, Virginia.
    United States Foreign Affairs Oral History Collection

Bancroft Library. Berkeley, California.
    Bernard Nietschmann Papers
    David Brower Papers
    Nicaragua Information Center Files
    Tecnica Papers

Biblioteca Álvaro Argüello Hurtado S.J. Instituto de Historia de Nicaragua y Centro-america. Managua, Nicaragua.

British National Archives. London, England.
    Foreign & Commonwealth Office
    Prime Minister's Office

Brown University Digital Repository.
    Documenting U.S.-Brazil Relations, 1960s–1980s

Chief George Manuel Memorial Online Library.

Declassified Documents Reference System.

Emory University, Manuscript, Archives, and Rare Book Library. Atlanta, Georgia.
    David M. Jessup Papers
    Ronald Radosh Papers

Franklin Delano Roosevelt Library. Hyde Park, New York.
    Adolf A. Berle Papers

Hoover Institution Archives, Stanford University. Stanford, California.
    Alfonso Robelo Files

John Koehler Files
Nicaragua Subject Files
Moises Hassan Papers
William J. Casey Papers
International Institute of Social History. Amsterdam, the Netherlands.
    Socialist International Papers
Jimmy Carter Library. Atlanta, Georgia.
    Carter Presidential Papers
    Remote Archives Capture Project
    Zbigniew Brzezinski Collection
John F. Kennedy Library. Boston, Massachusetts.
    National Security Files
    President's Office Files
Lyndon Baines Johnson Library. Austin, Texas.
    Administrative Histories
    National Security Files
    White House Central File
National Archives and Records Administration. College Park, Maryland.
    Record Group 59: General Records of the Department of State
        Bureau of Inter-American Affairs
        Central Foreign Policy Files
        Microfilm
        Policy Planning Staff
        Records of Anthony Lake, 1977–1981
        Records of Warren Christopher, 1977–1980
        Records Relating to the National Bipartisan Committee on Central America
            (Kissinger Commission), 1984–1987
    Record Group 286: Agency for International Development
        Bureau of Inter-American Affairs
        USAID Mission to Nicaragua
Princeton University Special Collections. Princeton, New Jersey.
    Sergio Ramírez Papers
Richard M. Nixon Library. Yorba Linda, California.
    National Security Council Files
    White House Tapes
Ronald Reagan Library. Simi Valley, California.
    Files of the Executive Secretary of the National Security Council
    Oliver North Files
    Roger Fontaine Files
    WHORM Subject Files
Rutgers University Special Collections. New Brunswick, New Jersey.
    Frances R. Grant Papers
    Robert J. Alexander Papers
Swarthmore College Peace Collection. Swarthmore, Pennsylvania.

Universidad Centroamericana. Managua, Nicaragua.
    Instituto de Historia de Nicaragua y Centroamérica Collection
        Colección Carlos Alemán Ocampo
        Colección Somoza
Universidad Centroamericana, Biblioteca "P. Florentino Idoate, S. J." San Salvador,
    El Salvador.
    Colección Salvadoreña
University of California, Berkeley, Graduate Theological Union Archive. Berkeley,
    California.
    Gustav Schultz Sanctuary Collection
    Northern California Ecumenical Council Collection
    Pledge of Resistance Collection
    Robert McAfee Brown Collection
University of Miami Special Collections. Miami, Florida.
    Dante B. Fascell Congressional Papers
University of Texas at Austin, Benson Latin American Collection. Austin, Texas.
    Ernesto Cardenal Papers
    Pablo Antonio Cuadra Papers
Woodrow Wilson Center History and Public Policy Program Digital Archive.
World Bank Group Digital Archives. Washington, DC.

Newspapers and Periodicals

Akwesasne Notes
Barricada
Cambio Político
Commentary
Confidencial
El Ex-Becario Nicaragüense
El Nuevo Diario
El Tiempo
FRIDE Comment
International Business Times
La Prensa
Los Angeles Times
Mother Jones
NACLA Report
New Republic
New York Times
New Yorker
Nuevo Amanecer Cultural
Oikos Semanario
Radio La Primerisima

resistencia
Revista Envío
Semana Comica
Semanario
Revista Conservadora
Washington Post
Wrecking and Salvage Journal

Works of Fiction

Aguirre, Erick, *Un sol sobre Managua*. Managua: HISPAMER, 1998.

Bard, Samuel A. *Waikna; or, Adventures on the Mosquito Shore*. London: Sampson Low, 1855.

Belli, Gioconda *Waslala, memorial del futuro: la búsqueda de una civilización perdida*. Barcelona: Seix Barral, 2006.

Cardenal, Ernesto, *El estrecho dudoso*. Managua: Nicarao, 1991.

Chamorro Cardenal, Pedro Joaquín, *El enigma de las alemanas*. Managua: El Pez y la Serpiente, 1977.

———. *Richter 7*. Managua: Ediciones El Pez y la Serpiente, 1976.

Galich, Franz, *Managua, salsa city: ¡Devórame otra vez!* El Dorado, Panama: Editoria Géminis, 2000.

Mayorga, Francisco, *El filatelista*. Managua: Ediciones Albertus, 2014.

Ramírez, Sergio, *De tropeles y tropelías*. Managua: Editorial El Pez y la Serpiente, 1972.

———. *¿Te dió miedo la sangre?* Havana: Casa de las Américas, 1982.

Essays, Letters, Memoirs, Testimonios, Speeches

Aguirre, Erick. *La espuma sucia del río: sandinismo y transición política en Nicaragua*. Managua: CIRA, 2001.

Baker, James. *The Politics of Diplomacy: Revolution, War, and Peace, 1989–1992*. New York: Putnam, 1995.

Baltodano M., Mónica. *Memorias de la lucha sandinista*. Managua: Instituto de Historia de Nicaragua y Centroamérica de la Universidad Centroaméricana, IHNCA-UCA, 2010.

Barrios de Chamorro, Violeta. *Dreams of the Heart*. New York: Simon & Schuster, 1996.

Berle, Beatrice Bishop, and Travis Beale Jacobs, eds. *Navigating the Rapids: From the Papers of Adolf A. Berle*. New York: Harcourt, 1973.

Cabezas, Omar. *La montaña es algo más que una inmensa estepa verde*. Managua: Anamá Ediciones, 2007.

Cameron, Bruce P. *My Life in the Time of the Contras*. Albuquerque: University of New Mexico, 2007.

Cardenal, Ernesto. *In Cuba*. New York, New Directions, 1974.

———. *La revolución perdida: memorias III*. Madrid: Trotta, 2004.

———. *Las ínsulas extrañas: memorias II*. Mexico City: Fondo de Cultura Económica, 2012.

Cardenal, Fernando. *Sacerdote en la revolución: memorias.* Managua: Anamá Ediciones, 2008.

Castro, Fidel. *Second Declaration of Havana.* Havana: Impr. Nacional, 1962.

Chamorro Cardenal, Jaime. *La Prensa: The Republic of Paper.* New York: Freedom House, 1988.

Chamorro, Pedro Joaquín. *Diario Político.* Managua: Editorial Nueva Nicaragua, 1990.

———. *La patria de Pedro: el pensamiento nicaragüense de Pedro Joaquín Chamorro.* Managua: La Prensa, 1981.

Christopher, Warren. *In the Stream of History: Shaping Foreign Policy for a New Era.* Stanford, CA: Stanford University Press, 1998.

Clarridge, Duane R. *A Spy for All Seasons: My Life in the CIA.* New York: Scribner, 2014.

Coronel Kautz, Ricardo. *El espíritu de mis padres: notas autobiográficas.* Managua: Ediciones Graphic, 2016.

Coronel Urtecho, José. *Conversación con Carlos.* Managua: Editorial Vanguardia, 1986.

———. *Reflexiones sobre la historia de Nicaragua: de la colonia a la independencia.* Managua: Fundación Vida, 2001.

———. *Tres conferencias a la empresa privada.* Managua: Ediciones El Pez y La Serpiente, 1974.

Council for Inter-American Security, *A New Inter-American Policy for the Eighties.* Washington, DC: Council for Inter-American Security, 1980.

Cruz, Arturo J. *Crónicas de un disidente.* Managua: Lea Grupo Editorial, 2010.

Cruz Jr., Arturo. *Memoirs of a Counterrevolutionary.* New York: Doubleday, 1989.

Cruz, Ernesto. *INCAE: los años formativos.* Managua: Editorial Hispamer, 2017.

Cuadra, Pablo Antonio. *Breviario imperial.* Madrid: Cultura Española, 1940.

———. *El hombre: un dios en exilio.* Managua: Fundación Vida, 2002.

———. *El nicaragüense.* Managua: Editorial Hispamer, 2007.

———. *Ensayos I.* Managua: Fundación Vida, 2003.

———. *Entre la cruz y la espada.* Madrid, Instituto de Estudios Políticos, 1946.

———. *Hacia la cruz del sur.* Buenos Aires: Comisión Argentina de Publicaciones e Intercambio, 1938.

———. *Otro rapto de Europa: notas de un viaje.* San José, Costa Rica: Libro Libre, 1986.

Dunbar Ortiz, Roxanne. *Blood on the Border: A Memoir of the Contra War.* Cambridge, MA: South End Press, 2005.

Guido, Clemente. *Noches de tortura: consejo de guerra de 1956.* Managua, 1965.

Hassan, Moisés. *La Maldición del Güegüense.* Managua: PAVSA, 2009.

Lacayo Oyanguren, Antonio. *La difícil transición Nicaragüense: en el gobierno con Doña Violeta.* Managua: Fundación Uno, 2005.

López Portillo, José. *Mis tiempos: biografía y testimonio político.* Mexico City: Fernández, 1988.

Martínez Cuenca, Alejandro. *Sandinista Economics in Practice: An Insider's Critical Reflections.* Boston: South End Press, 1992.

Means, Russell. *Where White Men Fear to Tread: The Autobiography of Russell Means.* New York: St. Martin's Griffin, 1995.

Moynihan, Daniel P., and Steven R. Weisman. *Daniel Patrick Moynihan: A Portrait in Letters of an American Visionary.* New York: Public Affairs, 2010.

Nietschmann, Bernard. *Caribbean Edge: The Coming of Modern Times to Isolated People and Wildlife.* Indianapolis: Bobbs-Merrill, 1979.

Pezzullo, Lawrence. *At the Fall of Somoza*. Pittsburgh: University of Pittsburgh Press, 1993.

Ramírez, Sergio. *Adiós Muchachos: A Memoir of the Sandinista Revolution*. Durham, NC: Duke University Press, 2012.

———. *Confesión de amor*. Managua: Ediciones Nicarao, 1991.

Reyes, Reynaldo, and J. K. Wilson. *Rafaga: The Life Story of a Nicaraguan Miskito Comandante*. Norman: University of Oklahoma, 1992.

Sandoval, Jesse, ed. *From the Monastery to the World: The Letters of Thomas Merton and Ernesto Cardenal*. Berkeley: Counterpoint, 2018.

Vegas-Latapie, Eugenio. *Memorias políticas: el suicidio de la monarquía y la segunda república*. Barcelona: Planeta, 1983.

White, Steven F. *Culture & Politics in Nicaragua: Testimonies of Poets and Writers*. New York: Lumen Books, 1986.

Government Documents, NGO Reports, Conference Proceedings

A Decade of Development: A Report on the Eighth National Conference on International Economic and Social Development. Washington, DC: USAID, 1961.

Academia de Ciencias de Nicaragua. *El canal oceánico por Nicaragua*. Managua: Serie Ciencia, Técnica y Sociedad, 2014.

Bandow, Doug, ed. *U.S. Aid to the Developing World: A Free Market Agenda*. Washington, DC: Heritage Foundation, 1985.

Bartolome, Miguel Alberto. *Declaration of Barbados*. Copenhagen: International Work Group for Indigenous Affairs, 1971.

Centro de Investigaciones y Documentación de la Costa Atlántica. *Ethnic Groups and the Nation State: The Case of the Atlantic Coast in Nicaragua*. Stockholm: University of Stockholm, 1987.

Clapp, Cynthia. *Significant Cases in Integrated Rural Development Experience*. Washington, DC: USAID, 1978.

Commission on United States-Latin American Relations. *The Americas in a Changing World: A Report of the Commission on United States-Latin American Relations*. New York: Quadrangle/New York Times, 1975.

Executive Seminar on Social and Civic Development: Title IX of the United States Foreign Assistance Act, Antigua, Guatemala, June 1–6, 1969. Washington, DC: Brookings Institution 1969.

Foreign Relations of the United States, 1969–1976. Vol. I, *Foundations of Foreign Policy, 1969–1972*. Washington, DC: GPO, 2005.

———. Vol. IV, *Vietnam, 1969–1976*. Washington, DC: GPO, 2006.

———. Vol. XII, *Foreign Relations 1961–1963—American Republics*. Washington, DC: GPO, 1996.

———. Vol. XXXI, *Foreign Relations 1964–1968—South and Central America; Mexico*. Washington, DC: GPO, 2004.

———. Vol. E–10, *Documents on American Republics, 1969–1972*. Washington, DC: GPO, 2009.

————. Vol. E–15, part 2, *Documents on Western Europe, 1973–1976.* Washington, DC: GPO, 2014.

Gobierno de México. *Las razones y las obras: gobierno de Miguel de la Madrid: crónica del sexenio 1982–1988.* Mexico City: Fondo de Cultura Económica, 1985.

Gobierno de Nicaragua. *Concertación Económica y Social, Fase II.* Managua, 1991.

Hapgood, David, ed. *The Role of Popular Participation in Development.* Cambridge, MA: MIT Press, 1969.

Heard, John. *Fundación Nicaragüense de Desarrollo (FUNDE), An Evaluation of Experience, Capability, and Potential, June 1980.* Washington, DC: USAID, 1980.

Horkan-Lopez, Kathleen. "USAID Support for Development Finance Institutions in Central America." Washington, DC: USAID, September 29, 1998.

Horn, Abigail. *Lessons Learned: Accountability, Transparency, and Hurricane Mitch.* Washington, DC: USAID, 2001.

Implementing Programs of Human Development. Washington, DC: World Bank, 1980.

Informe nacional de Nicaragua: reunión regional Caracas, Venezuela, presentado por vice ministro de planificación urbana Iván Osorio Peters. Managua: Vice Ministerio de Planificacion Urbana, 1976.

Institución Nacional Tecnológico. *La microempresa en Nicaragua y su potencial de desarrollo.* Managua: OIT / INATEC, 1992.

Instituto Centroamericano de Administración de Empresas. *Competitiveness in Central America: Preparing Companies for Globalization.* San José, Costa Rica: Latin American Center for Competitiveness and Sustainable Development, 1996.

————. *Estudio del sector privado de Centro América y Panamá.* USAID, November 1981.

Inter-American Economic and Social Council. *The Charter of Punta del Este.* Washington, DC: Agency for International Development, 1961.

Joeckes, Susan, and Roxana Moayedi. *Women and Export Manufacturing: A Review of the Issues and AID Policy.* Washington, DC: USAID, 1987.

John F. Kennedy: Containing the Public Messages, Speeches, and Statements of the President. Washington, DC: GPO, 1962.

Mann, Lawrence. *Evaluation of Managua Reconstruction Planning.* Washington, DC: USAID, 1975.

Mann, Lawrence, and Wilhelm von Moltke. *Report on a Process of Planning and Urban Design for the Reconstruction and Development of Managua.* Cambridge, MA: Harvard University Graduate School of Design, 1973.

Moscoso, Teodoro. *The Alliance for Progress: Its Program and Goals.* Washington, DC: USAID, 1963.

Nathan Associates, Inc. *Assistance to Resource Institutions for Enterprise Support: Mainstreaming Women in Enterprise Development.* Washington, DC: USAID, 1990.

New Partnerships Working Group, *New Partnerships in the Americas: The Spirit of Rio* Washington, DC: USAID, 1994.

Nicaragua, Ministerio de Acción Social. *Propuesta Política Nacional de Población.* Managua: MAS-FNUAP, 1994.

Pfeiffer, Jack B. *Official History of the Bay of Pigs Operation,* vol. II, *Participation in the Conduct of Foreign Policy.* Washington, DC: Central Intelligence Agency, 1979.

Pillsbury, Michael. *A.I.D. and Economic Policy Reform: Origins and Case Studies.* Washington, DC: USAID, 1993.

President's Task Force on International Private Enterprise. *Report to the President.* Washington, DC: GPO, 1984.

Ríos, Martha Regina. *Concertación de actores locales para el desarrollo integral del municipio de Totogalpa; sistematización de experiencia, 2002–2004.* Managua: Red Nicaragüense por la Democracia y Desarrollo Local, 2005.

Rockefeller, Nelson A. *The Rockefeller Report on the Americas.* Chicago: Quadrangle Books, 1969.

Sánchez S., Felipe, and Eduardo Terán G. *Sobre la descentralización.* Managua: INCAE, 1973.

Serrano Caldera, Alejandro. *La Nicaragua posible: por un proyecto nacional: 4 Foro de Política Nacional, realizado en la Universidad el 13 y 14 de marzo de 1992.* Managua: Univ. Nacional Autónoma de Nicaragua (UNAN), 1992.

Solórzano, Mario Arce, Catalina Ruiz Muñoz, and Jimmy Membreño Rivera. *Nicaragua, un destino turístico: breve historia del turismo y ecoturismo nicaragüense, 1936–2003.* Managua: Ediciones Centro de Investigaciones Turísticas Nicaragüenses, 2004.

Torres, F. "El Concepto de Sostenibilidad en el Desarrollo Agropecuario," in *Seminario Agricultura Sostenible en las Laderas Centroamericanas.* San José, Costa Rica: Instituto Interamericano de Cooperación para la Agricultura, 1991.

US Agency for International Development. *Activity Design Document (redacted version): SO2, IR 2.2.* Washington, DC: USAID, 2005.

———. *AID Congressional Presentation Fiscal Year 1983, Annex III, Latin America and the Caribbean.* Washington, DC: USAID, 1982.

———. *A.I.D. Loan No. 524-L-028—Program Loan.* Washington, DC: USAID, 1977.

———. *Audit of the Nicaragua Assistance Program Funded by Public Law 101–302 and Fiscal Year 1991 Appropriations as of September 30, 1991.* Washington, DC: USAID, 1992.

———. *Case Report: Nicaragua—Earthquake, December 1972.* Washington, DC: USAID, 1973.

———. *Community Development—Nicaragua.* Washington, DC: USAID, 1974.

———. *Development Assistance Program, Central America, Book 5, Chapter X—Nicaragua.* Washington, DC: USAID, 1973.

———. *Displaced Children and Orphans in Nicaragua.* Washington, DC: USAID, 1993.

———. *Implementation of "New Directions" in Development Assistance: Report to the Committee on International Relations on Implementation of Legislative Reforms in the Foreign Assistance Act of 1973.* Washington, DC: GPO, 1975.

———. *Land-Use Programming and Control for Intermediate-size Cities in the Developing Areas—An Experimental Project in Leon, Nicaragua, by PADCO, Inc.* Washington, DC: USAID, 1976.

———. *Nicaragua Project Paper: Natural Resources Management.* Washington, DC: USAID, 1991.

———. *Nicaragua Project Paper: Strengthening Democratic Institutions.* Washington, DC: USAID, 1991.

———. *Nicaragua—Rural Development Sector Loan.* Washington, DC: USAID, 1975.

———. *Nicaragua—Rural Education Development Program*. Washington, DC: USAID, 1977.

———. *Nicaragua Urban Sector Loan—Managua. Reconstruction*. Washington, DC: USAID, 1974.

———. *Proposal and Recommendations for the Review of the Development Loan Committee, Nicaragua—Program Loan, 1-31-73*. Washington, DC: USAID, 1973.

———. *PVO Child Survival Grants Program*. Washington, DC: USAID, 1992.

———. *Theory and Practice in Sustainability and Sustainable Development*. Washington, DC: USAID, 1994.

———. *U.S. Overseas Loans and Grants: Obligations and Loan Authorizations, July 1, 1945–September 30, 2015*. Washington, DC: USAID, 2015.

———. *Women in Development Technical Assistance Project, Economic Opportunities and Labor Conditions for Women: Perspectives from Latin America: Guatemala, El Salvador, Honduras*. Washington, DC: USAID, 2003.

US Agency for International Development/El Salvador. *The Caribbean Basin Initiative in El Salvador: A Plan for Private Sector Development*. San Salvador: USAID, July 1982.

US Agency for International Development/Nicaragua. *Action Plan FY 95–FY 96*. Washington, DC: USAID, 1994.

———. *Annual Budget Submission*. Washington, DC: USAID, 1993.

———. *Country Development and Strategy Statement*. Washington, DC: USAID, 1991.

———. *Semi-annual Project Status Report April 1, 1994–September 30, 1994*. Washington, DC: USAID, 1994.

US Congress House of Representatives Committee on Appropriations, Subcommittee on Foreign Operations and Related Agencies. *Foreign Assistance and Related Agencies Appropriations for 1975*, 93rd Cong., 2nd sess., 1974.

US Congress House of Representatives Committee on Foreign Affairs, Subcommittee on Inter-American Affairs. *The Caribbean Basin Policy*, 97th Cong., 1st sess., July 14, 21, and 28, 1981.

———. *Foreign Assistance Act of 1973*. Washington, DC: GPO, 1973.

US Congress House of Representatives Committee on Foreign Affairs, Subcommittee on Western Hemisphere Affairs, *Democracy and Reconciliation in Nicaragua: A Critical Assessment*, 103rd Cong., February 4, 1993.

US Congress House of Representatives Committee on International Relations, Subcommittee on International Development. *Rethinking United States Foreign Policy toward the Developing World: Nicaragua*, 95th Cong., 1st sess., October 18, 1977.

US Congress House of Representatives Committee on International Relations, Subcommittee on International Organizations. *Foreign Assistance Legislation for Fiscal Year 1979 (Part 4)*, 95th Cong., March 7, 1978.

———. *Human Rights in Nicaragua, Guatemala, and El Salvador: Implications for US Policy*, 94th Cong., 2nd sess., June 8 and 9, 1976, appendix 7.

US Congress House of Representatives Committee on International Relations, Subcommittee on International Resources, Food, and Energy. *Managing International Disasters—Guatemala: Hearings and Markup on H.R. 12046*, 94th Cong., 2nd sess., February 18 and March 4, 1976.

US Congress House of Representatives Committee on International Relations, Subcommittee on the Western Hemisphere. *An Evaluation of Democracy in Nicaragua*, 104th Cong., 1st sess., November 8, 1995.

———. *Latin America and the United States in the 1990's*, 101st Cong., 1st sess., March 1, 1989.

US Congress House of Representatives Subcommittee of the Committee on Appropriations, *Foreign Assistance and Related Agencies Appropriations for 1978, Part 3, Special Hearings of Public Witnesses*, 95th Cong., 1st sess., 1977.

US Congress Senate Committee on Foreign Relations. *Nicaragua Today: A Republican Staff Report to the Committee on Foreign Relations*. Washington, DC: GPO, 1992.

———. *Nomination of Warren M. Christopher to Be Secretary of State*, 103rd Cong., January 13th and 14th, 1993.

US Congress Senate Committee on Foreign Relations, Subcommittee on Western Hemisphere Affairs. *Latin America*, 95th Cong., October 4, 1978.

US Department of State. *From Revolution to Repression: Human Rights in Nicaragua under the Sandinistas*. Washington, DC: GPO, 1986.

US Government Accountability Office. *Aid to Nicaragua: U.S. Assistance Supports Economic and Social Development*. Washington DC: GPO, 1992.

Wardlaw, Andrew B. "The Operations of the Central American Common Market." Washington, DC: USAID, 1966.

World Commission on Environment and Development. *Our Common Future*. Oxford: Oxford University Press, 1987.

Secondary Sources

Acosta, Maria Luisa. "Encroaching upon Indigenous Land: Nicaragua and the 'Dry Canal.'" In *Indigenous Peoples: Resource Management and Global Rights*, ed. Svein Jentoft, Henry Minde, and Ragnar Nilsen. Delft: Eburon, 2003.

Aguirre, Eric. *Subversión de la Memoria: Tendencias en la Narrativa Centroamericana de Postguerra*. Managua: Centro Nicaragüense de Escritores, 2005.

Alba, Victor. *Alliance without Allies: The Mythology of Progress in Latin America*. New York: Praeger, 1966.

Allcock, Thomas Tunstall. "Becoming 'Mr. Latin America': Thomas C. Mann Reconsidered." *Diplomatic History* 38 (December 2014): 1017–1045.

Alvarez Montálvan, Emilio. *Cultura política nicaragüense*. Managua: HISPAMER, 2000.

Ameringer, Charles D. *The Caribbean Legion: Patriots, Politicians, Soldiers of Fortune, 1946–1950*. University Park: Pennsylvania State University Press, 1996.

———. *The Democratic Left in Exile: The Antidictatorial Struggle in the Caribbean, 1945–1959*. Coral Gables, FL: University of Miami Press, 1974.

———. *Don Pepe: A Political Biography of José Figueres of Costa Rica*. Albuquerque: University of New Mexico Press, 1978.

Anderson, Perry. *The Origins of Postmodernity*. London: Verso, 1998.

Annis, Sheldon. *Poverty, Natural Resources, and Public Policy in Central America*. New Brunswick, NJ: Transaction Publishers, 1992.

Arellano, Jorge Eduardo. *Pablo Antonio Cuadra: Aproximaciones a su Vida y Obra*. Managua: Ministerio de Educación, 1994.

Assmann, Hugo, ed. *El juego de los reformismos: frente a la revolución en Centroamérica*. San José, Costa Rica: Departamento Ecuménico de Investigaciones, 1981.

Babb, Florence. *After Revolution: Mapping Gender and Cultural Politics in Neoliberal Nicaragua*. Austin: University of Texas Press, 2001.

Bakan, Abigail B. David Cox, and Colin Leys, eds. *Imperial Power and Regional Trade: The Caribbean Basin Initiative*. Waterloo, Ontario: Wilfrid Laurier University Press, 1993.

Baracco, Luciano. "From Developmentalism to Autonomy: The Sandinista Revolution and the Atlantic Coast of Nicaragua." In *National Integration and Contested Autonomy: The Caribbean Coast of Nicaragua*, ed. Luciano Baracco. New York: Algora, 2011.

———. *Nicaragua: The Imagining of a Nation*. New York: Algora, 2005.

———. "The Nicaraguan Literacy Crusade Revisited: The Teaching of Literacy as a Nation-Building Project." *Bulletin of Latin American Research* 23, no. 3 (July 2004): 339–354.

Bauer, P. T. *Equality, the Third World, and Economic Delusion*. Cambridge, MA: Harvard University, 1981.

Becker, Marc. *Indians and Leftists in the Making of Ecuador's Modern Indigenous Movements*. Durham, NC: Duke University Press, 2008.

Bendaña, Alejandro. "The Foreign Policy of the Revolution." In *Nicaragua in Revolution*, ed. Thomas Walker. New York: Praeger, 1982.

———. *Una tragedia campesina: testimonios de la resistencia*. Managua: Editora de Arte, 1991.

Benjamin, Walter. "Central Park," trans. Lloyd Spenser and Mark Harrington. *New German Critique* 34 (Winter 1985).

Berger, Mark T. *Under Northern Eyes: Latin American Studies and U.S. Hegemony in the Americas, 1898–1990*. Bloomington: Indiana University Press, 1995.

Bickford-Smith, Vivian. "Introduction: The Case for Studying Cities and Nationalisms." *Journal of Urban History* 38 (2012), 855.

Biddle, William Jesse, and John D. Stephens, "Dependent Development and Foreign Policy: The Case of Jamaica." *International Studies Quarterly* 33, no. 4 (December 1989): 411–434.

Blandón, Jesus Miguel. *Carlos Fonseca, sacrificado: ¿quienes le enviaron a la muerte?* Managua: Segovia Ediciones Latinoamericanas, 2013.

Bonner, Raymond. *Weakness and Deceit: U.S. Policy and El Salvador*. New York: Times Books, 1984.

Booth, John A. *The End and the Beginning: The Nicaraguan Revolution*. Boulder, CO: Westview Press, 1982.

Bourgois, Philippe, "Class, Ethnicity, and State among the Miskitu Amerindians of Northeastern Nicaragua." *Latin American Perspectives* 8 (Spring 1981): 22–39.

Bourgois, Philippe, and Jorge Grunberg. *La mosquitia en la revolución: informe de una investigación rural en la Costa Atlántica Norte*. Managua: INRA, 1980.

Bourgois, Philippe, and Charles Hale. "The Atlantic Coast of Nicaragua." In *Sandinista Nicaragua, Part 1: Revolution, Religion, and Social Policy*, ed. Neil Snarr. Ann Arbor, MI: Pierian, 1989.

Brandt, Willy. *North-South: A Programme for Survival*. London: Pan Books, 1983.

Brown, Timothy C. *Causes of Continuing Conflict in Nicaragua: A View from the Radical Middle*. Stanford, CA: Hoover Institution, 1995.

———. *The Real Contra War: Highlander Peasant Resistance in Nicaragua*. Norman: University of Oklahoma Press, 2001.

Brown, Wendy. *Undoing the Demos: Neoliberalism's Stealth Revolution*. New York: Zone Books, 2015.

Bryan, Joe, and Denis Wood. *Weaponizing Maps: Indigenous Peoples and Counterinsurgency in the Americas*. New York: Guilford Press, 2015.

Brysk, Alison. *From Tribal Village to Global Village: Indian Rights and International Relations in Latin America*. Stanford, CA: Stanford University Press, 2000.

Brzeziński, Zbigniew. *Between Two Ages: America's Role in the Technotronic Era*. Harmondsworth: Penguin Books, 1978.

Burbach, Roger, and Orlando Núñez Soto. *Fire in the Americas: Forging a Revolutionary Agenda*. London: Verso, 1987.

Buvollen, Hans Petter. "Autonomy: Tactic and Self-Determination: The Sandinista Policy towards the Indigenous Peoples of Nicaragua." *Caribbean Quarterly* 36 (June 1990): 98–112.

Carmon, Fernando, ed. *Nicaragua: la estrategia de la victoria*. Mexico City: Nuestro Tiempo, 1980.

Carothers, Thomas. "The End of the Transition Paradigm." *Journal of Democracy* 13, no. 1140 (January 2002).

———. *In the Name of Democracy: U.S. Policy toward Latin America in the Reagan Years*. Berkeley: University of California Press, 1999.

Caryl, Christian. *Strange Rebels: 1979 and the Birth of the 21st Century*. New York: Basic Books, 2013.

Castañeda, Jorge G., and Marco A. Morales. *Leftovers: Tales of the Latin American Left*. New York: Routledge, 2008.

———. *Nicaragua: contradicciones en la revolución*. Mexico City: Tiempo Extra Editores, 1980.

———. *Utopia Unarmed: The Latin American Left after the Cold War*. New York: Knopf, 1993.

Chamorro Cardenal, Pedro Joaquín. *Los Somoza: una estirpe sangrienta*. Mexico City: Editorial Diógenes, 1979.

Chandler, David. *Resilience: The Governance of Complexity*. New York: Routledge, 2014.

Charlip, Julie. *Cultivating Coffee: The Farmers of Carazo, Nicaragua, 1880–1930*. Athens: Ohio University Press, 2003.

Chasteen, John Charles. *Born in Blood and Fire: A Concise History of Latin America*. New York: Norton, 2001.

Chávez, Daniel. *Nicaragua and the Politics of Utopia: Development and Culture in the Modern State*. Nashville, TN: Vanderbilt University, 2015.

Chodor, Tom. *Neoliberal Hegemony and the Pink Tide in Latin America: Breaking up with TINA?* New York: Palgrave, 2015.

Christian, Shirley. *Nicaragua, Revolution in the Family*. New York: Random House, 1985.

Clark, Mary Alison. "Transnational Alliances and Development Strategies: The Transition to Export-Led Growth in Costa Rica, 1983–1990." PhD diss., University of Wisconsin-Madison, 1993.

Close, David. *Nicaragua: The Chamorro Years*. Boulder, CO: Lynne Rienner Publishers, 1999.

Cohen, Lizabeth. *A Consumer's Republic: The Politics of Mass Consumption in Postwar America*. New York: Knopf, 2003.

Conroy, Michael. *Nicaragua: Profiles of the Revolutionary Public Sector*. Boulder, CO: Westview Press, 1987.

Coronel Urtecho, José. *Reflexiones sobre la Historia de Nicaragua: de la Colonia a la Independencia*. Managua: Fundación Vida, 2001.

Coulthard, Glen Sean. *Red Skin, White Masks: Rejecting the Colonial Politics of Recognition*. Minneapolis: University of Minnesota, 2014.

Criquillon, Ana. "The Nicaraguan Women's Movement: Feminist Reflections from Within." In *New Politics of Survival: Grass-roots Movements in Central America*, ed. M. Sinclair. New York: Monthly Review Press, 1995.

Cruz, Arturo J. and José Luis Velázquez. *The Hungry World: America's Cold War Battle against Hunger in Asia*. Cambridge, MA: Harvard University Press, 2013.

———. *Nicaragua, regresión en la revolución*. San José, Costa Rica: Asociación Libro Libre, 1986.

Dahl, Robert A. *Polyarchy: Participation and Opposition*. New Haven, CT: Yale University Press, 1971.

"Debate: 'The Concept of Neoliberalism Has Become an Obstacle to the Anthropological Understanding of the Twenty-First Century.'" *Journal of the Royal Anthropological Institute* 21 (2015): 911–923.

Delgado Aburto, Leonel. *Márgenes recorridos: apuntes sobre procesos culturales y literatura nicaragüense del siglo XX*. Managua: Instituto de Historia de Nicaragua y Centroamérica: Universidad Centroamericana, 2002.

Denevan, William M. "Bernard Q. Nietschmann, 1941–2000: Mr. Barney, Geographer and Humanist." *Geographical Review* 92 (January 2002): 104–109.

Díaz-Polanco, Héctor, and Kelley Swarthout. "*Neoindigenismo* and the Ethnic Question in Central America." *Latin American Perspectives* 14 (Winter 1987): 87–100.

Diederich, Bernard. *Somoza and the Legacy of US Involvement in Central America*. New York: Dutton, 1981.

Dinges, John. *Our Man in Panama: How General Noriega Used the United States and Made Millions in Drugs and Arms*. New York: Random House, 1990.

Dore, Elizabeth. *Myths of Modernity: Peonage and Patriarchy in Nicaragua*. Durham, NC: Duke University, 2006.

Dosal, Paul J. "Natural Disaster, Political Earthquake: The 1972 Destruction of Managua and the Somoza Dynasty." In *Aftershocks: Earthquakes and Popular Politics in Latin America*, ed. Jurgen Buchenau and Lymon Johnson. Albuquerque: University of New Mexico, 2009.

Dosman, Edgar J. *The Life and Times of Raúl Prebisch, 1901–1986*. Montreal: McGill, 2014.

Durham, William. *Scarcity and Survival in Central America: Ecological Origins of the Soccer War.* Stanford, CA: Stanford University Press, 1979.

Eisenhower, Milton. *The Wine Is Bitter: The United States and Latin America.* Garden City, NY: Doubleday, 1963.

Engerman, David. *Modernization from the Other Shore: American Intellectuals and the Romance of Russian Development.* Cambridge, MA: Harvard University Press, 2003.

Escobar, Arturo. *Territories of Difference: Place, Movement, Life, Redes.* Durham, NC: Duke University Press, 2008.

Esgueva Gómez, Antonio. *Elecciones, reelecciones y conflictos en Nicaragua, 1821–1963* Managua: IHNCA, 2011.

Everingham, Mark. "Agricultural Property Rights and Political Change in Nicaragua." *Latin American Politics and Society* 43, no. 3 (Autumn 2001): 61–93.

———. *Revolution and the Multiclass Coalition in Nicaragua.* Pittsburgh: University of Pittsburgh Press, 1996.

Farhi, Farideh. *States and Urban-based Revolutions: Iran and Nicaragua.* Urbana: University of Illinois Press, 1990.

Farrell, Nell. *Nicaragua before Now: Factory Work, Farming, and Fishing in a Low-Wage Global Economy.* Albuquerque: University of New Mexico Press, 2010.

Feinberg, Richard, and Daniel Kurtz-Phelan. "Nicaragua between 'Caudillismo' and Modernity: The Sandinistas Redux?" *World Policy Journal* 23 (Summer 2006): 76–84.

Ferguson, James. *The Anti-Politics Machine: "Development," Depolitization, and Bureaucratic Power in Lesotho.* Cambridge: Cambridge University Press, 1994.

Ferrero Blanco, María Dolores. *La Nicaragua de los Somoza: 1936–1979.* Huelva, Spain: Universidad de Huelva, 2010.

Field, Thomas C., Jr. *From Development to Dictatorship: Bolivia and the Alliance for Progress in the Kennedy Era* Ithaca, NY: Cornell, 2018.

Fitzgerald, E. V. K. "An Evaluation of the Economic Costs to Nicaragua of U.S. Aggression: 1980–1984." In Rose Spalding, ed., *The Political Economy of Revolutionary Nicaragua.* Boston: Allen & Unwin, 1987.

Fleet, Michael. *The Rise and Fall of Chilean Christian Democracy.* Princeton, NJ: Princeton, 1985.

Fonseca, Ana Mónica, "From the Iberian Peninsula to Latin America: The Socialist International's Initiatives in the First Years of Brandt's Presidency." In Bernd Rother and Klaus Larres, eds., *Willy Brandt and International Relations: Europe, the USA, and Latin America, 1974–1992.* New York: Bloomsbury Academic, 2019.

Foucault, Michel. *The Birth of Biopolitics: Lectures at the College de France, 1978–79.* New York: Palgrave Macmillan, 2008.

———. *The Order of Things: An Archaeology of the Human Sciences.* New York: Pantheon Books, 1971.

Frank, Andre Gunder. *Reflections on the World Economic Crisis.* New York: Monthly Review, 1981.

Fraser, Nancy. "Feminism, Capitalism and the Cunning of History." *New Left Review* 56 (March–April 2009): 97–117.

Freeman, James. "From the Little Tree, Half a Block toward the Lake: Popular Geography and Symbolic Discontent in Post-Sandinista Managua." *Antipode* 42, no. 2 (2010): 336–373.

Frühling, Pierre, Miguel González, and Hans Petter Buvollen. *Etnicidad y Nación: El desarrollo de la autonomía de la Costa Atlántica de Nicaragua 1987–2007*. Guatemala City: F&G Editores, 2007.

Gabbert, Wolfgang. "The Kingdom of Mosquitia and the Mosquito Reservation." In *National Integration and Contested Autonomy*, ed. Luciano Baracco. New York: Algora, 2011.

Gambone, Michael. *Capturing the Revolution: The United States, Central America, and Nicaragua, 1961–1972*. Westport, CT: Praeger, 2001.

Garrard-Burnett, Virginia, Mark A. Lawrence, and Julio Moreno. *Beyond the Eagle's Shadow: New Histories of Latin America's Cold War*. Albuquerque: University of New Mexico Press, 2013.

Gilbert, Dennis. *Sandinistas: The Party and the Revolution*. New York: Blackwell, 1988.

Gilman, Nils. *Mandarins of the Future: Modernization Theory in Cold War America*. Baltimore: Johns Hopkins University Press, 2003.

Gobat, Michel. *Confronting the American Dream: Nicaragua under U.S. Imperial Rule*. Durham, NC: Duke University Press, 2005.

———. *Empire by Invitation: William Walker and Manifest Destiny in Central America*. Cambridge, MA: Harvard University Press, 2018.

Goett, Jennifer. *Black Autonomy: Race, Gender, and Afro-Nicaraguan Activism*. Stanford, CA: Stanford University Press, 2017.

Gómez, Juan Pablo. *Autoridad/cuerpo/nación: batallas culturales en Nicaragua 1930–1943* Managua: IHNCA, 2015.

González, Felipe. "The Experience of the Inter-American Human Rights System." *Victoria University of Wellington Law Review* 40, no. 1 (June 2009): 103–125.

Gould, Jeffrey. *To Die in This Way: Nicaraguan Indians and the Myth of Mestizaje, 1880–1965*. Durham, NC: Duke University, 1998.

———. *To Lead as Equals: Rural Protest and Political Consciousness in Chinandega, Nicaragua, 1912–1979*. Chapel Hill: University of North Carolina Press, 1990.

———. "On the Road to "El Porvenir": Revolutionary and Counterrevolutionary Violence in El Salvador and Nicaragua." In *A Century of Revolution: Insurgent and Counterinsurgent Violence during Latin America's Long Cold War*, ed. Gilbert M. Joseph and Greg Grandin. Durham, NC: Duke University, 2010.

Grabendorff, Wolf. "International Support for Democracy in Contemporary Latin America: The Role of the Party Internationals." In *The International Dimensions of Democratization: Europe and the Americas*, ed. Laurence Whitehead. New York: Oxford University Press, 2001.

Grandin, Greg. *Empire's Workshop: Latin America, the United States, and the Rise of the New Imperialism*. New York: Metropolitan Books, 2006.

———. "Your Americanism and Mine: Americanism and Anti-Americanism in the Americas." *American Historical Review* 111, no. 4 (1 October 2006): 1042–1066.

Grandin, Greg, and Gilbert Joseph, eds. *A Century of Revolution: Insurgent and Counterinsurgent Violence during Latin America's Long Cold War.* Durham, NC: Duke University, 2010.

Greenberg, Amy S. *Manifest Manhood and the Antebellum American Empire.* Cambridge: Cambridge University Press, 2005.

Grunwald, Joseph, Michael Wionczek, and Martin Conroy, eds. *Latin American Integration and U.S. Policy.* Washington, DC: Brookings Institution, 1972.

Guardia, Gloria. *Pablo Antonio Cuadra, Poeta y Pensador Cristiano.* San José, Costa Rica: Promesa, 2007.

Guerra, Lillian. *Visions of Power in Cuba: Revolution, Redemption, and Resistance, 1959–1971.* Chapel Hill: University of North Carolina, 2014.

Guilhot, Nicolas. *The Democracy Makers: Human Rights and the Politics of Global Order.* New York: Columbia University Press, 2005.

Guillermoprieto, Alma. *The Heart that Bleeds: Latin America Now.* New York: Knopf, 1994.

Haas, J. E., R. W. Kates, and M. J. Bowden, eds. *Reconstruction Following Disaster.* Cambridge, MA: MIT Press, 1977.

Hale, Charles R. "Does Multiculturalism Menace? Governance, Cultural Rights and the Politics of Identity in Guatemala." *Journal of Latin American Studies* 34, no. 3 (August 2002): 485–524.

———. *Resistance and Contradiction: Miskitu Indians and the Nicaraguan State, 1894–1987.* Stanford, CA: Stanford University Press, 1994.

———. "'Wan Tasbaya Dukiara': Contested Notions of Land Rights in Miskitu History." In *Remapping Memory: The Politics of TimeSpace,* ed. Jonathan Boyarin. Minneapolis: University of Minnesota Press, 1994.

Hansen, Roger D. *Central America: Regional Integration and Economic Development.* Washington, DC: National Planning Association, 1967.

Harmer, Tanya. *Allende's Chile and the Inter-American Cold War.* Chapel Hill: University of North Carolina Press, 2011.

Harrington, Michael. *The Long-Distance Runner: An Autobiography.* New York: Paragon House, 1991.

Hartmann, Hauke. "US Human Rights Policy under Carter and Reagan, 1977–1981." *Human Rights Quarterly* 23 (May 2001): 402–430.

Harvey, David. *A Brief History of Neoliberalism.* Oxford: Oxford University Press, 2005.

Heilbroner, Robert L. *The Great Ascent: The Struggle for Economic Development in Our Time.* New York: Harper & Row, 1963.

Helms, Mary. *Asang: Adaptations to Culture Contact in a Miskito Community.* Gainesville: University of Florida Press, 1971.

Henighan, Stephen. *Sandino's Nation: Ernesto Cardenal and Sergio Ramírez Writing Nicaragua, 1940–2012.* Montreal: McGill-Queen's University Press, 2016.

Hinton, Elizabeth. *From the War on Poverty to the War on Crime: The Making of Mass Incarceration in America.* Cambridge, MA: Harvard University, 2016.

Hodge, Joseph Morgan. "Writing the History of Development (Part 1: The First Wave)." *Humanity* 6, no. 3 (Winter 2015).

Honey, Martha. *Hostile Acts: U.S. Policy in Costa Rica in the 1980s.* Gainesville: University of Florida, 1994.

Horton, Lynn. *Peasants in Arms: War and Peace in the Mountains of Nicaragua.* Athens: Ohio University Center for International Studies, 1998.

Hunt, Michael H. *Ideology and U.S. Foreign Policy.* New Haven: Yale University Press, 1987.

Huntington, Samuel P. "The Bases of Accommodation." *Foreign Affairs* (July 1968).

Iber, Patrick. *Neither Peace nor Freedom: The Cultural Cold War in Latin America.* Cambridge, MA: Harvard University Press, 2015.

Iber, Patrick J. "'Who Will Impose Democracy?': Sacha Volman and the Contradictions of CIA Support for the Anticommunist Left in Latin America." *Diplomatic History* 37, no. 5 (November 2013): 995–1028.

Immerwahr, Daniel. *Thinking Small: The United States and the Lure of Community Development.* Cambridge, MA: Harvard University Press, 2015.

Incer Barquero, Jaime, and Jaime Wheelock Román. *Desastres naturales de Nicaragua: guía para conocerlos y prevenirlos.* Managua: HISPAMER, 2000.

Ingersoll, Jasper. "Anthropologists and the Agency for International Development (A.I.D.): An Old Hate Relationship and a New Love Affair," in "Anthropology and the Public Sector," special issue, *Anthropological Quarterly* 50, no. 4 (October 1977): 199–203.

Isbester, Katherine. "Nicaragua 1996–2001: Sex, Corruption, and Other Natural Disasters." *International Journal* 56 (Autumn 2001): 632–648.

Jameson, Fredric. *The Political Unconscious: Narrative as a Socially Symbolic Act.* Ithaca, NY: Cornell University Press, 1981.

Jamieson, Mark. "Territorial Demarcation and Indigenous Rights in Eastern Nicaragua: The Case of Kakabila." In *National Integration and Contested Autonomy: The Caribbean Coast of Nicaragua,* ed. Luciano Baracco. New York: Algora, 2011.

Jarquín Calderón, Edmundo. *Pedro Joaquín: ¡juega!* Managua: Anama Ediciones Centroamericanas, 1998.

Jenkins Molieri, Jorge. *El desafío indígena en Nicaragua: el caso de los Mískitos.* Mexico City: Editorial Katún, 1986.

Johnson, Samuel. *A Dictionary of the English Language: In Which the Words Are Deduced from Their Originals: to Which Are Prefixed a History of the Language and an English Grammar: Stereotyped Verbatim from the Last Folio Edition Corrected by the Doctor.* London: Robinson, 1830.

Jones, Daniel Stedman. *Masters of the Universe: Hayek, Friedman, and the Birth of Neoliberal Politics.* Princeton, NJ: Princeton University Press, 2012.

Joseph, Gilbert, Catherine Legrand, and Ricardo Salvatore, eds. *Close Encounters of Empire: Writing the Cultural History of U.S.-Latin American Relations.* Durham, NC: Duke University Press, 1998.

Kagan, Robert. *A Twilight Struggle: American Power and Nicaragua, 1977–1990.* New York: Free Press, 1994.

Kampwirth, Karen. *Feminism and the Legacy of Revolution: Nicaragua, El Salvador, Chiapas.* Athens: Ohio University, 2004.

————. *Latin America's New Left and the Politics of Gender: Lessons from Nicaragua*. New York: Springer, 2011.

————. "The Mother of the Nicaraguans: Doña Violeta and the UNO's Gender Agenda," in "Women in Latin America, Part 2," *Latin American Perspectives* 23: (Winter 1996): 67–86.

Kates, R., J. E. Haas, D. J. Amaral, R. A. Olson, R. Ramos, and R. Olson. "Human Impact of the Managua Earthquake." *Science* 182 (December 7, 1973).

Kaul, Inge, et al., eds. *The New Public Finance: Responding to Global Challenges*. London: Oxford University Press, 2005.

Kay, Cristóbal. *Latin American Theories of Development and Underdevelopment*. New York: Routledge, 1989.

Keys, Barbara J. *Reclaiming American Virtue: The Human Rights Revolution of the 1970s*. Cambridge, MA: Harvard University Press, 2014.

Kinzer, Stephen. *Blood of Brothers: Life and War in Nicaragua*. New York: Putnam, 1991.

Kirkendall, Andrew J. *Paulo Freire and the Cold War Politics of Literacy*. Chapel Hill: University of North Carolina Press, 2010.

Kirkpatrick, Jeane. *Dictatorships and Double Standards: Rationalism and Reason in Politics*. New York: Simon and Schuster, 1982.

Kornbluh, Peter. "The Covert War." In *Reagan versus the Sandinistas: The Undeclared War on Nicaragua*, ed. Thomas W. Walker. Boulder, CO: Westview Press, 1987.

Kreimer, Alcira. "Post-Disaster Reconstruction Planning: The Cases of Nicaragua and Guatemala." *Mass Emergencies* 3 (1978): 23–40.

Krippner, Greta. *Capitalizing on Crisis: The Political Origins of the Rise of Finance*. Cambridge, MA: Harvard University Press, 2012.

Kunzle, David. "Nicaragua's *La Prensa*—Capitalist Thorn in Socialist Flesh." *Media, Culture & Society* 6 (April 1984): 151–176.

Lafeber, Walter. *Inevitable Revolutions: The United States in Central America*. New York: Norton, 1983.

————. *The New Empire: An Interpretation of American Expansion*. Ithaca, NY: Cornell University Press, 1963.

Laínez, Francisco. *Terremoto '72: elites y pueblo*. Managua: Editorial Unión, 1976.

Lake, Anthony. *Somoza Falling*. Boston: Houghton Mifflin, 1989.

Lancaster, Roger. *Life Is Hard: Machismo, Danger, and the Intimacy of Power in Nicaragua*. Berkeley: University of California Press, 1992.

————. *Thanks to God and the Revolution: Popular Religion and Class Consciousness in the New Nicaragua*. New York: Columbia University Press, 1988.

Lara, Jorge Bautista. *La urbanización de Managua*. Managua: PAVSA, 2008.

Latham, Michael. *Modernization As Ideology: American Social Science and "Nation Building" in the Kennedy Era*. Chapel Hill: University of North Carolina Press, 2000.

————. *The Right Kind of Revolution: Modernization, Development, and U.S. Foreign Policy from the Cold War to the Present*. Ithaca, NY: Cornell University Press, 2011.

Lefebvre, Henri. *The Production of Space*. Cambridge: Blackwell, 1991.

Lehman, David. *Democracy and Development in Latin America: Economics, Politics and Religion in the Post-War Period*. Philadelphia: Temple University, 1990.

Leiva, Fernando. *Latin American Neostructuralism: The Contradictions of Post-Neoliberal Development*. Minneapolis: University of Minnesota, 2008.

LeoGrande, William M. *Our Own Backyard: The United States in Central America, 1977–1992*. Chapel Hill, NC: University of North Carolina Press, 1998.

Leon, Madeline B., and William Leons. "The Utility of Pluralism: M. G. Smith and Plural Theory." *American Ethnologist* 4 (August 1977): 559–575.

Lerner, Daniel. *The Passing of Traditional Society: Modernizing the Middle East*. New York: Free Press, 1958.

Levinson, Jerome I., and Juan de Onís. *The Alliance that Lost its Way: A Critical Report on the Alliance for Progress*. Chicago: Quadrangle, 1970.

Li, Tania. *The Will to Improve: Governmentality, Development, and the Practice of Politics*. Durham, NC: Duke University, 2007.

Lievesley, Geraldine, and Steve Ludlam, eds. *Reclaiming Latin America: Experiments in Radical Social Democracy*. London: Zed Books, 2009.

Lipton, Michael. *Why Poor People Stay Poor: A Study of Urban Bias in World Development*. London: Temple-Smith, 1977.

López Castellanos, Nayar, and Sergio Ramírez. *La ruptura del Frente Sandinista*. Mexico City: Plaza y Valdés, 1996.

Lowenthal, Abraham. *Exporting Democracy: The United States and Latin America*. Baltimore: Johns Hopkins University Press, 1991.

———. "Foreign Aid as a Political Instrument: The Case of the Dominican Republic." *Public Policy* 14 (1965): 141–160.

Luciak, Ilja A. *After the Revolution: Gender and Democracy in El Salvador, Nicaragua, and Guatemala*. Baltimore: Johns Hopkins University Press, 2001.

———. "Gender Equality and Electoral Politics on the Left: A Comparison of El Salvador and Nicaragua." *Journal of Interamerican Studies and World Affairs* 40, no. 1 (Spring 1998).

Macdonald, Theodore. "The Moral Economy of the Miskito Indians: Local Roots of a Geopolitical Conflict." In *Ethnicities and Nations: Processes of Interethnic Relations in Latin America, Southeast Asia, and the Pacific*, ed. Remo Guidieri, Francesco Pellizzi, and Stanley J. Tambiah. Austin: University of Texas Press, 1988.

Macekura, Stephen J. *Of Limits and Growth: The Rise of Global Sustainable Development in the Twentieth Century*. New York: Cambridge University Press, 2015.

Maddick, Henry. *Democracy, Decentralisation and Development*. London: Asia Publishing House, 1963.

Maldonado, A. W. *Luis Muñoz Marín: Puerto Rico's Democratic Revolution*. San Juan: Universidad de Puerto Rico, 2006.

Mann, Gregory. *From Empires to NGOs in the West African Sahel: The Road to Nongovernmentality*. New York: Cambridge University Press, 2015.

Manuel, George. *The Fourth World: An Indian Reality*. Don Mills, Ontario: Collier-Macmillan Canada, 1974.

Martínez Cuenca, Alejandro; Roberto Pizarro; and María Rosa Renzi. *Sandinista Economics in Practice: An Insider's Critical Reflections*. Boston: South End Press, 1992.

McGuire, Mark F., and Vernon W. Ruttan. "Lost Directions: U.S. Foreign Assistance Policy since New Directions." *Journal of Developing Areas* 24 (January 1990): 127–180.

Mecham, J. Lloyd. *The United States and Inter-American Security, 1889–1960.* Austin: University of Texas Press, 1961.

Merkx, Gilbert W., and Karen L. Remmer. "Bureaucratic-Authoritarianism Revisited." *Latin American Research Review* 17 (1982): 3–40.

Mendieta Alfaro, Róger. *Olama y Mollejones.* Managua: Carqui, 1992.

Merton, Thomas. "Carta a Pablo Antonio Cuadra sobre los gigantes," from *El hombre: un dios en exilio,* in *Ensayos II.* Managua: Fundación Vida, 2002.

Metoyer, Cynthia Chavez. *Women and the State in Post-Sandinista Nicaragua.* Boulder, CO: Lynne Rienner, 2000.

Miller, Valerie Lee. *Between Struggle and Hope: The Nicaraguan Literacy Crusade.* Boulder, CO: Westview Press, 1985.

Millet, Richard. *Guardians of the Dynasty.* Maryknoll, NJ: Orbis, 1977.

Millikan, Max F., and W. W. Rostow. *A Proposal: Key to an Effective Foreign Policy.* Westport, CT: Greenwood, 1957.

Mirowski, Philip. *Never Let a Serious Crisis Go to Waste: How Neoliberalism Survived the Financial Meltdown.* New York: Verso, 2014.

Molina Jiménez, Iván, and David Díaz Arias, eds. *Ahí me van a matar: cultura, violencia y Guerra Fría en Costa Rica, 1979–1990.* San José, Costa Rica: EUNED, 2018.

Monte C., Antonio. "Patrimonialismo y Clientelismo del régimen somocista en la implementación del Mercado Común Centroamericano en Nicaragua (1960–1972)." *Revista de Historia* 29 (2013): 37–58.

Moulian, Tomás. *Chile actual: Anatomía de un mito.* Santiago, Chile: ARCIS Universidad, 1997.

Moyn, Samuel. "Do Human Rights Increase Inequality?" *Chronicle Review* (May 29, 2015).

———. *The Last Utopia: Human Rights in History.* Cambridge, MA: Belknap Press, 2010.

———. "A Powerless Companion: Human Rights in the Age of Neoliberalism." *Law & Contemporary Problems* 77, no. 4 (2015): 147–169.

Mujal-Leon, Eusebio. "European Socialism and the Crisis in Central America." In *Rift and Revolution: The Central American Imbroglio,* ed. Howard Wiarda. Washington, DC: American Enterprise Institute, 1984.

———. "The West German Social Democratic Party and the Politics of Internationalism in Central America." *Journal of Interamerican Studies and World Affairs* 29, no. 4 (Winter 1987–1988): 89–123.

Munck, Ronaldo. *Latin America: The Transition to Democracy.* London: Zed Books, 1989.

Muravchik, Joshua. *Uncertain Crusade: Jimmy Carter and the Dilemmas of Human Rights Policy.* Lanham, MD: Hamilton Press, 1986.

Murray, Santiago. "Building towards Reconciliation." *Américas* 44:3 (1992).

Mutchler, David E. "Adaptations of the Roman Catholic Church to Latin American Development: The Meaning of Internal Church Conflict." In *The Roman Catholic Church in Modern Latin America,* ed. Karl M. Smith. New York: Alfred A. Knopf, 1972.

Nellis, John R. "Algerian Socialism and Its Critics." *Canadian Journal of Political Science* 13 (September 1980): 481–507.

Nepstad, Sharon. *Convictions of the Soul: Religion, Culture, and Agency in the Central America Solidarity Movement.* New York: Oxford University Press, 2004.

Newfarmer, Richard. "A Look at Reagan's Revolution in Development Policy." *Challenge* 26 (October 1983): 34–43.

Nichols, Bruce. "Rubberband Humanitarianism." *Ethics in International Affairs* 1 (March 1987): 191–210.

Nietschmann, Bernard. *Between Land and Water: The Subsistence Ecology of the Miskito Indians, Eastern Nicaragua.* New York: Seminar, 1973.

———. "Economic Development by Invasions of Indigenous Nations." *Cultural Survival Quarterly* 10, no. 2 (1986): 2–12.

———. "The Miskito Nation and the Geopolitics of Self-Determination." In *The Ethnic Dimension in International Relations*, ed. Bernard Schechterman and Martin Slann. Westport, CT: Praeger, 1993.

———. *The Miskito Nation, Nicaragua, and the United States: The Unknown War.* New York: Freedom House, 1989.

———. "Protecting Indigenous Coral Reefs and Sea Territories, Miskito Coast, RAAN, Nicaragua." In *Conservation through Cultural Survival: Indigenous Peoples and Protected Areas*, ed. S. E. Stevens. Washington, DC: Island Press, 1997.

Niezen, Ronald. *The Origins of Indigenism: Human Rights and the Politics of Identity.* Berkeley: University of California Press, 2003.

Núñez Soto, Orlando. *La Guerra y el Campesinado en Nicaragua.* Managua: CIPRES, 1995.

———. *La Oligarquía en Nicaragua.* Managua, Nicaragua: CIPRES, 2006.

Nygren, Anja. "Nature as Contested Terrain: Conflicts over Wilderness Protection and Local Livelihoods in Rio San Juan, Nicaragua." In *Ethnographies of Conservation: Environmentalism and the Distribution of Privilege*, ed. David G. Anderson and Eeva Berglund. New York: Berghahn, 2003.

O'Donnell, Guillermo. *Modernization and Bureaucratic-Authoritarianism: Studies in South American Politics.* Berkeley: Institute of International Studies, University of California, 1973.

O'Donnell, Guillermo, Philippe C. Schmitter, and Laurence Whitehead, eds. *Transitions from Authoritarian Rule.* Baltimore: Johns Hopkins University Press, 1986.

Offner, Amy. *Sorting Out the Mixed Economy: The Rise and Fall of Welfare and Developmental States in the Americas.* Princeton, NJ: Princeton University, 2019.

Ortega R., Giselle. *Reconstrucción histórica y gráfica de Managua anterior al yerremoto de 1972.* Managua: Universidad Nacional Autónoma de Nicaragua, n.d.

Ortega Saavedra, Humberto. *La odisea por Nicaragua.* Managua: Lea Grupo Editorial, 2013.

Paige, Jeffery. *Coffee and Power: Revolution and the Rise of Democracy in Central America.* Cambridge, MA: Harvard University Press, 1997.

Pastor, Robert A. *Condemned to Repetition: The United States and Nicaragua.* Princeton, NJ: Princeton University Press, 1987.

———. *Not Condemned to Repetition: The United States and Nicaragua.* Boulder, CO: Westview Press, 2002.

Peace, Roger. *A Call to Conscience: The Anti-Contra War Campaign.* Amherst: University of Massachusetts Press, 2012.

Peattie, Lisa R. *Planning: Rethinking Ciudad Guayana*. Ann Arbor: University of Michigan Press, 1987.

Pee, Robert. *Democracy Promotion, National Security and Strategy: Foreign Policy under the Reagan Administration*. New York: Routledge, 2016.

Perlman, Janice E. *The Myth of Marginality: Urban Poverty and Politics in Rio de Janeiro* Berkeley: University of California, 1976.

Petras, James F., and Frank T. Fitzgerald. "Authoritarianism and Democracy in the Transition." *Latin American Perspectives* 15 (Winter 1988): 93–111.

Petras, James F., Frank T. Fitzgerald, and Morris H. Morley. *US Hegemony under Siege: Class, Politics, and Development in Latin America*. New York: Verso, 1990.

Pineda, Baron. *Shipwrecked Identities: Navigating Race on Nicaragua's Mosquito Coast*. New Brunswick, NJ: Rutgers, 2006.

Plehwe, Dieter. "The Origins of Neoliberal Development Discourse." In *The Road from Mont Pèlerin: The Making of the Neoliberal Thought Collective*, ed. Philip Mirowski and Dieter Plehwe. Cambridge, MA: Harvard University Press, 2009.

Prashad, Vijay. *The Poorer Nations: A Possible History of the Global South*. London: Verso, 2014.

Pritchett, Wendell. "Which Urban Crisis: Regionalism, Race, and Urban Policy, 1960–1974." *Journal of Urban History* 34 (2008): 266–286.

Rabe, Stephen G. *Eisenhower and Latin America: The Foreign Policy of Anticommunism*. Chapel Hill: University of North Carolina Press, 1988.

Rama, Angel. *La ciudad letrada*. Monterrey: Ediciones del Norte, 1984.

Ramírez, Sergio. *Balcanes y volcanes y otros ensayos y trabajos*. Managua: Editorial Nueva Nicaragua, 1983.

Randall, Margaret. *Sandino's Daughters*. Toronto: New Star, 1981.

Rao, Rahul. *Third World Protest: Between Home and the World*. New York: Oxford University, 2010.

Robinson, William. *A Faustian Bargain: U.S. Intervention in the Nicaraguan Elections and American Foreign Policy in the Post-Cold War Era*. Boulder, CO: Westview Press, 1992.

———. *Promoting Polyarchy: Globalization, U.S. Intervention, and Hegemony*. Cambridge, MA: Cambridge University Press, 1996.

———. *Transnational Conflicts: Central America, Social Change, and Globalization*. New York: Verso, 2003.

Robinson, William, and Kent Norsworthy. *David and Goliath: Washington's War against Nicaragua*. London: Zed, 1987.

Rodgers, Daniel. *Contested Truths: Keywords in American Politics Since Independence*. Cambridge, MA: Harvard University Press, 1987.

Rodgers, Dennis. "A Symptom Called Managua." *New Left Review* 49 (January–February 2008).

Roelofs, Joan. *Foundations and Public Policy: The Mask of Pluralism*. Albany: State University of New York Press, 2003.

Rondinelli, Dennis. *Secondary Cities in Developing Countries: Policies for Diffusing Urbanization*. London: Sage Library of Social Research, 1983.

Rose, Nikolas. *Powers of Freedom: Reframing Political Thought.* Cambridge: Cambridge University Press, 2004.

Rostow, Walt Whitman. *Politics and the Stages of Growth.* Cambridge: Cambridge University Press, 1971.

———. *The Stages of Economic Growth: A Non-Communist Manifesto.* New York: Cambridge University Press, 1960.

Rother, Bernd, and Klaus Larres, eds., *Willy Brandt and International Relations: Europe, the USA, and Latin America, 1974–1992.* New York: Bloomsbury Academic, 2019.

Ruttan, Victor. *United States Development Assistance Policy: The Domestic Politics of Foreign Economic Aid.* Baltimore: Johns Hopkins University Press, 1994.

Ryan, Phil. *Fall and Rise of the Market: Political Economy in Sandinista Nicaragua.* Ottawa: National Library of Canada, 1993.

Saldaña-Portillo, María Josefina. *The Revolutionary Imagination in the Americas and the Age of Development.* Durham, NC: Duke University Press, 2003.

Saldomando, Ángel. *El retorno de la AID: El caso de Nicaragua: condicionalidad y reestructuración conservadora.* Managua: Ediciones CRIES, 1992.

Santa-Cruz, Arturo. *International Election Monitoring, Sovereignty, and the Western Hemisphere: The Emergence of an International Norm.* Hoboken, NJ: Taylor and Francis, 2013.

Sartorius, Rolf H., and Vernon W. Ruttan. "The Sources of the Basic Human Needs Mandate." *Journal of Developing Areas* 23, no. 3 (April 1989).

Schild, Verónica. "Feminism and Neoliberalism in Latin America." *New Left Review* 96 (November–December 2015).

Schmitz, David F. *Thank God They're on Our Side: The United States and Right-Wing Dictatorships, 1921–1965.* Chapel Hill: University of North Carolina Press, 2009.

Schori, Pierre, *Escila y Caribdis: Olof Palme, la Guerra Fría y el poscomunismo.* Mexico City: Fondo de Cultura Económica, 1994.

Schoultz, Lars. *In Their Own Best Interest: A History of the U.S. Effort to Improve Latin Americans.* Cambridge, MA: Harvard University Press, 2018.

———. *That Infernal Little Cuban Republic: The United States and the Cuban Revolution.* Chapel Hill: University of North Carolina Press, 2011.

Schwarz, Jordan A. *Liberal: Adolf A. Berle and the Vision of an American Era.* New York: Free Press, 1987.

Scott, Catherine V. *Gender and Development: Rethinking Modernization and Dependency Theory.* Boulder, CO: Lynn Rienner, 1995.

Scott, David. *Conscripts of Modernity: The Tragedy of Colonial Enlightenment.* Durham, NC: Duke University Press, 2004.

Scott, James C. *Seeing Like a State: How Certain Schemes to Improve the Human Condition Have Failed.* New Haven, CT: Yale University Press, 1998.

Sellars, Kirsten. *The Rise and Rise of Human Rights.* Stroud, UK: Sutton, 2002.

Severin, Tim. *In Search of Robinson Crusoe.* New York: Basic Books, 2003.

Serrano Caldera, Alejandro. *La unidad en la diversidad: hacia la cultura del consenso.* Managua: Editorial San Rafael, 1993.

Sheppard, Randal. *The Persistent Revolution: History, Nationalism, and Politics in Mexico since 1968.* Albuquerque: University of New Mexico Press, 2016.

Shibusawa, Naoko. "Ideology, Culture, and the Cold War." In *The Oxford Handbook of the Cold War*, edited by Richard H Immerman and Petra Goedde. Oxford: Oxford University Press, 2013.

Sholk, Richard. "The National Bourgeoisie in Post-Revolutionary Nicaragua." *Comparative Politics* 16 (April 1984): 253–276.

Shoultz, Lars. *Human Rights and United States Policy toward Latin America*. Princeton, NJ: Princeton University Press, 1981.

Slobodian, Quinn. *Globalists: The End of Empire and the Birth of Neoliberalism*. Cambridge, MA: Harvard University Press, 2018.

Smith, Christian. *Resisting Reagan: The U.S. Central America Peace Movement*. Chicago: University of Chicago Press, 1996.

Solís, Pedro Xavier. *Pablo Antonio Cuadra, Itinerario*. Managua: Academia Nicaragüense de la Lengua, 2008.

Sommer, Doris. *Foundational Fictions: The National Romances of Latin America*. Berkeley: University of California Press, 1991.

Soto, Lily. *Nicaragua: El desarrollo histórico de los partidos políticos en la década del 60* Managua: Fondo Editorial CIRA, 2001.

Spalding, Rose J. *Capitalists and Revolution*. Chapel Hill: University of North Carolina, 1994.

———. *Contesting Trade in Central America: Market Reform and Resistance*. Austin: University of Texas Press, 2014.

Stoll, David. "The Nicaraguan Contras, Were They Indios?" *Latin American Politics and Society* 47 (Autumn 2005): 145–157.

Stone, Samuel Z. *The Heritage of the Conquistadors: Ruling Classes in Central America from the Conquest to the Sandinistas*. Lincoln: University of Nebraska Press, 1990.

Supple, Barry. "Revisiting Rostow." *Economic History Review* 37 (February 1984): 107–114.

Suri, Jeremi. *Henry Kissinger and the American Century*. Cambridge, MA: Belknap Press, 2009.

Svampa, Maristella. "Commodities Consensus: Neoextractivism and Enclosure of the Commons in Latin America." *South Atlantic Quarterly* 114 (2015): 65.

———. *Debates latinoamericanos: Indianismo, desarrollo, dependencia, populismo*. Buenos Aires: Edhasa, 2016.

Szulc, Tad. *Twilight of the Tyrants*. New York: Henry Holt, 1959.

Taffet, Jeffrey. *Foreign Aid as Foreign Policy: The Alliance for Progress in Latin America*. New York: Routledge, 2007.

Téfel, Reinaldo Antonio. *El infierno de los pobres: diagnóstico sociológico de los barrios marginales de Managua*. Managua: Distribuidora Cultural, 1978.

"Toward a History of the New International Economic Order." Special issue, *Humanity* 6, no. 1 (Spring 2015): 1–233.

Toynbee, Arnold J. *A Study of History*, vol. 8. New York: Oxford University Press, 1948.

Tresierra, Julio. "Mexico: Indigenous Peoples and the Nation States." In *Indigenous Peoples and Democracy in Latin America*, ed. Donna Lee Van Cott. New York: St. Martin's Press, 1994.

Vaky, Viron P. "Everything Is Part of Everything Else." *Foreign Affairs* 59, no. 3 (1980): 617–647.

Valdez, Fernando. *La fascinación por la Moncloa: del pacto entre élites al acuerdo socia: hablan líderes de Chile, El Salvador y Guatemala*. Guatemala City: Universidad Rafael Landívar, Instituto de Investigaciones y Gerencia Política, 2009.

Van der Post, JanGeert. *El Largo y Sinuoso Camino*. Managua: IHNCA, 2014.

Vanden, Harry E., and Gary Prevost. *Democracy and Socialism in Sandinista Nicaragua*. New York: St. Martin's Press, 1997.

Vargas, Armando, ed. *La crisis de la democracia en Costa Rica*. San José, Costa Rica: EUNED, 1981.

Vasconcelos, José. *La Raza cósmica*. Baltimore: Johns Hopkins University Press, 1997.

Velázquez, José Luis. *Nicaragua: sociedad civil y dictadura*. San José, Costa Rica: Libro Libre, 1986.

Vilas, Carlos M. *Between Earthquakes and Volcanos: Market, State, and Revolution in Central America*. New York: Monthly Review Press, 1995.

———. *Estado, clase y etnicidad: la costa atlántica de Nicaragua*. Mexico City: Fondo de Cultura Económica, 1992.

———. *El legado de una década*. Managua: Lea Grupo Editorial, 2005.

———. "Family Affairs: Class, Lineage and Politics in Contemporary Nicaragua." *Journal of Latin American Studies* 24, no. 2 (May 1992): 309–341.

———. "Nicaragua: A Revolution That Fell from Grace of the People." *Socialist Register* 27 (1991): 302–321.

———. *The Sandinista Revolution: National Liberation and Social Transformation in Central America*. New York: Monthly Review, 1986.

———. *State, Class, and Ethnicity in Nicaragua: Capitalist Modernization and Revolutionary Change on the Atlantic Coast*. Boulder, CO: Lynne Rienner Publishers, 1989.

Walker, Thomas W. *The Christian Democratic Movement in Nicaragua*. Tucson: University of Arizona Press, 1970.

Walker, William. *The War in Nicaragua*. Tucson: University of Arizona Press, 1985.

Wall, David. "City Profile: Managua." *Cities* 13 (1996).

Walter, Knut, *El régimen de Anastasio Somoza, 1936–1956*. Managua: IHNCA, 2004.

Watts, Michael J. "Now and Then: The Origins of Political Ecology and the Rebirth of Adaptation as a Form of Thought." In *The Routledge Handbook of Political Ecology*, ed. Tom Perreault, Gavin Bridge, and James McCarthy. New York: Routledge, 2015.

Way, John T. *The Mayan in the Mall: Development, Globalization, and the Making of Modern Guatemala*. Durham, NC: Duke University Press, 2012.

Weber, Clare. *Visions of Solidarity: U.S. Peace Activists in Nicaragua from War to Women's Activism and Globalization*. Lanham, MD: Lexington Books, 2006.

Wellinga, Klaus. *Entre la poesía y la pared: política cultural sandinista, 1979–1990*. San José, Costa Rica: FLACSO, 1994.

West, Paige. *Conservation Is Our Government Now: The Politics of Ecology in Papua New Guinea*. Durham, NC: Duke University, 2006.

Westad, Odd Arne. *The Global Cold War: Third World Interventions and the Making of Our Times*. New York: Cambridge University Press, 2007.

Wheelock Román, Jaime. *Nicaragua, imperialismo y dictadura*. Havana: Editorial de Ciencias Sociales, 1980.

——. *Raíces indígenas de la lucha anticolonialista en Nicaragua: de Gil González a Joaquín Zavala, 1523 a 1881*. Mexico City: Siglo Veintiuno, 1980.

Whisnant, David E. *Rascally Signs in Sacred Places: The Politics of Culture in Nicaragua*. Chapel Hill: University of North Carolina, 2000.

——. "Rubén Darío as a Focal Cultural Figure in Nicaragua: The Ideological Uses of Cultural Capital." *Latin American Research Review* 27 (July 1992): 7–49.

White, Stephen F. *El mundo más que humano en la poesía de Pablo Antonio Cuadra: un estudio ecocrítico*. Managua: Asociación Pablo Antonio Cuadra, 2002.

——. "An Interview with Pablo Antonio Cuadra." *Northwest Review* 23 (1985): 74–91.

Whitehead, Laurence. *The International Dimensions of Democratization: Europe and the Americas*. Oxford: Oxford University Press, 1996.

Whyte, Jessica. "The Fortunes of Natural Man: Robinson Crusoe, Political Economy, and the Universal Declaration of Human Rights." *Humanity* 5, no. 3 (Winter 2014): 301–321.

Wiarda, Howard J. *Corporatism and Comparative Politics: The Other Great "Ism."* Armonk, NY: M.E. Sharpe, 1997.

——. *Corporatism and National Development in Latin America*. Boulder, CO: Westview, 1981.

Williams, Gareth. *The Other Side of the Popular: Neoliberalism and Subalternity in Latin America*. Durham, NC: Duke University, 2002.

Williams, William Appleman. *The Tragedy of American Diplomacy*. New York: Dell Publishing, 1962.

Wood, Bryce. *The Making of the Good Neighbor Policy*. New York: Columbia University Press, 1961.

Wright, Bruce. *Theory in the Practice of the Nicaraguan Revolution*. Athens: Ohio University Center for International Studies, 1995.

Yashar, Deborah. *Contesting Citizenship in Latin America: The Rise of Indigenous Movements and the Postliberal Challenge*. New York: Cambridge University Press, 2005.

Zorn, Jean G., and Harold Mayerson. "The Caribbean Basin Initiative: A Windfall for the Private Sector." *Lawyer of the Americas* 14 (Winter 1983): 523–556.

Index

CPSIA information can be obtained
at www.ICGtesting.com
Printed in the USA
LVHW091555260721
693702LV00012B/700/J